Karen Morrison and Nick Hamshaw
Tabitha Steel, Coral Thomas, Mark Dawes and Steven Watson

Cambridge IGCSE®
Mathematics
Extended

Problem-solving Book

CAMBRIDGE
UNIVERSITY PRESS

University Printing House, Cambridge CB2 8BS, United Kingdom

One Liberty Plaza, 20th Floor, New York, NY 10006, USA

477 Williamstown Road, Port Melbourne, VIC 3207, Australia

314–321, 3rd Floor, Plot 3, Splendor Forum, Jasola District Centre,
New Delhi – 110025, India

79 Anson Road, #06–04/06, Singapore 079906

Cambridge University Press is part of the University of Cambridge.

It furthers the University's mission by disseminating knowledge in the pursuit of education, learning and research at the highest international levels of excellence.

www.cambridge.org
Information on this title: www.cambridge.org/9781316643525

© Cambridge University Press 2017

This publication is in copyright. Subject to statutory exception
and to the provisions of relevant collective licensing agreements,
no reproduction of any part may take place without the written
permission of Cambridge University Press.

First published 2017

20 19 18 17 16 15 14 13 12 11 10 9 8 7 6 5

Printed in Great Britain by CPI Group (UK) Ltd, Croydon CR0 4YY

A catalogue record for this publication is available from the British Library

ISBN 978-1-316-64352-5 Paperback

Cambridge University Press has no responsibility for the persistence or accuracy of URLs for external or third-party internet websites referred to in this publication, and does not guarantee that any content on such websites is, or will remain, accurate or appropriate. Information regarding prices, travel timetables, and other factual information given in this work is correct at the time of first printing but Cambridge University Press does not guarantee the accuracy of such information thereafter.

®IGCSE is the registered trademark of Cambridge International Examinations.

All exam-style questions and sample answers have been written by the authors.

Cover image: Mickael Fontaneau/EyeEm/Getty Images

....

NOTICE TO TEACHERS IN THE UK
It is illegal to reproduce any part of this work in material form (including photocopying and electronic storage) except under the following circumstances:
(i) where you are abiding by a licence granted to your school or institution by the Copyright Licensing Agency;
(ii) where no such licence exists, or where you wish to exceed the terms of a licence, and you have gained the written permission of Cambridge University Press;
(iii) where you are allowed to reproduce without permission under the provisions of Chapter 3 of the Copyright, Designs and Patents Act 1988, which covers, for example, the reproduction of short passages within certain types of educational anthology and reproduction for the purposes of setting examination questions.

Contents

Introduction — iv

Problem-solving strategies:

1. Draw a diagram — 1
2. Work back from what you know — 16
3. Change your point of view — 28
4. Simplify the problem — 42
5. Consider different cases — 53
6. Make connections — 62
7. Use logical reasoning — 74
8. Use equations, formulae or ratios — 85
9. Organise data and work systematically — 96
10. Guess, test and improve — 104
11. Put it together — 114

Worked solutions:

1. Draw a diagram — 117
2. Work back from what you know — 135
3. Change your point of view — 148
4. Simplify the problem — 166
5. Consider different cases — 176
6. Make connections — 189
7. Use logical reasoning — 202
8. Use equations, formulae or ratios — 210
9. Organise data and work systematically — 226
10. Guess, test and improve — 237
11. Put it together — 251

Introduction

In today's world, information is easy to access. You can find facts and content easily on the internet and from other sources. This has meant that the focus in education and in the employment market has shifted, and students are expected to develop a range of skills to apply and use information, including problem-solving skills. Creative thinking and the ability to find solutions to complex problems are highly valued in all areas of life. At school, this means that you are now expected to solve unfamiliar and sometimes complex problems and to show how you found the solutions. To do this you need to know basic skills, but you also have to be able to make decisions and communicate your thinking. Learning problem-solving strategies can help you become a better mathematician and also help you meet the demands of the 21st-century workplace.

What is mathematical problem-solving?

In primary school the word 'problems' is often used to describe worded questions or 'story sums'. For example: Josh and Khanye have 37 marbles between them. Josh has three more than Khanye. How many marbles does each boy have?

As you learn more mathematics, the story and the situations might become more complex. For example: Mr Smith and Ms Khan earned the same amount of money although one person worked six shifts more than the other. Mr Smith earned $72 per shift and Ms Khan earned $120 per shift. How many shifts did each person work? In reality, the problems themselves are similar.

For many students, the main difficulty with these types of questions is not the mathematics involved, it is that they don't know what the question is asking them to do. Once they work out what is being asked, the solution is fairly clear to them.

In this book, we consider a 'problem' to be a question or situation where the solution is not immediately clear or obvious. Some of these might be worded problems, but problem-solving in mathematics also involves shape and space and graphical problems that are not dependent on stories (word problems).

So, for our purposes, a problem exists when you have to find a solution and it is not immediately clear how to do that.

Problem-solving is the process that you go through to find the solution. It is generally accepted that there are four main steps in the process:

- understanding the problem
- devising a plan to solve it
- carrying out the plan
- looking back.

You already know how to work through these steps and you have solved problems in real life and mathematics for many years. In this book we are going to focus on a range of strategies to make the first two steps in the process more familiar and easier to work through. The strategies are practical methods for making sense of problems. Once you are familiar with them, you will find it much easier to devise a plan for solving problems that look difficult or impossible at first glance.

Step 3 generally involves fairly straightforward mathematical techniques such as finding the highest common factor, solving a quadratic equation or drawing a Venn diagram. We do not teach these skills in this book. You will learn and practise these techniques as part of your IGCSE Mathematics course. If you are unsure of any of the mathematical techniques used in the solution section, it will be helpful to refer to the relevant chapter of your coursebook.

The strategies – your toolkit

The strategies that we introduce and use in this book are intended to help you devise a plan for solving different types of problems. Some strategies are better suited to particular types of problems. Our aim is to give you experience and practice in selecting and using the different strategies. Research shows this is the best way of developing your problem-solving skills.

The key strategies are:

- draw a diagram
- work back from what you know
- change your point of view
- simplify the problem
- consider different cases
- make connections
- use logical reasoning
- use equations, formulae or ratios
- organise data and work systematically
- guess, test and improve.
- put it together

How this book is organised

Chapters 1 to 10 are organised around the strategies listed above. Each chapter introduces a strategy and shows you how to use it. Once you have read through the sample problems and understood how the strategy can be used, you can then work through the graded problems.

Chapter 11 provides you with a range of mixed problems and you should devise a plan using the strategy that you think is best. The aim here is to consolidate what you have learnt and to apply your skills without the guidance given in the earlier chapters.

Cambridge IGCSE Mathematics Extended Problem-solving Book

The problems are graded with stars.

★☆☆ These are entry level problems that are useful for practising the strategy if you are not completely confident.

★★☆ When you have worked through and mastered at least some of the entry level problems, try these questions to develop your experience and skills.

★★★ These are modelled on the unstructured questions you will come across in mathematics at this level. Many of these draw on different strands and you will be expected to apply your mathematical skills in unfamiliar or mixed situations.

You can use your calculator as you work through the problem unless you see the 'no calculator' symbol . For these questions you need to find the solution using pen and paper methods.

> **Tip**
> There are tip boxes alongside the questions to give you clues and to link the problem to mathematics you already know.

The colour wheel 🎨 which contains the question number shows you which strand of mathematics the problem comes from. These are:

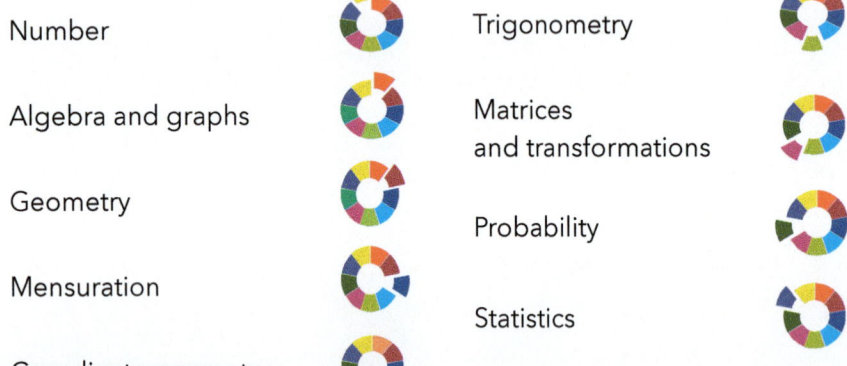

Number

Algebra and graphs

Geometry

Mensuration

Coordinate geometry

Trigonometry

Matrices and transformations

Probability

Statistics

The exploded pieces of the colour wheel tell you what strands of maths each question covers.

Worked solutions

In the second part of the book, detailed worked solutions are given for each problem using the strategy taught, or the one identified as most helpful. The boxes alongside the solution guide you through the steps and explain how the strategy was applied.

Chapter 1
Draw a diagram

You might have heard the saying 'a picture is worth a thousand words'. This means that a picture can show a lot of information without using language. Different types of graphs, Venn diagrams, maps, scale drawings, tree diagrams and two way tables are all mathematical 'pictures' that can show mathematical information in a clear way.

Drawing a picture is a very useful problem-solving strategy. You can use pictures to help you 'see' a problem and to work out what you need to do to solve it.

When you are given a word problem, you can 'translate' it into a more visual form (a diagram, graph, rough sketch or table) to help you see the problem more clearly. You can also use your picture to organise the information you are given and work out what you need to do to solve the problem.

For some problems a diagram will be provided. If so, remember that you can write on the diagram and add information to it to help you solve the problem.

When no diagram is provided you can draw your own.

Decide what type of picture will be most useful. Then draw a clear diagram that is large enough to work on. You can use different colours and highlighters to make it easier to see what you are doing. Rough sketches are acceptable but your sketch should look like the thing it describes. If there is a triangle in the problem, then your shape should be a triangle. If there is supposed to be a straight line, then your line should be straight. The actual sizes of sides and angles are not important in a rough sketch.

Label your diagram. If there is information provided in the question (such as the lengths of sides, or the sizes of angles) then write these on your diagram. This will often help when you are solving a problem.

Add new information that you work out. When you work out something new, add this to the diagram too.

So, in summary:

- draw a clear diagram
- label it
- add new information that you work out.

Here are three examples where drawing diagrams could help you:

Tip

When we use the word 'diagram' here, we mean any visual representation of a problem. This can include rough sketches, graphs, number lines, tree diagrams, possibility diagrams, two way tables and Venn diagrams.

Tip

Drawing is a useful strategy to consider for problems involving combined probabilities, sets, loci, area and perimeter, ratio and proportion, fractional sharing, growth and decay, vectors, transformations, angles, distances and statistics.

Problem 1.1: A canteen offers a 'meal deal' that allows customers to choose a main course of fish, chicken or vegetables and a side order of either rice, fries, noodles or salad.

How many different meal combinations can you choose?

You could work systematically and create a list, but a diagram would also help.

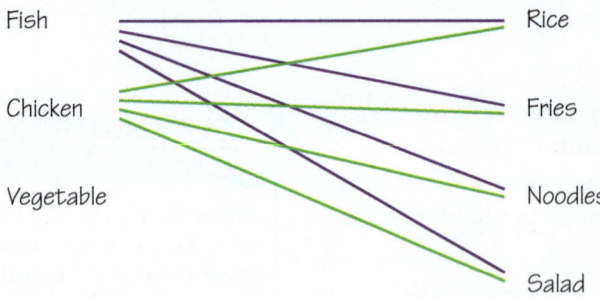

The diagram above shows all the options and the lines show some of the possible combinations.

There are four purple lines from fish to the four side options and four green lines from chicken to the four side options. This shows you that there are four choices for each main. You don't need to draw in the other lines to work out that there are 12 possible combinations.

You could use a possibility diagram like the one below to solve this problem.

Each tick, or each cell on the grid, represents one possibility. There are 12 ticks, so there are 12 possible meal combinations.

	Rice	Fries	Noodles	Salad
Fish	✓	✓	✓	✓
Chicken	✓	✓	✓	✓
Vegetable	✓	✓	✓	✓

Problem 1.2: A rectangle has sides of 10 cm and 8 cm to the nearest centimetre.

a What are the limits of accuracy for the area of this rectangle?

b What is the difference between the minimum and maximum values for:

  i the lengths of the sides

  ii the area?

Draw a rough sketch of a rectangle. Label the sides and find the upper and lower bound of each measurement. This is the error interval.

$9.5 \leqslant L < 10.5$
10 cm

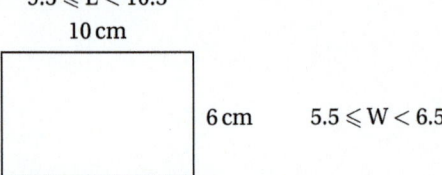

6 cm $5.5 \leqslant W < 6.5$

Tip

It can be useful to use a ruler to draw straight lines, even in sketches.

Sketch the smallest and greatest rectangles and find the area of each.

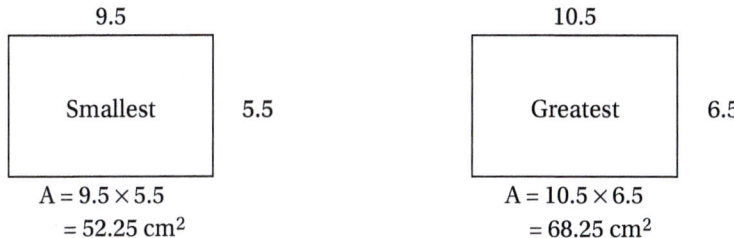

$A = 9.5 \times 5.5$
$= 52.25 \text{ cm}^2$

$A = 10.5 \times 6.5$
$= 68.25 \text{ cm}^2$

Write the values as an error interval for the area, A, of the rectangle using the correct notation.

a The limits of accuracy for the area are $52.25 \text{ cm}^2 \leqslant A < 68.25 \text{ cm}^2$

Your sketches show that the difference between the minimum and maximum values of the length and width is 1 cm.

You can subtract to find the difference between the minimum and maximum area.

b i 1 cm   **ii** 16 cm²

Here is an example where a table with highlighting is useful:

Problem 1.3: Amman says, "If I write out numbers in rows of six, all of the prime numbers will either be in the column that has 1 at the top, or in the column that has 5 at the top".

Can you tell if he is right?

You need to have some numbers to look at here so a diagram will be important.

Highlight a few prime numbers.

The table shows that the numbers in each column increase by six as you move down.

You know that 2 is the only even prime number. So you can eliminate all numbers in the 2nd, 4th and 6th columns, except for the 2 in the first row. (Adding six to an even number will always give an even answer.)

Adding six is the same as adding two threes, so all the numbers in the column with 3 at the top must multiples of 3 and therefore not prime, except for the 3 in the first row.

This means that besides the first row, any prime numbers must be in the first or fifth columns so Amman is right.

1	2	3	4	5	6
7	8	9	10	11	12
13	14	15	16	17	18
19	20	21	22	23	24
25	26	27	28	29	30
31	32	33	34	35	36

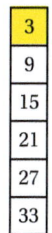

Cambridge IGCSE Mathematics Extended Problem-solving Book

In the local cement factory, the cement bags are placed on pallets made of planks of wood and bricks.

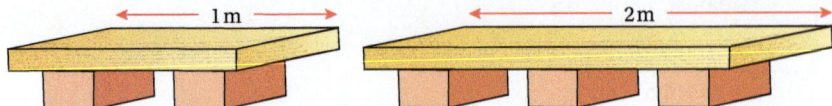

The number of bricks needed to make the pallet is calculated as 'one more than the length of the plank in metres'.

a What length of pallet uses five bricks?

b If the pallet is 7 m long, how many bricks are used in it?

The factory needs pallets with a total length of 15 m for the next batch of cement. It has planks of wood that are 4 m long and 3 m long.

c What combinations of planks can they have?

d How many bricks would be needed for each combination?

Sanjita wants to plant a cherry tree in her garden. She needs to make sure there is a circular area of lawn with diameter 3 m around the base of the tree, so that all of the fruit will fall onto the lawn area.

Here is a sketch, not drawn to scale, of Sanjita's garden.

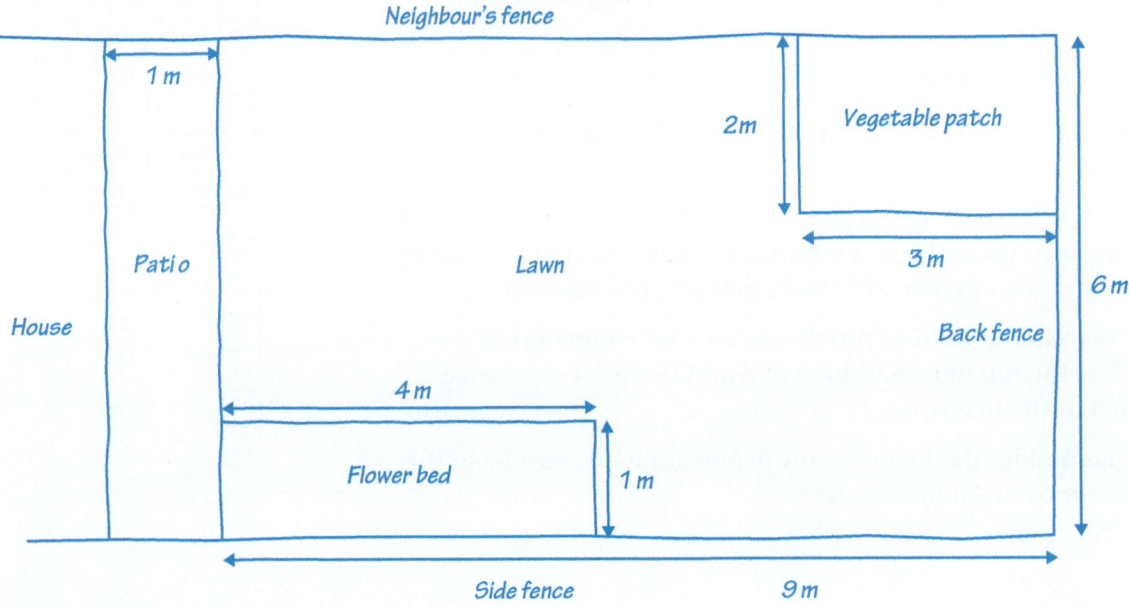

Where could the tree be planted to meet her conditions?

Chapter 1: Draw a diagram

 3

The diagram represents towns A and B in a mountainous region.

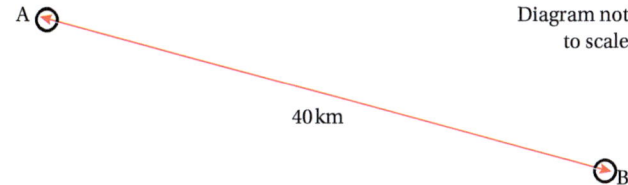

The mountain rescue helicopters from both towns will always be sent to rescue any casualty within a radius of 25 km of town A or town B. The fire and rescue team from town B will travel to any accident scene closer to town B than town A.

Shade the region that the helicopters and town B's fire and rescue team will both cover.

A rectangle has length $(2x + 3)$ and width $(x - 1)$.

a Write an expression for the perimeter of the rectangle.

b Write an expression for the area of the rectangle.

The area of the rectangle is $250\,\text{cm}^2$.

c How long is the longest side?

d What is the perimeter of the rectangle?

Tip

$253 = 23 \times 11$

The probability that Hamza catches the 6.30 am train to the city is 0.7.

If he misses the train he will be late for work.

The probability the train will be late is 0.15.

If the train is late he will be late for work.

What is the probability Hamza will be on time for work on a particular day?

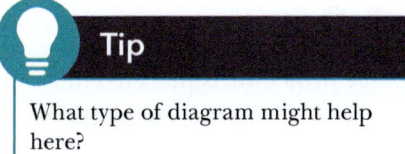

Tip

What type of diagram might help here?

Two five-sided spinners are numbered 1 to 5. When the arrows are spun, your total score is calculated by adding the two numbers that the spinners land on.

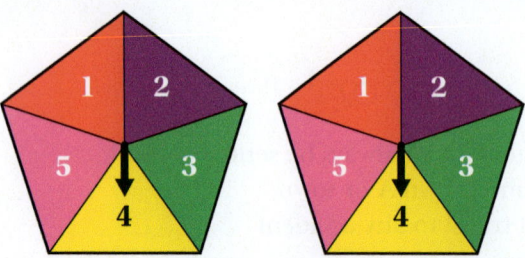

a Draw a suitable diagram to show all possible outcomes when spinning these spinners.

b What is the highest score you could get?

c What is the probability of getting a total score of 8?

The vertices of a quadrilateral are A, B, C and D.

A has coordinates (2, 1).

$\overrightarrow{AB} = \begin{pmatrix} 2 \\ 3 \end{pmatrix}$, $\overrightarrow{BC} = \begin{pmatrix} 4 \\ 0 \end{pmatrix}$, $\overrightarrow{AD} = \begin{pmatrix} 4 \\ 0 \end{pmatrix}$

a Write a column vector for $\overrightarrow{CD}$.

b Compare $\overrightarrow{CD}$ with $\overrightarrow{AB}$. What do you notice? Can you explain?

c What type of quadrilateral is ABCD?

>  **Tip**
>
> Use squared paper to draw your diagram.

A projector is placed 1 m from a screen. When the projector is turned on, the image produced is only 20 cm high.

How far back should the projector be moved to produce an image that exactly fills the screen, which is approximately 1.5 m in height?

(Assume that no other adjustments are made to the projector.)

9

A factory manager planned to install a new hot drinks machine for the factory workers. He thought tea would be the most popular hot drink.

The workers did a survey to check what the preferred hot drink was among them. Each person could choose one drink from hot chocolate, tea or coffee.

Eight women wanted hot chocolate.

A total of 16 workers wanted tea, of which seven were men.

10 men and 12 women chose coffee.

There were 25 men in total.

Was tea the most popular hot drink?

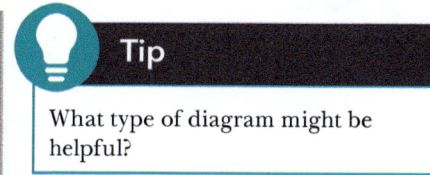

Tip

What type of diagram might be helpful?

10

A ship sails 17.6 km on a bearing of 270° and then 15.4 km due south.

What is the shortest distance back to where it started?

11

Maria needs to make a long-distance journey. She is looking for the cheapest car hire.

Whacky Wheels has a standard charge of $35, then 15¢ for every kilometre driven.

Wheelies Rentals has a charge of 23¢ per kilometre travelled, but no standard charge.

  a Complete the charges graph for both car hire companies.

  b Maria thinks the return journey will be 300 km. Which company would be cheaper to use?

  c Maria made a mistake in her route plan and the return journey was 500 km. How much money would Maria have saved by using the other hire company?

Tip

In this question you can use the axes that are given to help you draw the diagram.

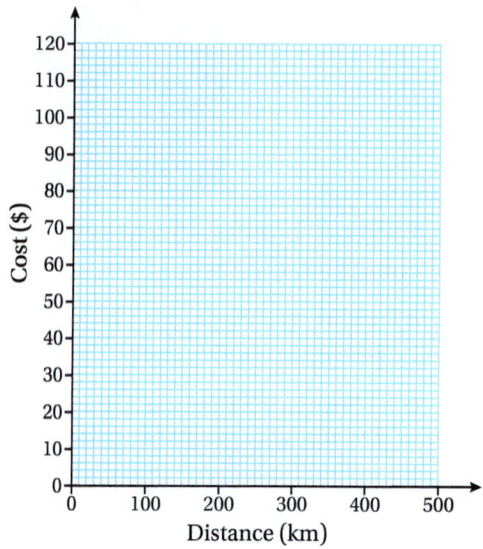

12 ★★☆

ABCD is a field surrounded by fences AB, BC, CD and DA.

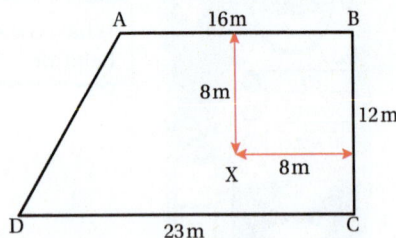

A goat is tied to the spike X on a rope measuring 3 m.

A bull is tied by an 8 m rope to the top of post A.

Find a route from corner D to corner B that would avoid both the bull and the goat.

13 ★★☆

This patchwork quilt is made from scraps of fabric.

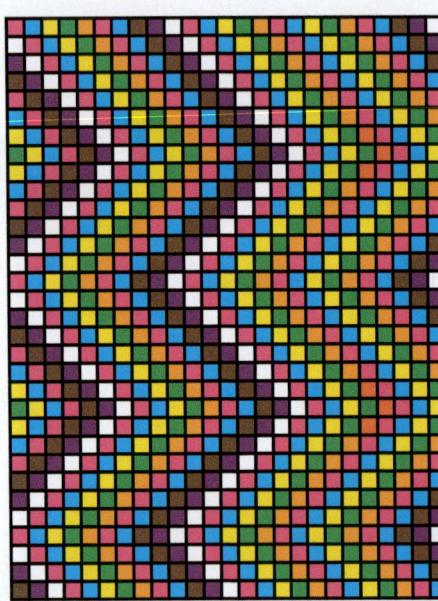

> **Tip**
>
> The diagram in the question is very detailed. Could a simpler diagram help?

Each patch is $(2x - 3)$ cm long and $(x + 3)$ cm wide. The area of the completed quilt is 2.8 m².

a There are 25 patches in each row. Write a possible expression for the width of the quilt.

b There are 32 patches in each column. Write a possible expression for the length of the quilt.

Chapter 1: Draw a diagram

c Write an expression for the area of the quilt, in the form $m(ax^2 + bx + c)$ where m is a constant.

d What are the dimensions of each patch? Give your answers in centimetres.

> **Tip**
>
> $2.8\,m^2 = 28\,000\,cm^2$. It might be easier to work in centimetres.

A square-based food container has a capacity of $1440\,cm^3$.

The base of the container has length x cm.

a Write an equation for the height of the container in terms of x.

The inside of the container (base and four sides) is to be lined with grease-proof paper with no overlaps.

b What is the formula, in terms of x, for the area of grease-proof paper needed?

c If the height of the container is 10 cm, what is the area of the base?

d What is the area of grease-proof paper needed?

A rectangular swimming pool is surrounded by a path made of mosaic tiles. The width of the path is x. It cost $3196.80 to have the path tiled, at a rate of $30 per square metre.

The pool itself measures 35 m by 30 m.

a Write an expression for the area of the tiled path in terms of x.

b Find the width of the path to the nearest centimetre.

Serrianne has taken up golf and goes to practise at the golf range twice a week. She uses one bucket of balls each time. In every bucket of 25 balls there are always 3 yellow balls; the rest are white.

Serrianne hits one ball (chosen at random) at a time.

a What is the probability that the first 3 balls she uses will all be yellow?

b What is the probability that the first 3 balls she uses will all be white?

c Calculate the probability that the first 3 balls Serrianne uses are a mixture of two yellows and one white.

Cambridge IGCSE Mathematics Extended Problem-solving Book

17

To make the journey to work Abu must drive through two sets of traffic lights.

The probability of the first set being green is 0.7. If the first set is green, the probability of the second set also being green is 0.8. But if the first set is not green, the probability of the second set being green is 0.4.

a What is the probability that Abu does not have to stop on his journey to work tomorrow?

b What is the probability that Abu only has to stop once on his journey to work tomorrow?

18

Kalima and Jiao are very competitive and often have badminton and squash matches. The probability of Kalima winning at badminton is 0.85 and the probability of Kalima winning at squash is 0.35.

a What is the probability that the next time they play both matches, Kalima wins both?

b What is the probability that Kalima loses at badminton but wins at squash?

c What is the probability that both girls win one match each?

19

On a commercial flight to Tanzania the passengers were questioned about their malaria precautions. Only 70% of the passengers had obtained and started a course of anti-malaria tablets. The chances of getting malaria are $\frac{1}{200}$ if you take the tablets but $\frac{1}{50}$ if you are not taking the tablets. What is the probability that one passenger selected randomly will contract malaria?

Tip

What type of diagram would be helpful?

The owner of a bookshop carried out a survey to find the most popular school subjects in Year 10 to help decide how many revision guides to stock. A total of 200 students were asked whether they were studying Chemistry, Physics or Maths.

43 of the students surveyed did not study any of these 3 subjects.

A total of 92 were studying Chemistry.

There were 23 studying both Chemistry and Maths, but not Physics.

There were 19 studying both Physics and Maths, but not Chemistry.

29 were only studying Physics, and there were a total of 74 who studied Physics.

53 of the students studied 2 of these 3 subjects.

a Display the information in an appropriate diagram.

b If one person was chosen at random, what is the probability they only studied maths?

c If one person was chosen at random, what is the probability they studied at least two of the subjects?

The point A has coordinates (2, 2).
$\overrightarrow{AB} = \begin{pmatrix} 2 \\ 5 \end{pmatrix}$
$\overrightarrow{BC} = \begin{pmatrix} 3 \\ 0 \end{pmatrix}$

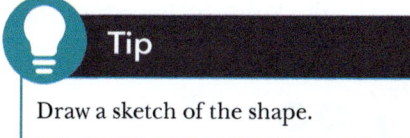

Draw a sketch of the shape.

a Find a possible pair of coordinates for D, if ABCD is an isosceles trapezium.

b Write $\overrightarrow{AC}$ as a column vector.

c Find the coordinates of E, if $\overrightarrow{AE} = 4\overrightarrow{BC}$.

d Using these coordinates for E, write $\overrightarrow{BE}$ as a column vector.

a Amira has a challenge for her classmate, Janet:

"I'm thinking of a triangle…

It has a right angle. It has one angle of 40°. It has one side that has a length of 5 cm.

Draw my triangle."

   i Accurately construct a triangle that satisfies Amira's conditions.

   ii Demonstrate that there is more than one triangle that Amira could be thinking of.

   iii How could Amira alter her challenge so that only one triangle is possible?

b Janet comes up with a challenge for Amira:

"I'm thinking of a triangle…

It has one side of length 4 cm. It has another side of length 7 cm. The angle in between these two sides is 55°.

Draw my triangle."

   i How many triangles satisfy Janet's conditions? Explain your answer.

   ii Find the length of the third side.

Tip

To construct an accurate triangle you need to use a ruler, protractor and a pair of compasses.

Tip

Before you start your accurate construction, make some rough sketches to show the positions of the sides and angles you are given.

Raj took a photo of his mother on holiday. Later, when Raj looked at the picture, he saw that his mother seemed to be the same height as a hill in the background.

Raj stood approximately 3 m away from his mother when he took the photo, and they were about 2 km away from the hill. Raj's mother is 15 cm taller than him.

Approximately how high is the hill?

When enlarging photographs, the increase in width and length must be directly proportional to each other or the photos will be distorted.

A photo has width 40 cm and length 55 cm.

   a An enlargement of this photo has width 112 cm. Find the length for this photo poster.

b Another enlargement of the original photo has length 148.5 cm. What must the width be for this enlargement?

c A third photo with length 15 cm and area 127.5 cm² is enlarged to a poster of width 25.5 cm. What is the area of this poster?

Suki and Fleur do some swimming every morning. They swim a total of 45 lengths each. They always start together but never finish together. They swim at different speeds for different swimming strokes.

Suki always swims 45 lengths of breaststroke in 30 minutes, completing each one at the same speed.

Fleur always does 30 lengths of front crawl in the first 12 minutes, then the remaining 15 lengths at a speed of one length per 40 seconds.

a After ten minutes, how many lengths has Suki completed?

b How long does it take Fleur to complete her final 15 lengths?

c What is Suki's speed in lengths per minute?

d How long must Fleur wait for Suki to finish?

e Roughly, on average, how many lengths does Fleur swim each minute?

f If Suki continued swimming for another 10 minutes, in theory how many lengths should she complete in total? Explain why this figure might not be correct.

You can use the three transformations listed below:

A Reflect in the line $y = x$

B Translate by $\begin{pmatrix} 1 \\ 0 \end{pmatrix}$

C Enlarge by scale factor $\frac{1}{2}$ about the point (2, 3)

a Carry out all three transformations, in order, on a starting shape of your choice.

b How does the resulting image change if the transformations are applied in reverse order? C ⟶ B ⟶ A

c How many different final images could be produced by changing the order in which the three transformations are applied?

Tip

You will find this question easier if you try it out. Think about how you can make it simpler by choosing shapes and side lengths that make the enlargement easier.

Two of the vertices of an equilateral triangle are located at points with coordinates (0, 0) and (6, 0).

a Work out the possible coordinates of the third vertex.

b If two of the vertices of a different equilateral triangle are located at (−3, 2) and (5, −4), what is its area?

An astronomer wants to calculate the distance to one of our closest stars, Proxima Centauri. To do this, she takes two angle measurements, six months apart. The two angles measured by the astronomer are shown in the diagrams below.

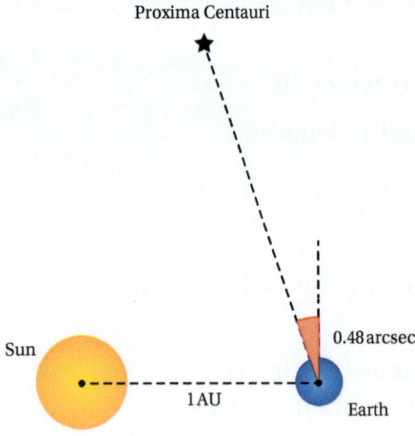

Six months later…

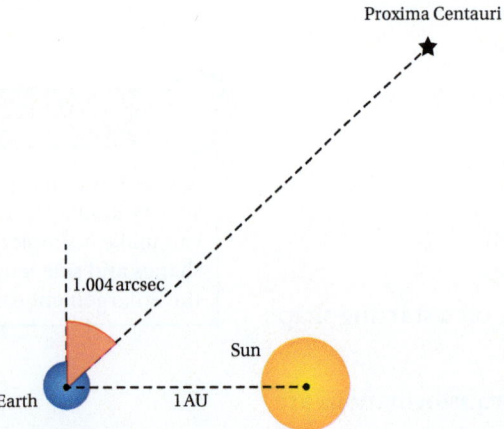

Key facts:

$1 \text{ AU} \approx 1.5 \times 10^8 \text{ km}$

$1 \text{ arcsec} = \left(\dfrac{1}{3600}\right)^\circ$

Use the astronomer's measurements to calculate the approximate distance to Proxima Centauri.

Find the area of the triangle enclosed by the *x*-axis and the straight lines with equations $3x + 2y = 15$ and $y - 2x = 4$.

Tip

Work out where the lines cross the axes and use these coordinates to help you draw a diagram.
It is helpful to consider one more point when calculating the area of the triangle. How will you find the coordinates of this point?

Rectangle ABCD has width 1 cm and length *k* cm, where *k* is greater than 1. AB = 1 cm and BC = *k* cm. The rectangle is divided into a square and a smaller rectangle by drawing a line parallel to the side AB. The smaller rectangle is mathematically similar to the rectangle ABCD. Calculate the value of *k*.

Tip

Draw a diagram. You need to be able to work out the length and width of the smaller rectangle.

Two circles, one larger than the other, have the same centre. A chord is drawn joining two points on the circumference of the larger circle. This chord is also a tangent to the smaller circle. The chord has length 20 cm. Find the area of the ring enclosed between the circles.

Give your answer as an exact multiple of π.

Tip

You do not need to know the radius of either circle to answer this question, but you do need to find a relationship between the two radii. What can you draw on the circle to help you?

Chapter 2
Work back from what you know

Many problems don't have obvious solutions. Your first step should be to read the problem carefully to try to make sense of it. Next you have to consider what you already know, what information you have been given and what connections and relationships you can use to work towards solving it. Working logically and systematically with what you have been given and what you already know will often help you to find the solution.

When a solution or method of working is not obvious:

- read the problem again
- focus on the key information you are given and pay attention to details that could be useful
- use what you know and what you can work out to narrow down the problem
- record your work so that you can retrace your steps and verify or change your method.

Work through the two examples here carefully to see how to approach a problem when the solution is not immediately obvious.

Tip

With some problems, focusing on the answer doesn't help. Instead it is sometimes easier to work out what you **can** do rather than the thing you **want** because, sometimes, you will find you have got the answer almost by accident!

Problem 2.1: In the diagram below, a square and an isosceles triangle are drawn on a straight line.

Work out the size of angle A.

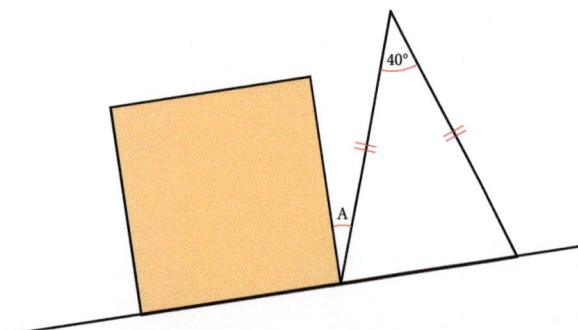

You can't work out angle A immediately. But there are some things you **do** know.

There is a square in the diagram, so you can put in some right angles.

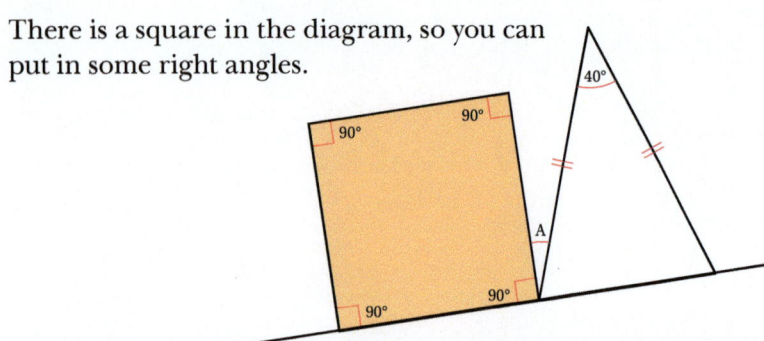

Some of these might not be helpful, but as there are only a few angles on the diagram, you are already narrowing down the problem.

You also know the triangle is isosceles. That means the base angles are equal and you can make an equation to work out the size of the unknown angles.

Let each base angle be x.

$2x + 40 = 180$ (angle sum of triangle)

$\therefore 2x = 140$

$\therefore x = 70$

Now mark those angles on the diagram.

> **Tip**
>
> Remember angles on a straight line add up to 180°.

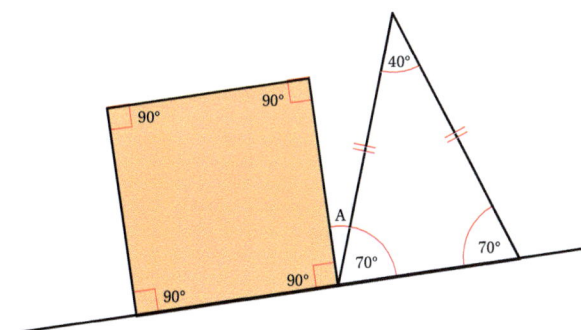

Now you can find A using angles on a line.

$A + 90 + 70 = 180$ (angle on a line)

$A = 180 - 160$

$A = 20°$

Look back at the steps in the example.

In this case, you will see that we have used all of the information provided in the question.

In this diagram a square (*you used the fact that angles in a square are 90°*) **and an isosceles triangle** (*you used the facts that base angles in an isosceles triangle are equal and that angles in a triangle add up to 180°*) **are drawn on a straight line** (*you used the fact that angles on a straight line add up to 180°*). **Work out the size of angle A.** (*You've done that*).

The key points are: start with the diagram, work out the things you can, and then write this new information on the diagram.

> **Problem 2.2:** This diagram consists of a square with four semicircles drawn inside.
>
> What fraction of the square is shaded?
>
>

Cambridge IGCSE Mathematics Extended Problem-solving Book

You don't have a formula for finding the shaded area and you aren't given any measurements so you will need to use letters (variables).

You do know that the sides of the square form the diameter of the semicircles.

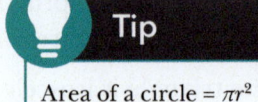

Tip

Area of a circle = πr^2

So, consider one semicircle to start with.

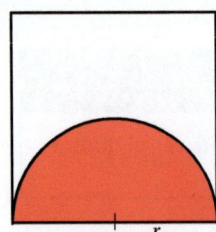

Call the radius of the circle r. The area of the semicircle is $\frac{1}{2}\pi r^2$.

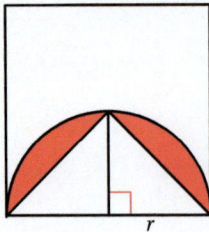

You don't need the area of the entire semicircle. You can draw the diagonals of the square to make half of each 'petal'.

If you subtract the area of the triangle formed inside the semicircle you can find the area of one of the petals.

Area of the triangle = $\frac{1}{2}bh$

$$= \frac{1}{2}(2r)(r)$$

$$= r^2$$

That means the area of one petal is $\left(\frac{1}{2}\pi r^2 - r^2\right)$.

The fraction of the original diagram (which is a square of side $2r$) that is shaded is $\dfrac{4(\frac{1}{2}\pi r^2 - r^2)}{(2r)^2}$.

The numerator can be factorised to give $\dfrac{4r^2(\frac{1}{2}\pi - 1)}{4r^2}$ which is $\frac{1}{2}\pi - 1$.

You can check this is sensible because you know it must be between 0 and 1.

$\frac{1}{2}\pi - 1 \approx 0.57$

So, by starting with something you can work out (the area of a semi-circle), you have solved the problem.

The following problems may be solved using more than one method; however, the worked solutions provided at the back of this book are based on the method introduced above.

Without using a calculator, decide whether the statement below is true or false.

 $10\sqrt{70} < 80$

Explain your answer.

a Find a formula in terms of *x* for the area of the shape shown below.

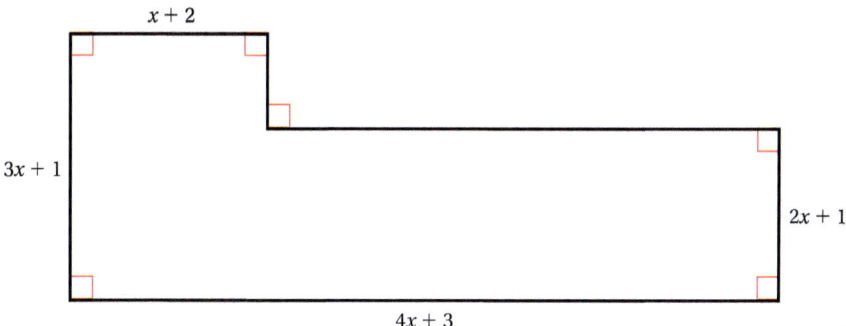

The actual length of the side labelled $(3x + 1)$ is 16 metres.

b What is the area of the shape? Give your answer in square metres.

The shape is the plan of a field. The farmer wants to put a fence around the field.

He intends to put three lengths of wire between wooden posts around the field, as shown in the diagram.

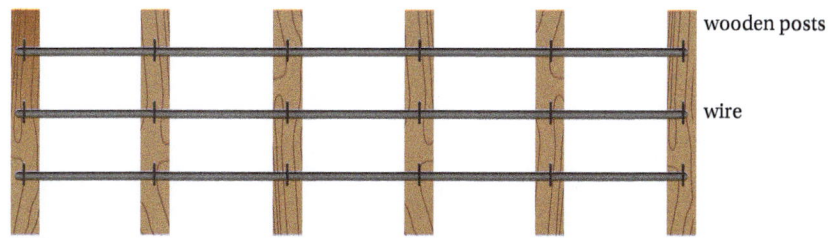

The wooden posts will be placed one metre apart.

c How many wooden posts will the farmer need in total?

d What length of wire will the farmer require for three lengths, as shown in the diagram?

Posts cost $18.50 each and wire is sold for $2.30 per metre.

e How much is it going to cost the farmer to fence the field?

Abassi paid $2.90 for three mangoes and two pawpaws at the market.

Oban paid $5.50 for five mangoes and four pawpaws at the same market.

What is the price of a mango and the price of a pawpaw?

Cambridge IGCSE Mathematics Extended Problem-solving Book

The maximum safe load of Jabu's van is 840 kg, correct to the nearest 10 kg.

Jabu is going to transport large stone slabs for his next garden project.

The slabs each weigh 16 kg correct to the nearest kg.

Jabu doesn't want to risk damaging his van.

What is the maximum number of slabs Jabu can safely transport in one trip in his van?

Sandra wants to make a triangular prism (as shown in diagram on the right):

She draws the diagram below, cuts it out, folds it up and tapes it together.

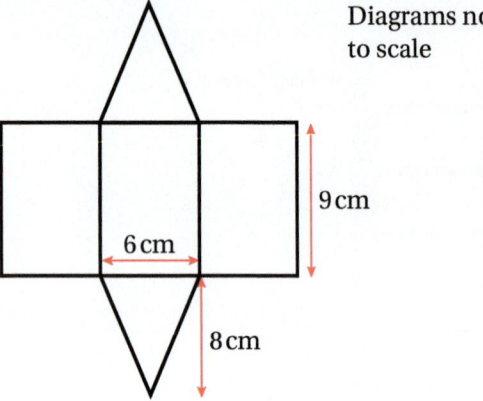

Diagrams not to scale

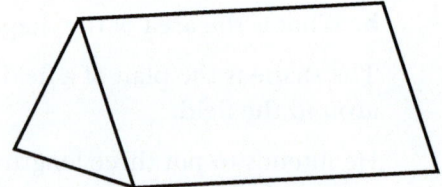

a What is the volume of the triangular prism?

b Kristof makes a different prism (as shown in diagram on the right):

The pentagonal faces each have an area of 36 cm².

The volume of Kristof's prism is the same as the volume of Sandra's prism.

Calculate the length of this prism.

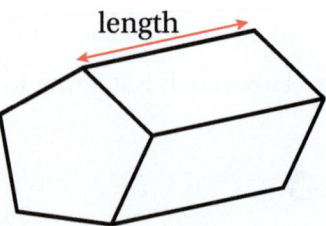

Jeff takes a full 500 ml bottle of water and pours himself a drink into the glass shown to the right. He fills the glass to 2 cm below the top.

How much water is left in the bottle?

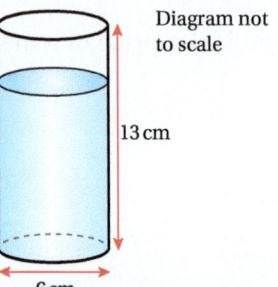

Diagram not to scale

Mrs Nelson and Miss Choudhury are writing tests for maths classes.

Each test will have 32 questions split in the ratio of 3 : 5 for non-calculator to calculator questions.

There will eventually be 15 tests.

Miss Choudhury will write all of the non-calculator questions for the 15 tests and some of the calculator questions so she and Mrs Nelson will each write the same number of questions.

a How many non-calculator questions will each test contain?

b How many calculator questions must be written in total?

c What fraction of the total questions written by Miss Choudhury will be calculator questions?

A bag contains green, yellow and white balls. The probability of picking a green ball out of the bag is 0.64. The probability of picking a white ball is the same as the probability of picking a yellow ball.

a What is the probability of picking out a white ball?

b If there are nine yellow balls, what is the total number of balls in the bag?

Mie, Sue, Frances and Anisha are all running in a 5 km sponsored road race.

The probability of each of them finishing first out of the four of them is shown in the table below:

Mie	0.23
Sue	0.46
Frances	0.15
Anisha	x

What is the probability that either Sue or Anisha finishes first?

The mean of five numbers is 12. The numbers are in the ratio 1 : 1 : 3 : 4 : 6.

Find the largest number.

Cambridge IGCSE Mathematics Extended Problem-solving Book

A maths teacher has a dice but doesn't know whether it is biased or not. 20 students each throw the dice 10 times. The number of times each student rolls a six is shown below.

Is the dice biased? Explain your ideas.

Student	Number of sixes in 10 rolls	Student	Number of sixes in 10 rolls
A	7	K	4
B	4	L	5
C	3	M	6
D	6	N	4
E	4	O	5
F	3	P	7
G	4	Q	0
H	5	R	3
I	5	S	3
J	3	T	2

The area of the rectangle is the same as the area of the square. All measurements are given in cm.

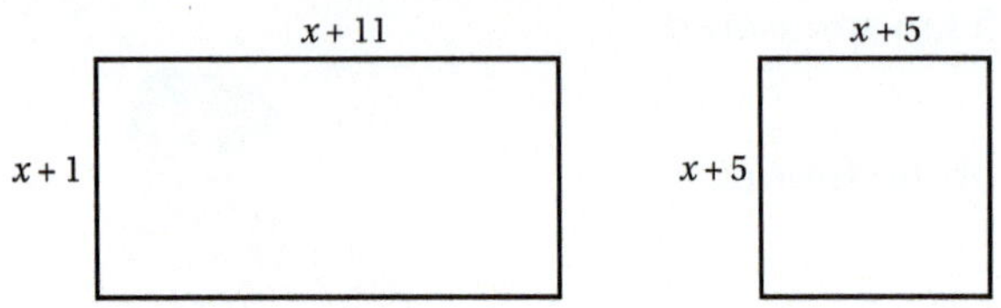

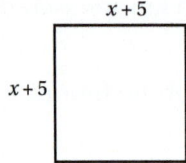

$x + 11$

$x + 1$

$x + 5$

$x + 5$

Diagrams not to scale

How many centimetre squares are needed to cover the rectangle?

A shape is formed by cutting a square from the corner of a larger square, as shown in the diagram.

a Write an expression for the blue area.

b If the area of the blue shape is 1944 cm², find the perimeter of the blue shape.

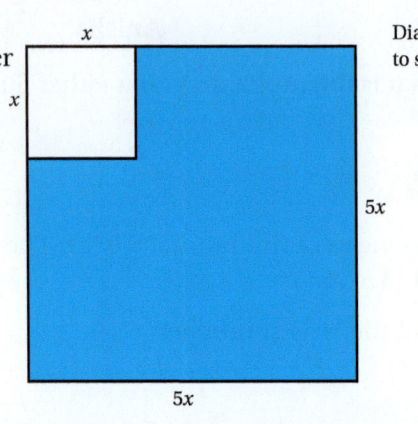

Diagram not to scale

x

x

$5x$

$5x$

Farieda is planning to make a patchwork quilt for her niece. She has decided to include the flower pattern shown below as part of her design. The centre piece of this flower is a regular hexagon.

Tip

What do you know about a regular hexagon? What angles can you work out? What about a regular pentagon?

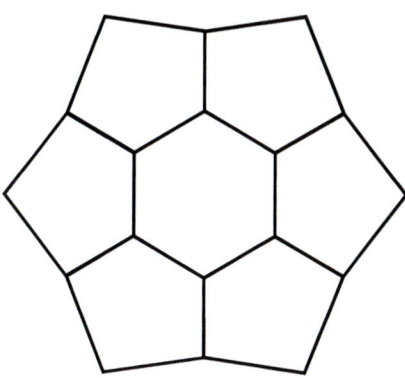

a Show that Farieda cannot produce this pattern by using regular pentagons.

b She still wants to use a regular hexagon for the centre piece. Are there any regular polygons that she could put around the edge to form the petals?

c If she wanted to use regular pentagons for the petals, which regular polygon would she need in the centre?

Jenny makes a kite. She starts with a square piece of paper, like this.

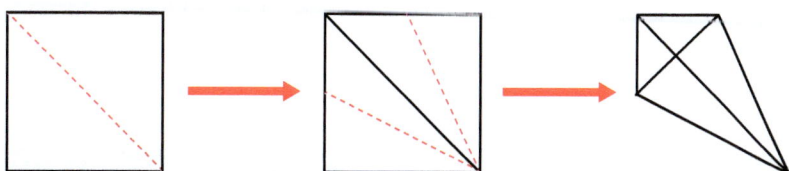

Jenny makes more kites and puts them together around a point. The start of this pattern is shown in the diagram. How many kites does she need altogether so they fit together without any gaps?

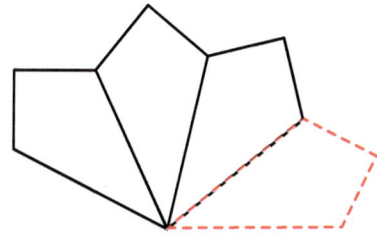

Cambridge IGCSE Mathematics Extended Problem-solving Book

16 ⭐⭐☆

$\frac{4}{5}$ of the rectangle on the right is shaded.

a How many extra square units must be shaded to increase this fraction to $\frac{5}{6}$?

The $\frac{4}{5}$-shaded rectangle is put next to a congruent rectangle that is $\frac{2}{3}$ shaded.

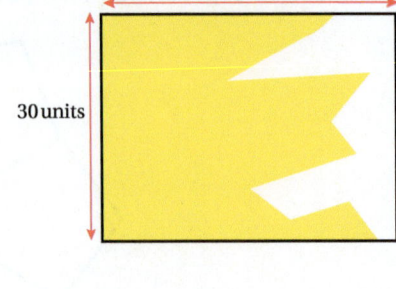

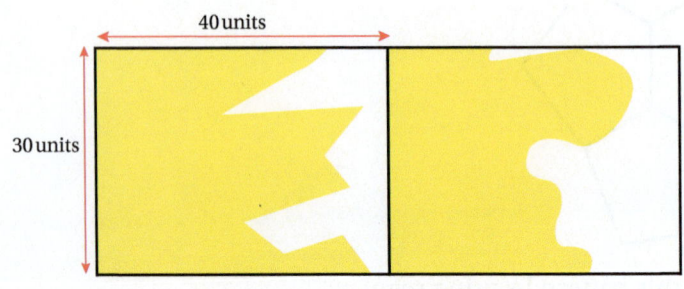

b What fraction of the resulting large rectangle is shaded?

c How many square units need to be shaded to increase the fraction so that exactly $\frac{3}{4}$ of the large rectangle is shaded?

Tip

You could draw a diagram showing the shading in a 'neater' way.

17 ⭐⭐☆

A young boy uses his calculator to work out $6 \div 0.5$ and is surprised that he gets such a big answer. He tries $6 \div 0$ and doesn't understand why it won't tell him the answer.

How could you explain the answers to this boy?

Tip

Think about how you might do this in a way that someone younger than you would understand. Remember, you have to be clear enough to change their mind!

18 ⭐⭐☆

An average-sized roll of toilet paper is 10.5 cm wide and has a diameter of 12 cm. The hole in the centre has a diameter of 5 cm.

A good-quality paper has thickness 0.5 mm and each sheet is 10 cm long.

A company advertise their toilet rolls as the best on the market, with each roll containing at least 200 good-quality sheets.

Is their claim true?

Tip

What can you work out? Can you find the volume of a sheet of toilet paper? What about the volume of the toilet roll?

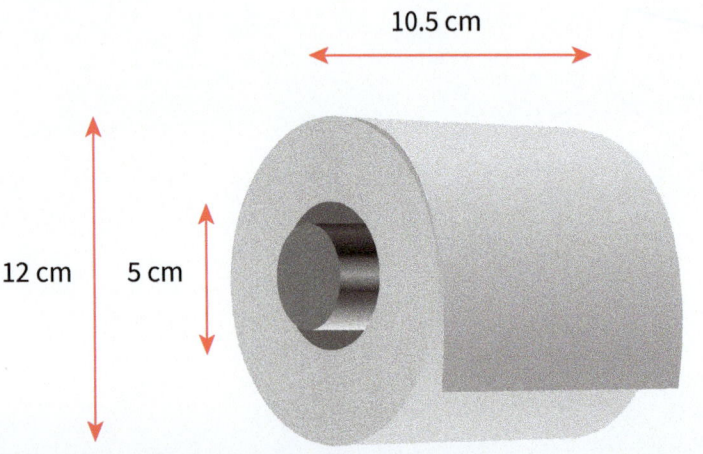

Patience says: "I think tan θ is equal to sin θ ÷ cos θ."

Using the values in the table below to justify your response, decide whether Patience is correct.

θ	sin θ	cos θ	tan θ
0°	0	1	
30°	$\frac{1}{2}$	$\frac{\sqrt{3}}{2}$	
45°	$\frac{\sqrt{2}}{2}$	$\frac{\sqrt{2}}{2}$	
60°	$\frac{\sqrt{3}}{2}$	$\frac{1}{2}$	
90°	1	0	

In the diagram, AC is a diameter of the circle and AD = BC.

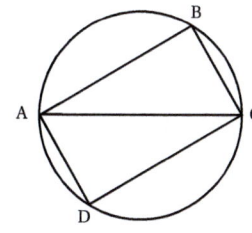

 Tip

What do you know about the triangles? Consider how knowing about congruent triangles might help you with this question.

Show that quadrilateral ABCD is a rectangle.

A trapezium is inscribed in a circle with centre O. ∠BOC is 50° and ∠AOB is 75°.

a Calculate the size of ∠COD.

b What does this tell you about trapezium ABCD?

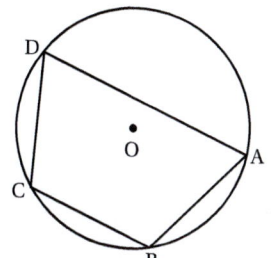

Diagram not to scale

 **Tip**

Draw a clear diagram and write on it the information you are given.
a What is special about the angles?
b What other angles can you calculate?

 Tip

What are the properties of a trapezium? How could you use these to help you to answer this question?

Cambridge IGCSE Mathematics Extended Problem-solving Book

22 Nadine has kept woodlice in the Biology lab for a year. They have survived well in their plastic habitat, but Nadine knows that she should only keep approximately 150 woodlice in a habitat of that size. She thinks it's getting close to the time when she should let some of the woodlice go free, so she decides to count them by using a capture-mark-release counting method.

Nadine catches 16 woodlice and marks each one with a dot. She then places them back in their habitat. Two days later Nadine catches 16 woodlice again and discovers she has recaptured two with dots.

Based on the information given, does she need to set any free?

Tip
You can't immediately solve the problem, but you do know what fraction of woodlice have a dot: $\frac{2}{16}$ $(=\frac{1}{8})$. So each time Nadine catches 16 woodlice, she gets about $\frac{1}{8}$ of all the woodlice.

23 Five equilateral triangles are drawn on the edges of a regular pentagon.

Show that the polygon created by joining points F, G, H, I and J is also a regular pentagon.

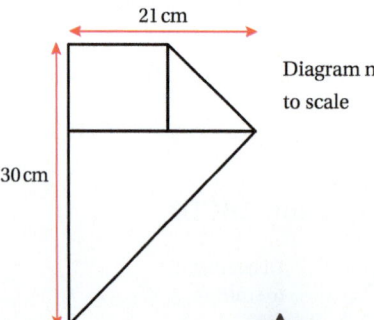

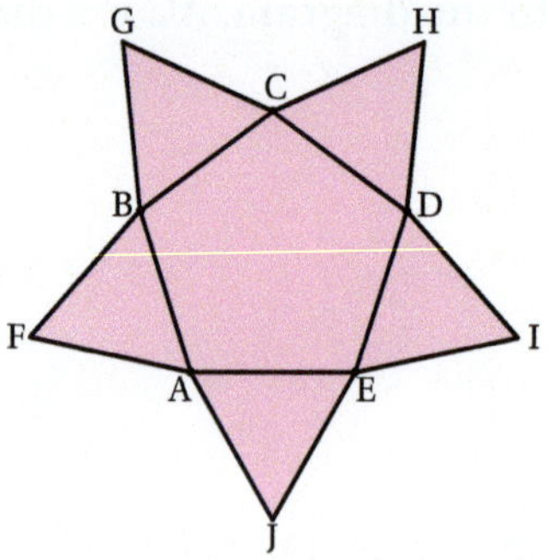

24 Jo creates a quadrilateral by folding a rectangular piece of paper as shown in the diagram below.

a What is the area of the quadrilateral?

b What fraction of the original rectangle does the quadrilateral represent?

21 cm, 30 cm, Diagram not to scale

Tip
For part **b** you could give your answer as a fraction, decimal or percentage. If you choose to use a fraction, make sure you give it in its simplest form.

25 Saskia wants to make a medieval-style hat for a school play. She will buy a sheet of black card, big enough for her to be able to make the whole hat from a single piece of card.

The hat will be conical in shape with a radius of 9 cm and slant height of 36 cm.

What size card must Saskia buy?

Tip
What shape will the net of the hat be? Think about how this could help you.

Chapter 2: Work back from what you know

26 ★★★

Tomato soup contains 59 kcalories per 100 ml. Martin has decided to use a smaller bowl to help him reduce his portion sizes. The images show Martin's original bowl and the smaller bowl he will now use. Martin always fills his bowl as close to the brim as possible.

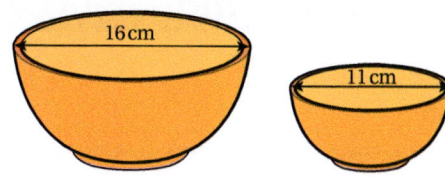

Assuming the two bowls are perfect hemispheres, how many kcalories will he save by eating tomato soup from the smaller bowl? Give your answer to the nearest kcalorie.

27 ★★★

Many astronomical distances are measured in light years. A light year is the distance that light travels in a vacuum in one year.

Light travels at approximately 2.99×10^5 km/sec.

The distance to Proxima Centauri is approximately 4.22 light years.

How many laps of a standard 400 m running track is this equivalent to?

Tip

What can you work out? How far does light travel in a minute/hour/year?

28 ★★★

Look at the two triangles drawn on this coordinate grid.

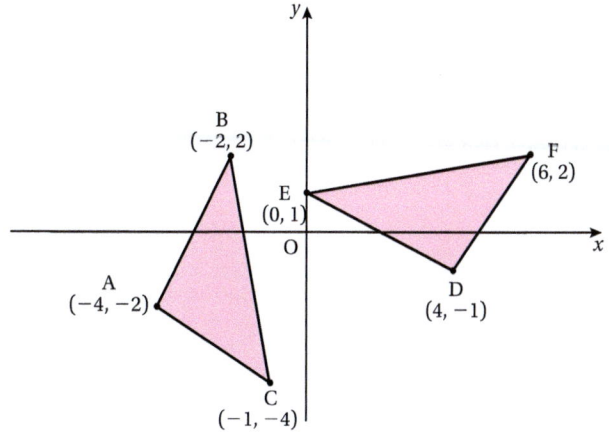

Show that the two triangles are congruent.

Tip

You can't say straight away if they are congruent, but you can calculate the lengths of some sides. Remember to refer to the conditions for congruence.

29 ★★★

The hare and the tortoise are having a race. The hare is confident and offers the tortoise a shortcut across the middle of the field.

If the tortoise totters along at 0.1 m/s, what is the lowest speed the hare could run and still win the race?

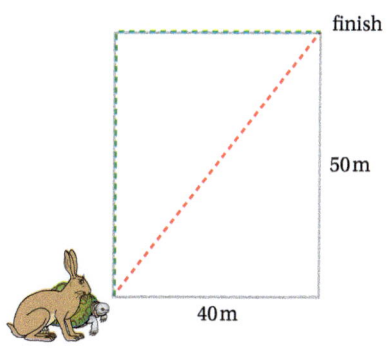

Chapter 3
Change your point of view

Sometimes the best way to solve a problem is to change your point of view. In other words, change how you see the problem. For example, you could change fractions to decimals to work with them or you could rewrite terms and factorise expressions to see them in a different way.

Many of the problems you solve in geometry, graphs and measurement topics will involve diagrams. You can add information, including useful lines to these diagrams to help you see the problem from a different point of view.

Some mathematically useful lines are:

- lines parallel to given lines
- perpendiculars, including bisectors
- axes of symmetry (mirror lines)
- lines that join two or more points
- radii and diameters
- loci.

Deciding which type of line or information is going to be useful will depend on the context of the problem as well as what you know about the properties of the lines. Practice and experience will allow you to make choices that lead towards solutions.

Consider the problem below.

In the diagram, two parallel lines are shown. Work out the size of angle a.

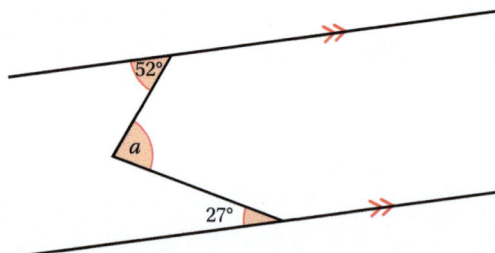

There are different ways of viewing this problem. Here are three options, all of which involve adding extra lines to the given diagram to help you to see the problem in a different way.

Option 1

Add a line that is parallel to the other two lines and that passes through the angle you want to work out:

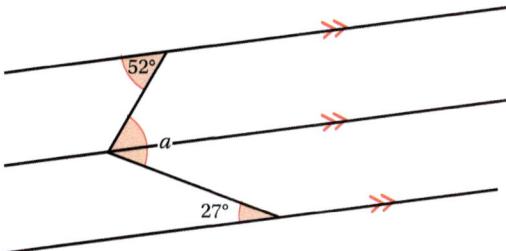

This changes how you view the problem - now you can see how to solve it using alternate angles.

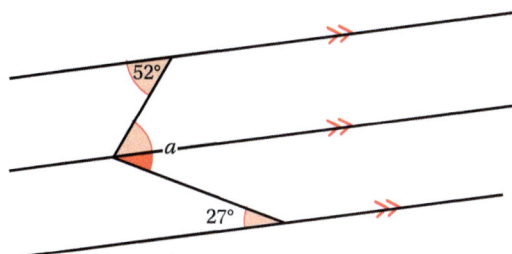

The angle shown in red is equal to 27° because it is alternate to the 27° angle. Similarly, the other part of angle a is 52° because it is alternate to the 52° angle.

So angle $a = 27 + 52 = 79°$

Option 2

Add a line that is perpendicular to the parallel lines and that passes through the vertex of angle a, as shown below.

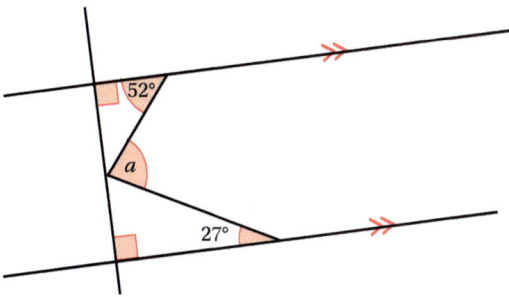

You now have two right-angled triangles and you can view this as an 'angle sum of triangles' problem. Once you've found the missing angles in each triangle, you can use angles on a line to find a.

Cambridge IGCSE Mathematics Extended Problem-solving Book

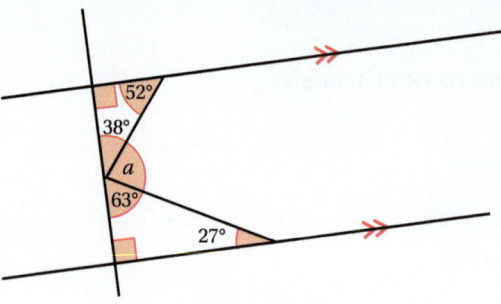

$a + 38 + 63 = 180$

$a = 79°$

Option 3

Add a line that is perpendicular to the parallel lines and that passes through the vertex of the 27° angle as shown in the diagram here.

> **Tip**
> You might need to try out several ideas before one works!

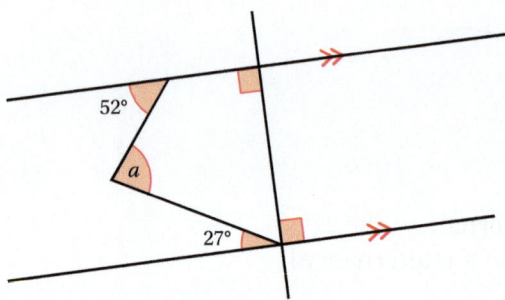

You can now see a quadrilateral in the diagram. You can also 'see' what to do to solve the problem, because you can work out three of the angles in the quadrilateral and you know that all of the angles add up to 360°.

There are lots of different lines you could have drawn on this diagram that wouldn't have helped you find a solution. For example, this line in the below diagram to change how you see the problem doesn't do anything special and is not helpful.

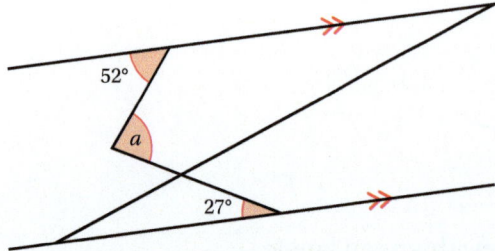

The following problems may be solved using more than one method; however, the worked solutions provided at the back of this book are based on the method of changing how you view the problem introduced above.

Chapter 3: Change your point of view

1 ★☆☆

The perimeter of the shape shown is 2.28 km.

Calculate the value of *a*. Give your answer in kilometres (km).

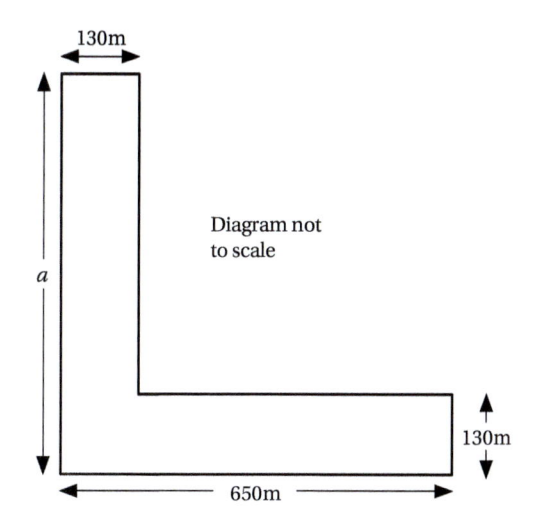

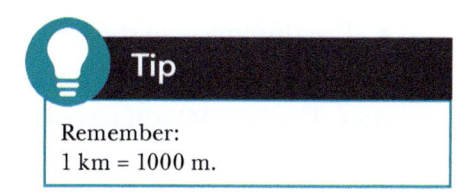

130m

Diagram not to scale

a

130m

650m

Tip

Remember:
1 km = 1000 m.

2 ★☆☆

Marco is designing a template for an art project. He plans to cut a regular octagon in half through two vertices and place them side by side, as shown.

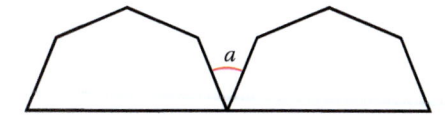

a

Marco is trying to calculate the size of the angle labelled *a*.

Show two ways in which he could do this.

3 ★☆☆

Mandeep is investigating patterns in circles. He draws eight dots equally spaced around a circle.

He draws a triangle by connecting three of the dots. The line AC passes through the centre of the circle, O.

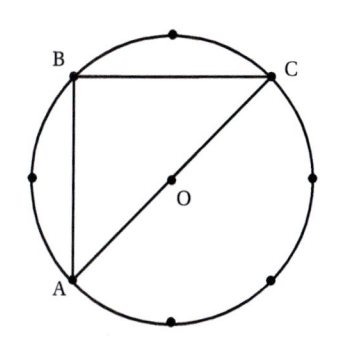

B
C
O
A

Diagrams not to scale

Tip

Drawing extra lines on the diagrams can help you to answer questions like this. Think carefully about which line to draw.

a Use this image to show that ∠ABC is a right angle.

He draws another triangle by connecting a different set of three dots. The line AC still passes through the centre of the circle.

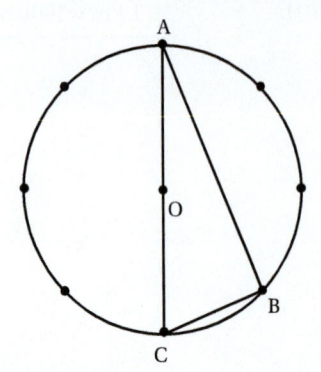

b Is ∠ABC a right angle?

Mandeep draws a different circle and marks ten dots equally spaced around its circumference. Once again, he draws a triangle by connecting three of these dots. The line AC passes through the centre of the circle.

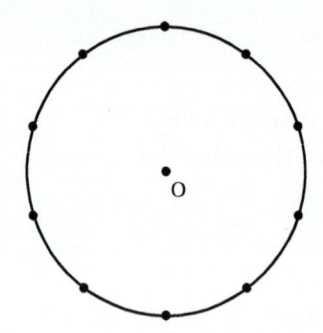

c Show that for a triangle of your choice that meets these conditions, the sum of ∠BAC and ∠BCA is 90°.

Students taking part in a mathematical challenge are shown this image.

They are asked the question: "What proportion of the outer (large) triangle is coloured purple?"

After some thought, the teams hand in their answers. Four of these answers are shown below:

Team A: 24 cm²

Team B: $\frac{3}{4}$

Team C: $\left(\frac{3}{4}\right)^2$

Team D: 0.5625

The question is marked out of 4 marks. How many marks would you award each team?

Justify your decisions.

5

Gerry has a swimming pool at his home. He needs to put a fence around the pool for safety reasons.

He wants the fence to surround the pool completely, at a distance of 1 m from the edge.

a Calculate the length of fencing that Gerry will need to buy. Give your answer correct to 3 s.f. (significant figures).

Arjun also needs to build a fence around his pool, but it is a different shape from Gerry's. Arjun would like to build his fence 1.5 m from the edge of the pool.

b Will Arjun need to buy more fencing than Gerry? Explain your answer.

6

Show how this shape could be divided into:

a three congruent shapes

b four congruent shapes.

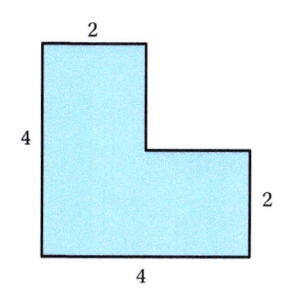

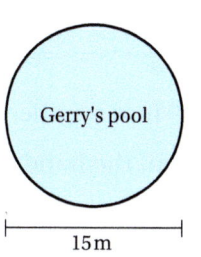

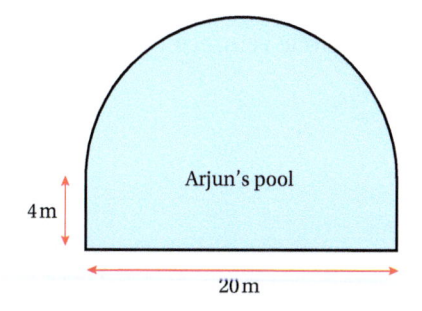

> **Tip**
>
> Make several copies of the diagram and try out your ideas.

7 ★☆☆

Charlie's house has two floors connected by a staircase. The vertical distance between the two floors is 3.6 m. Each step in the staircase is 18 cm high and 28 cm deep.

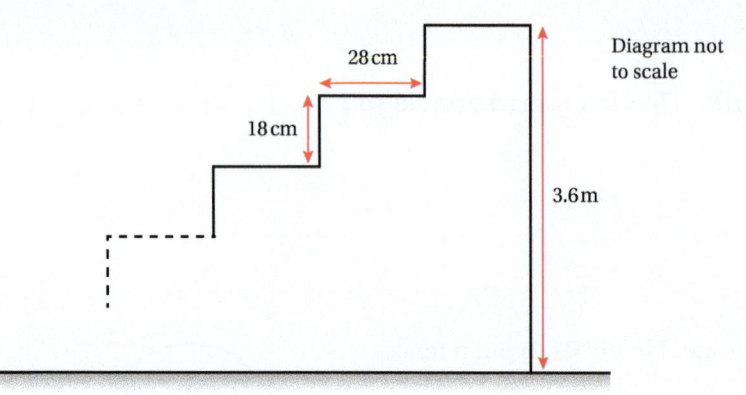

Diagram not to scale

a How many steps are there in the staircase?

b How long will the hand rail be?

8 ★★☆

A circle is inscribed in a triangle as shown below. What is the value of x?

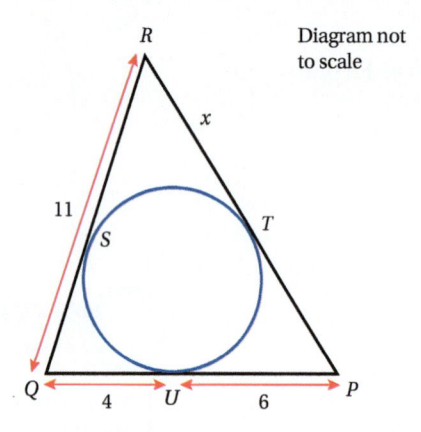

> **Tip**
>
> Join the centre of the circle to the three points of contact with the tangents.

9 ★★★

A rectangular tabletop has a perimeter of 12 m. The width of the table is x m.

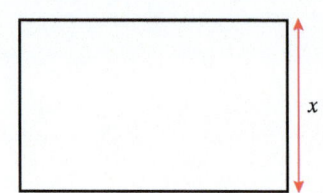

a Write an expression in terms of x for the area of the tabletop.

The area of the tabletop is 6.3 m².

b Would a tablecloth measuring 2.2 m by 3.1 m cover this tabletop?

10 ★☆☆

Lin looks up at the clock on her office wall. She is disappointed to see that it is not yet five o'clock, which is the time she can go home.

Tip

Remember that on an analogue clock, the hour hand and the minute hand both move continuously. What angle does each hand turn through in one hour?

a Through how many degrees must the clock's minute hand turn before Lin can leave work?

b Through what angle must the hour hand turn before Lin can leave work?

11 ★★☆

The graphs of two quadratics are shown below.

The blue parabola is symmetrical about the line $x = 2$ and has roots at A and B.

The blue parabola has been reflected in the x-axis to create the red parabola. The red parabola has roots at C and D.

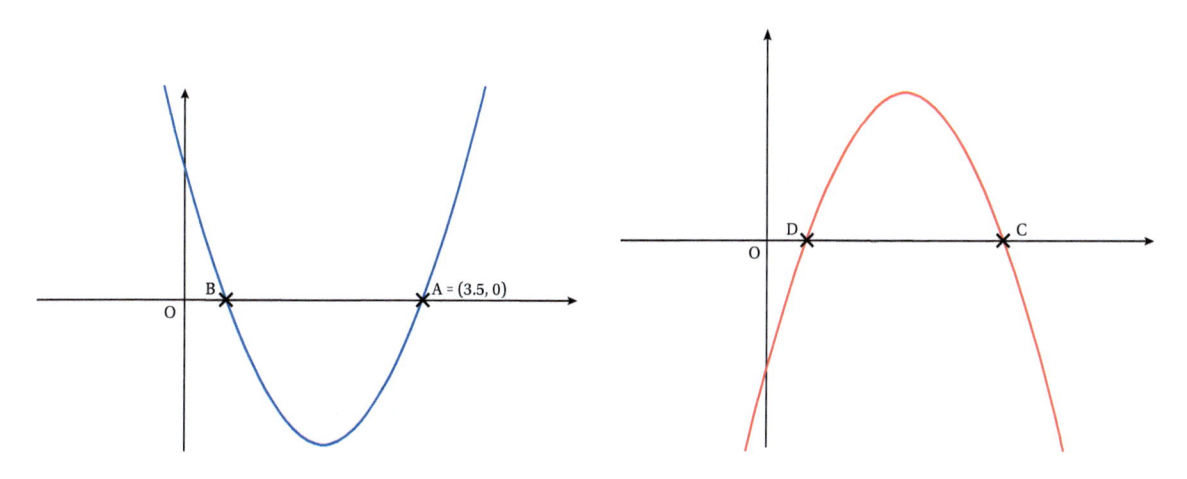

Work out the coordinates of points B, C and D.

12 ★★★

As shown in the diagram,

$\overrightarrow{SW} = 3\mathbf{v}$, $\overrightarrow{ST} = 2\mathbf{u}$

$\overrightarrow{SR} = -\dfrac{1}{2}\mathbf{u}$, $\overrightarrow{SX} = -2\mathbf{v}$

$\overrightarrow{SP}$ is the diagonal of parallelogram SWPT and $\overrightarrow{SZ}$ is the diagonal of parallelogram SRZX.

Are Z, S and P collinear?

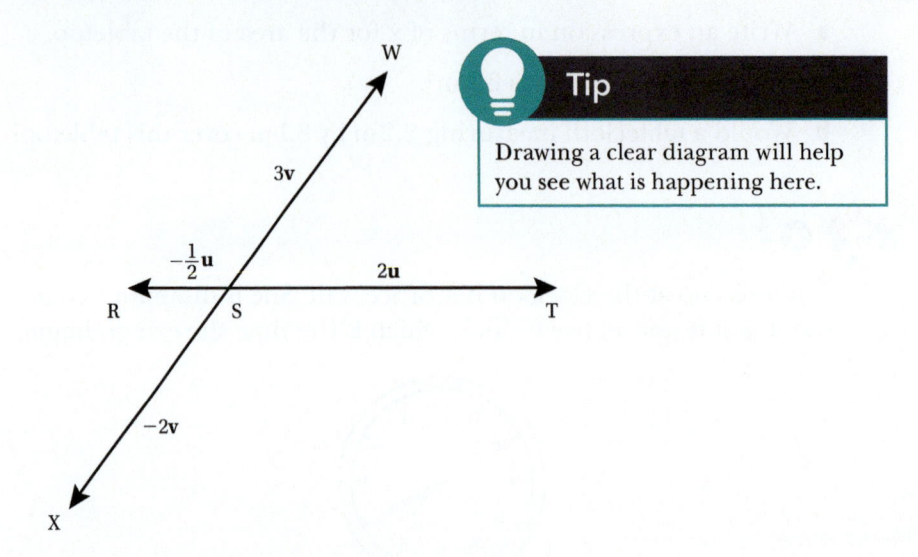

Tip

Drawing a clear diagram will help you see what is happening here.

13 ★★★

A large paperclip is placed against a ruler as shown below. The curved ends are semicircles.

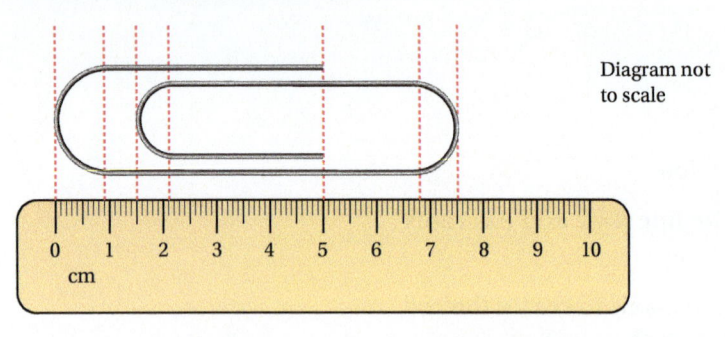

Diagram not to scale

a Calculate the length of wire needed to make this paperclip. Give your answer correct to 1 d.p. (decimal point).

A second paperclip is placed against the ruler.

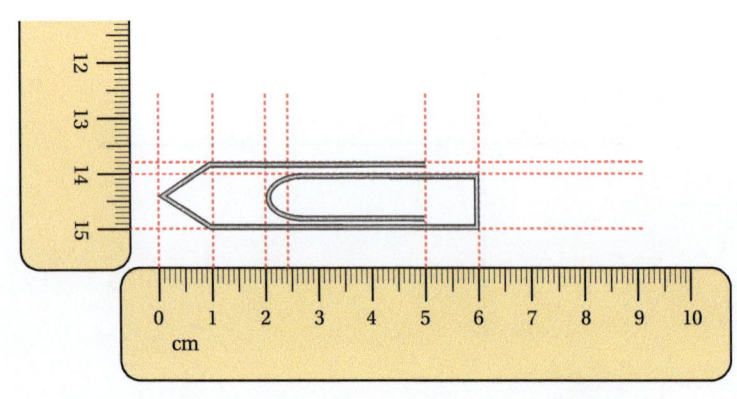

b Which paperclip uses the greater length of wire?

Tip

You might need to use Pythagoras' theorem in this question.

14 ★★☆

In an isosceles triangle the lengths of the sides are given as $(2x-1)$ cm and $(2x-4)$ cm.

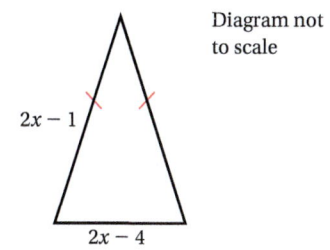

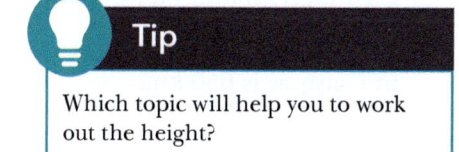

Diagram not to scale

$2x-1$

$2x-4$

> **Tip**
>
> Which topic will help you to work out the height?

a Work out an algebraic expression for the perpendicular height of this triangle.

b If the perpendicular height of the triangle is 12 cm, find the area of the triangle.

15 ★★☆

Students on a field trip are told they can use a clever trick to estimate the height of a tall tree. They are told to point their arm at an angle of approximately 45° and to look along it. They then walk backwards until their arm is pointing to the top of the tree.

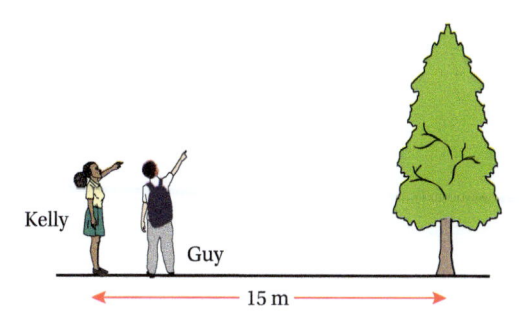

Kelly

Guy

15 m

The distance from the student to the tree trunk is then approximately the same as the height of the tree, plus the student's own height.

a Explain why this method gives a rough answer.

Two students, Kelly and Guy, (who are the same height) try this out. Guy ends up standing 3 m in front of Kelly.

b If Kelly's angle is exactly 45°, at what angle must Guy be holding his arm?

Keisha is travelling from London to Glasgow to attend university. There are two options for getting to Glasgow.

She can travel by bus direct from London to Glasgow. Alternatively, she can travel by train to Glasgow. She will have to change trains in Birmingham and wait one hour 45 minutes for the second train.

The distance from Victoria station in London to Buchanan Station in Glasgow is 650 km.

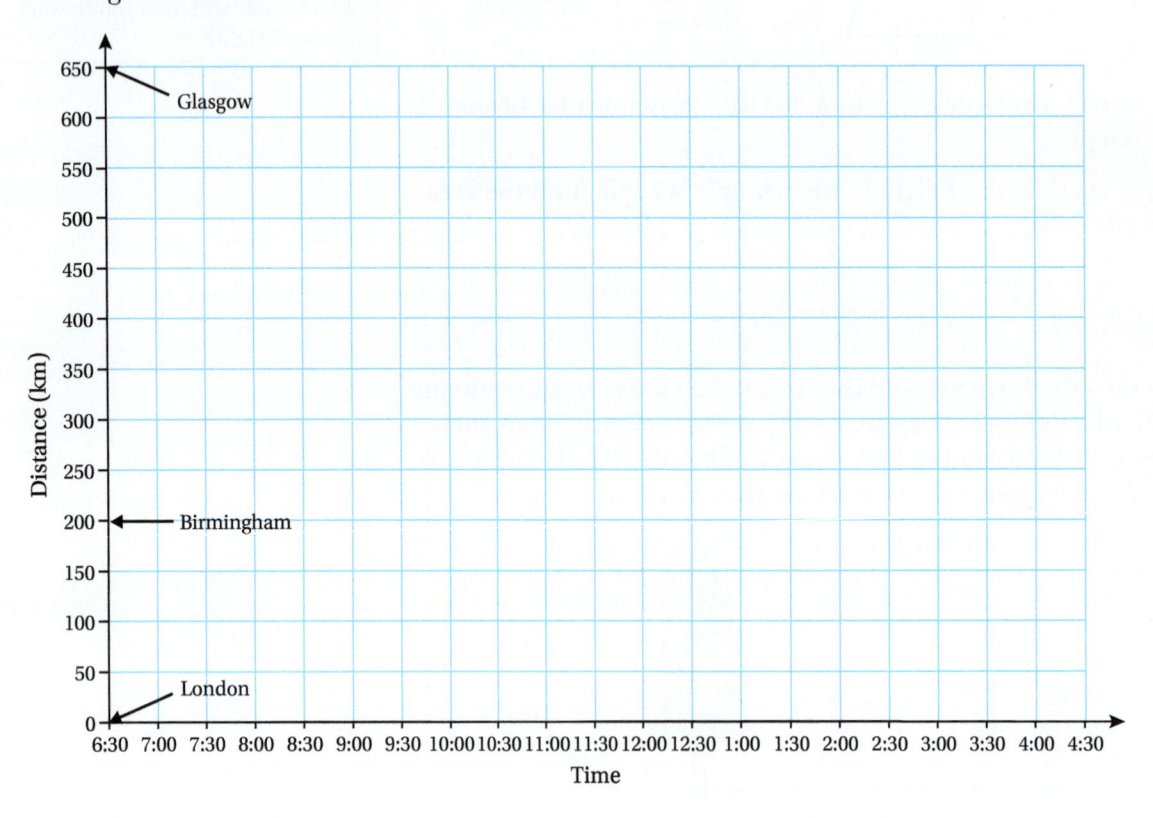

The bus leaves at 6.30 am and takes exactly eight hours to arrive in Glasgow.

If Keisha goes by train, she would leave Victoria station at 7 am and arrive in Birmingham at 8.40 am.

The train journey from Birmingham to Glasgow should then take four hours and 15 minutes.

a What is the average speed for the bus journey?

b What is the average speed for the train journey?

17 ★★★

Six cylindrical candles are held together in a plastic sleeve in the formation shown. Each candle has a radius of 2.7 cm.

Calculate the length of plastic needed to hold the candles tightly. Give your answer correct to 2 d.p.

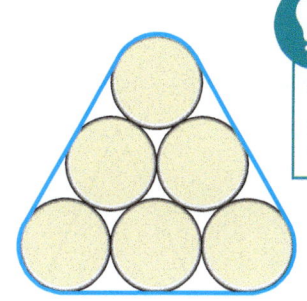

Tip

Think about the plastic being wrapped around just one candle. What about two candles?

18 ★★★

The circle has radius 5 and is centred on the origin. The point (3, 4) lies on the circle.

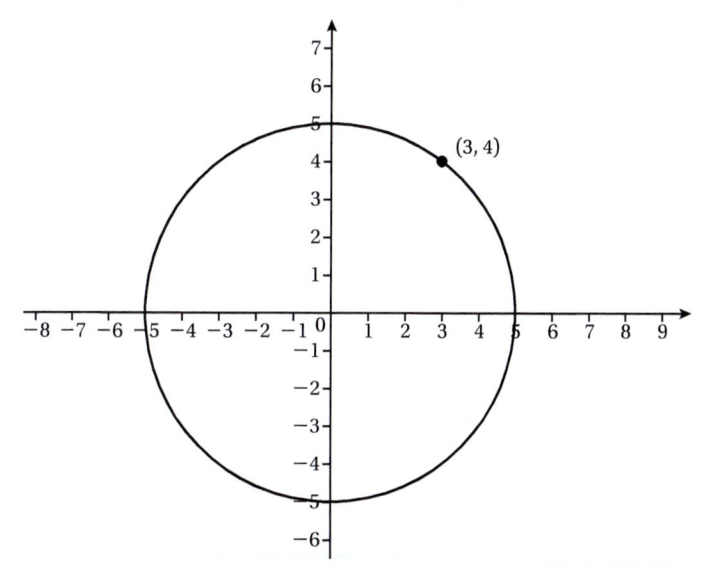

a Find the equation of the tangent to the circle at this point.

b Use your answer to part **a** to write down the equation of another tangent to the circle.

19 ★★★

ABCDEF is a regular hexagon.

A has coordinates (2, 1).

The column vector for $\overrightarrow{AB} = \begin{pmatrix} 0 \\ 2 \end{pmatrix}$

a What is the column vector for $\overrightarrow{DE}$

b Find the coordinates of C.

c What is the column vector for $\overrightarrow{BC}$

d What is the column vector for $\overrightarrow{FC}$

e What is the column vector for $\overrightarrow{AE}$

f What is the column vector for $\overrightarrow{AC}$

g What is the column vector for $\overrightarrow{EF}$

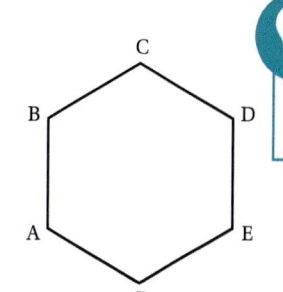

Tip

Some of your answers will involve surds.

20 ★★★

Two triangles are shown below.

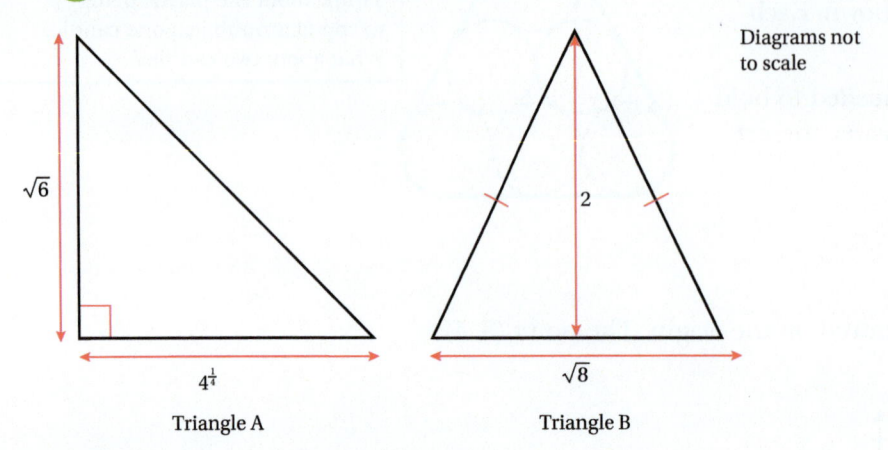

Diagrams not to scale

Triangle A: right triangle with vertical side $\sqrt{6}$ and horizontal side $4\frac{1}{4}$.

Triangle B: isosceles triangle with height 2 and base $\sqrt{8}$.

Without using a calculator, explain which triangle has:

a the greater perimeter

b the greater area.

21 ★★★

A square is inscribed inside a circle of radius 1 cm as shown below.

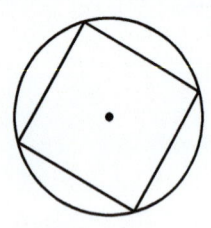

a Calculate the area of the square.

An equilateral triangle is inscribed in a circle.

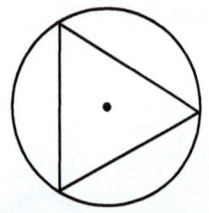

b Show that the ratio of the area of the triangle to the area of the square in part **a**, is approximately $2:3$.

A regular pentagon is inscribed in a circle.

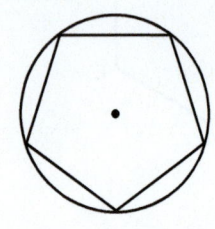

c Show that the area of the pentagon is approximately $\frac{6}{5}$ the area of the square in part **a**.

Chapter 3: Change your point of view

22 ✪✪✪

Two straight lines are drawn from a point A outside a circle to two points, B and C, on the circumference of the circle. The lengths of the four arcs created are marked in the diagram in terms of x.

Calculate the size of ∠BAC.

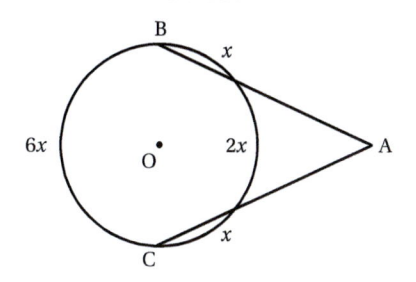

Diagram not to scale

Tip

Are there any useful lines that you can draw to make this problem look more 'friendly'?
Why have you been told the arc lengths? What does this have to do with angles in the circle?

23 ✪✪✪

A line joins the points A(2, 2) and B(5, 6). Find the shortest distance of the point C(3, 6) from the line AB. Give your answer as an exact fraction.

Tip

Questions that combine coordinates with distances use triangles. Draw a diagram and think about which triangles might be useful.

24 ✪✪✪

The diagram shows a triangular prism ABCDEF.

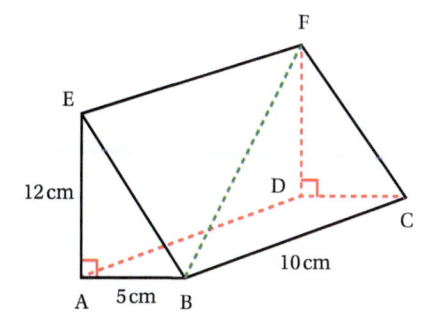

The base of the prism ABCD is a rectangle with AB = 5 cm and BC = 10 cm. The cross-section of the prism is a right-angled triangle with base AB and height AE = 12 cm. Calculate the angle that the line BF makes with the plane ABCD. Give your answer to 1 decimal place.

Tip

When dealing with trigonometry in three dimensions you must always decide which lines are perpendicular to which other lines and planes. Draw right-angled triangles in separate diagrams to help you.

25 ✪✪✪

In the quadrilateral ABCD, AB = 18 cm and CD = 16 cm. Angle ABC = 90°, angle ADC = 80° and angle BAC = 40°.

Calculate angle ACD giving your answer to 1 decimal place.

Tip

This question uses techniques from all of chapters 1–3. You must draw a diagram and be prepared to calculate things that you have not been asked for. To do this you need to add a line that has not been mentioned in the question.

Chapter 4
Simplify the problem

When you are faced with a difficult or very complicated problem it is useful to begin by solving a simpler (but similar) problem. Solving the simpler problem won't give you the answer, but it will allow you to find a method that you can apply to solve the more complicated problem.

There are different ways of simplifying problems. One method involves replacing clumsy or large numbers from the original problem with rounded or smaller numbers to make calculation easier.

Solving a series of simpler versions of the problem might lead you to a pattern that you can apply to solve the original problem. It is easier to find patterns if you work systematically and make lists or tables to keep track of your results.

Simplifying the problem is also useful for complicated shape and space problems as it allows you to break down a spatial problem into smaller components and use the pattern established to solve the more complex problem.

You might have seen problems like the first one below that involve finding the number of overlapping squares.

Problem 4.1: How many squares are there in this diagram?

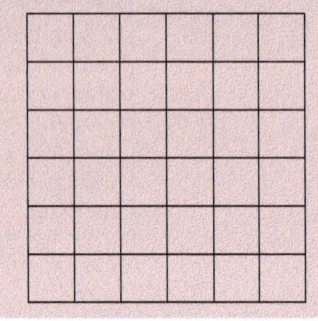

Simplifying this problem involves using smaller grids that allow you to find a pattern of consecutive square numbers that can be generalised to any similar problem.

1		2×2 unit square
4		1×1 unit squares

$1 + 4$ is a sum of consecutive square numbers.

$1^2 + 2^2$

1		3×3 unit square
4		2×2 unit squares
9		1×1 unit squares

1 + 4 + 9 is a sum of consecutive square numbers.

$1^2 + 2^2 + 3^2$

The largest number squared is equal to the number of units per side of the diagram.
So, if there are six units per side, the total number of squares is:

$1^2 + 2^2 + 3^2 + 4^2 + 5^2 + 6^2 = 91$ squares

> **Problem 4.2:** George climbs a flight of 10 stairs. He can go from one stair to the next one (1-step), or can miss out a stair and go up two at once (2-step). How many different ways can he go up the 10 stairs?

You could start by drawing a diagram using lines to show the movements from step to step, but you will quickly produce a picture that has too many lines on it.

You could also start to systematically list the different possibilities, using 1 to stand for '1-step' and 2 to stand for '2-step'.

So:

1111111111

1211212

22222

and so on.

But again, this gives too many possibilities and it is easy to repeat or miss out some options.

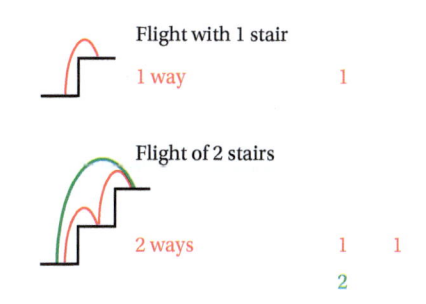

Try simplifying the problem. Start with the very simplest option. Imagine that George wants to climb a flight of stairs that has 1 stair in it. This is easy: 1 way (if he tries to do a 2-step he will only actually go up one step). Now try a flight with 2 stairs in it. There are two ways. The diagram shows the working.

You could now look at the pattern of answers to see if that will help, as shown in this table.

Flight with 1 stair

1 way   1

Flight of 2 stairs

2 ways   1   1
          2

Number of stairs	Number of ways of climbing them
1	1
2	2
3	3
4	5
5	8

> **Tip**
>
> The Fibonacci sequence is one of the number sequences you should know and recognise. Other useful sequences are square, cube and prime numbers.

Do you recognise the number sequence in the second column?

1, 2, 3, 5, 8 is part of the Fibonacci sequence, where you add the two previous numbers to get the next one. 1 + 2 = 3, 2 + 3 = 5, 3 + 5 = 8.

If this is the right sequence then the next one will be 5 + 8 = 13. You don't want to draw this out, so instead think about why this might be sensible.

When you look at the numbers written next to each flight of stairs you can see some similarities.

Here are the routes up the 5-stair flight:	If you remove the final digit of each number you get this sequence:
11111	1111
2111	211
221	22
212	21
1211	121
122	12
1112	111
1121	112

and these are the ways of climbing a 3-stair and a 4-stair flight!

Why does that make sense?

Well, if you want to climb a 5-stair flight of stairs, you could go up 4 stairs and then do a 1-step to get to the top. So you need all of the ways of climbing a 4-stair flight and can then put a 1 at the end. Alternatively, you can get to stair 3 and then do a 2-step to get to the top, so you need all of the ways of climbing a 3-stair flight with a 2 after them. This means you really are adding the previous two numbers together.

To climb a 10-stair flight you need to continue the sequence and get: 1, 2, 3, 5, 8, 13, 21, 34, 55, 89. So, there are 89 ways to climb the ten stairs.

Here, simplifying the problem meant you could get started and could see what was going on.

Problem 4.3: What is the smallest number that can be divided (with no remainder) by all of the numbers from 1 to 20?

What do you know already?

Clearly the number will have to end with a zero (to make it divisible by 10). It will have to be even so it is divisible by 2 (but if it ends with a zero then that is already the case).

One strategy that might be useful is to make the problem simpler.

Change the problem so it now says this:

What is the smallest number that can be divided by all of the numbers from 1 to 3?

If you do 2 × 3 = 6 then you know that can be divided by 1, by 2 and by 3. Is it the smallest number? Yes.

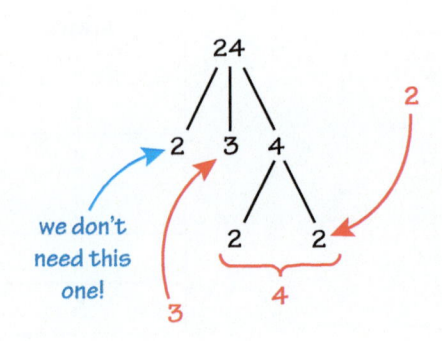

Another change:

What is the smallest number that can be divided by all of the numbers from 1 to 4?

If you do 2 × 3 × 4 = 24 then you know that can be divided by 1, by 2, by 3 and by 4. But there is a smaller number that works. 12 can be divided by 1, by 2, by 3 and by 4. Why didn't 2 × 3 × 4 give you the right answer? To make it divisible by 4 you didn't need to multiply the previous answer by 4, because there was already a 2 involved. If you had just multiplied that previous answer by 2 that would have given you something that is divisible by 4.

Therefore the answer is 2 × 3 × 2 = 12

Do you notice that these numbers are prime numbers?

Try the next one:

What is the smallest number that can be divided by all of the numbers from 1 to 5?

You currently have 2 × 3 × 2, which is not helpful if you want it to be divisible by 5. The trick that you used with 4 (splitting it into 2 × 2) won't work here because 5 is a prime number. To make it a multiple of 5 you will need to multiply by 5, giving you
2 × 3 × 2 × 5 = 60

You can see that the next one is easy.

What is the smallest number that can be divided by all of the numbers from 1 to 6?

60 is obviously already divisible by 6, and you can see that in the numbers because 2 × 3 is in there. 2 × 3 × 2 × 5 is divisible by all of the numbers from 1 to 6.

To make the smallest number divisible by 7 we need to include a 7, because you cannot make 7 by multiplying smaller numbers (7 is prime).

To make it divisible by 7 you therefore need to have 2 × 3 × 2 × 5 × 7

To make it divisible by 8 you only need an extra 2 because it is already divisible by 4, and to make it divisible by 9 you need an extra 3.

Then this is already divisible by 10.

Now you can finish off the problem by thinking about each of the numbers from 11 up to 20 as shown in the table below.

11	Needed, prime number	16	You have 8, so just need extra 2
12	Have already (2 × 2 × 3)	17	Needed, prime number
13	Needed, prime number	18	Have already (2 × 3 × 3)
14	Have already (2 × 7)	19	Needed, prime number
15	Have already (3 × 5)	20	Have already (2 × 2 × 5)

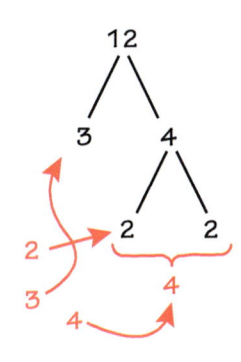

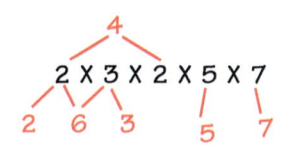

Your final answer is therefore:

$2 \times 2 \times 2 \times 2 \times 3 \times 3 \times 5 \times 7 \times 11 \times 13 \times 17 \times 19 = 232\,792\,560$

The following problems may be solved using more than one method; however, the worked solutions provided at the back of this book are based on the method introduced above.

1

Sanne knows that she can create a heart shape from a triangle and two semicircles. She starts by cutting a heart shape out of a rectangle of red cardboard 9 cm by 13 cm, as shown below.

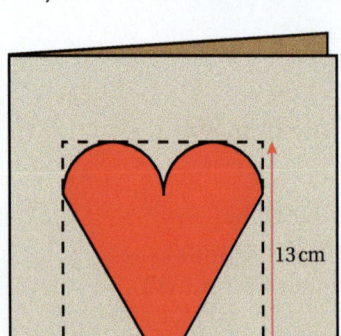

> **Tip**
>
> Start simply. Find the radius of the circle first. Does that help you find the areas you need?

What area of red cardboard has Sanne removed from the original piece to make the heart? Give your answer correct to 3 s.f.

2

Ahmed buys a piece of wood measuring 12 cm by 5 cm by 1 m for $5.

He uses the wood to make door wedges like this.

Diagram not to scale

a He made 40 wedges from the piece of wood he bought. What is the width x cm of these wedges?

b What is the lowest price Ahmed could sell the wedges for to make at least $30 profit?

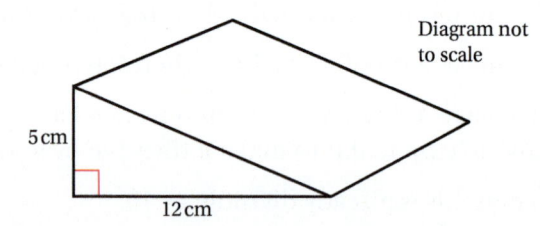

3

Paolo wants to invest $40 000 in a compound interest savings account.

ABC Bank offers 8% interest, compounded annually on your money if you invest more than $30 000 and it remains in the bank for at least ten years.

Paolo estimates that his money will more than double if he invests it for ten years.

a Is Paolo correct?

b What is the exact amount Paolo will have in his account at the end of ten years?

Paolo's mother also invests some money at the same rate. She wants to have a total of at least $75 000 at the end of the ten-year period.

c What is the smallest amount (to the nearest $1000) she must invest to have at least $75 000 at the end of ten years?

4

Is it possible for you to count aloud from one to one million in your lifetime?

> **Tip**
>
> Don't try this out! What easier version of this question could you try out? There isn't an exact counting speed, so you won't get an exact answer!

5

Zarah drives to work every day. On her journey there is a pedestrian crossing, a set of traffic lights and a traffic circle. At each of these she either must stop or is allowed to continue.

The probability of stopping at the pedestrian crossing is $\frac{1}{10}$.

The probability of stopping at the lights is $\frac{1}{4}$.

The probability of stopping at the traffic circle is $\frac{2}{3}$.

What is the probability that on Zarah's next journey to work she has to stop at least once?

6

Nilesh loves to go eagle-spotting in the mountains.

If he wakes up early and is able to be in the mountains before 7 am, the probability of him seeing an eagle is 0.7. If Nilesh wakes up late and does not arrive until after 7 am, his chance of spotting an eagle is 0.4.

The probability of Nilesh waking up early on the morning of one of his planned trips is 0.85.

a What is the probability that Nilesh will see an eagle on one of his trips?

Sometimes Nilesh takes his younger sister with him on his trip.

The probability of his sister waking up early enough to allow them to arrive before 7 am is 0.75.

b What is the probability that Nilesh will **not** see an eagle when his sister is on the trip with him?

c What happens to Nilesh's chances of seeing an eagle if his sister goes with him?

7

Consider each of the calculations below. Without using a calculator decide whether the answer is odd or even. Explain your reasoning.

a $4^3 + 3^4$

b $6^7 + 3^7$

8

Two almost identical logos are shown below. Both show a square of side length 10 cm with a second red square tilted inside it.

a Do they have the same total line length?

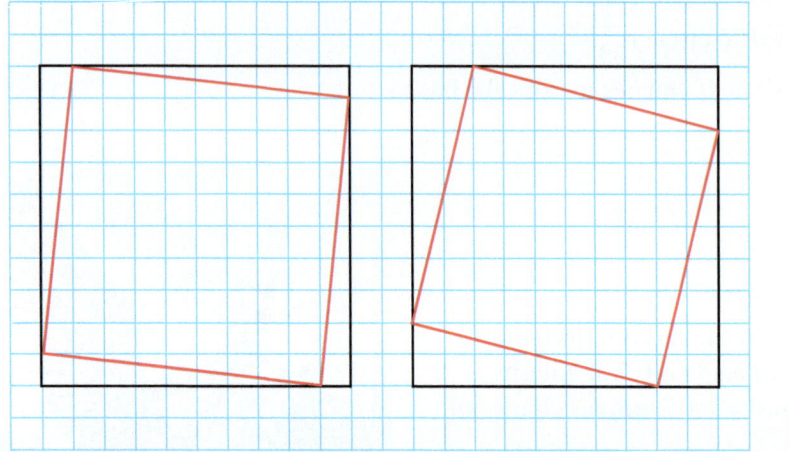

Scale
☐ = 1 cm²

A third logo is created in the same style. The tilted red square in the new logo has an area exactly half that of the original black square.

b Make an accurate drawing of this logo on squared paper.

9 ★★☆

Tygo is travelling 280 km from Town A to Town B. He is travelling by car and a graph of his journey is shown below.

Hazel is travelling from Town B to Town A on the same day as Tygo, but she rides a motorbike.

A graph of Hazel's journey is also shown.

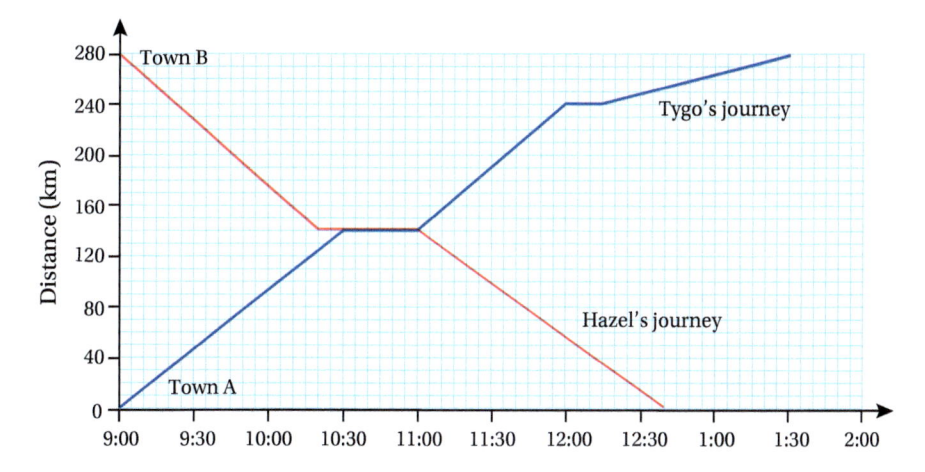

Both Tygo and Hazel set out on their journeys at 9:00 am.

a What was Tygo's speed for the first 140 km?

b What was Hazel's speed for the first stage of her journey?

c How long did Hazel have to wait before Tygo arrived at the service station where they were meeting for a coffee?

d Tygo got caught up in a traffic jam before he reached Town B. What time was this?

e How long did Tygo's journey take? What was his average speed?

f How long did Hazel's journey take? What was her average speed?

The speed limit is 70 miles per hour.

g Might either of them receive a speeding ticket for any stage of their journeys?

> **Tip**
> To convert kilometres to miles, divide by 8 and multiply by 5.

10 ★★☆

Who is the oldest?

- Pia — 14.2 years
- Ross — 169 months
- Jemima — 5293 days
- Arindam — 450 million seconds

Cambridge IGCSE Mathematics Extended Problem-solving Book

11 ★★★

Abu is starting a bakery. He wants to advertise nutritional information about his homemade cakes.

He follows this recipe and increases it to make a batch of 30 muffins:

Makes 12		
2 eggs	200 g sugar	250 ml milk
125 ml vegetable oil	400 g flour	1 tsp salt

1 Egg
Fat: 4.6 g
Sugar: Trace

Milk
Fat: 2%
Sugar: 5%

Vegetable oil
Fat: 100%
Sugar: 0%

Flour
Fat: $\frac{7}{500}$
Sugar: $\frac{1}{1000}$

Abu knows that 1 ml of liquid weighs about 1 g.

a What is the amount, in grams, of sugar and fat in each muffin?

The government advises that adults limit their fat intake to 70 g per day and sugar to 30 g per day.

b What should Abu advertise as the percentage of the GDA in each of his muffins?

12 ★★★

A garden centre sells two types of hanging basket.

One type is a cone shape and the other is a hemisphere.

Assuming that both types have the same diameter and that the height of the conical basket is also equal to its diameter, which basket has the greater volume?

> **Tip**
> This problem tells you what you can assume about the baskets. Without that information, you would not be able to solve it very easily.

> **Tip**
> Volume of a cone = $\frac{1}{3}\pi r^2 h$
> Volume of a sphere = $\frac{4}{3}\pi r^3$

Chapter 4: Simplify the problem

13 ★★★

The area of rectangle A is equal to the area of rectangle B.

Find the value of a.

Rectangle A: width a, height $\sqrt{2}$.
Rectangle B: width $2\sqrt{5}$, height $\sqrt{10}$.

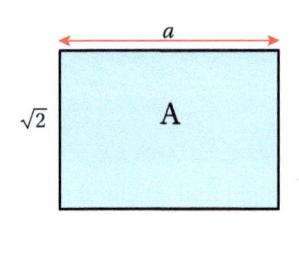

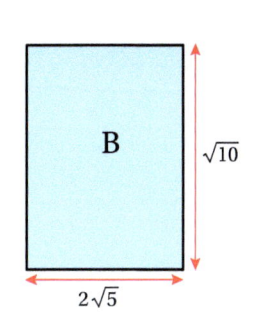

Diagrams not to scale

14 ★★★

A small rectangle is cut out of a larger rectangle. Calculate the proportion of the original rectangle that is left.

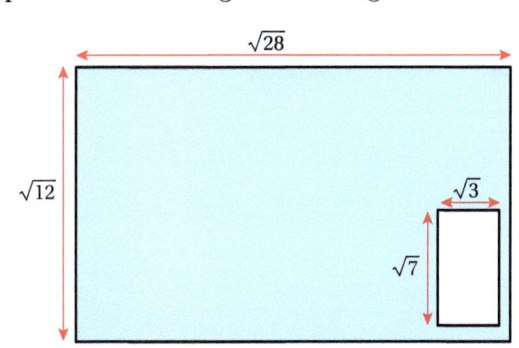

Larger rectangle: $\sqrt{28}$ by $\sqrt{12}$. Smaller rectangle cut out: $\sqrt{3}$ by $\sqrt{7}$.

Diagram not to scale

> **Tip**
> How would you solve it if the numbers weren't surds?

15 ★★★

A mug is printed with a chequerboard pattern made up of squares that have been rotated through 45°.

Exactly five of the white squares fit around the mug.

The diameter of the mug is 9 cm.

Calculate the perimeter of one square on the mug.

Give your answer correct to 3 s.f.

> **Tip**
> Think of the design as a rectangle that has been wrapped around the mug. Draw a diagram to show the net of the cup with the squares on it. How long will the rectangle be?

16 ★★★

a Factorise completely

$(x+y)^2(p-q)^3 + (x+y)^3(p-q)^2$

b Solve

$(x^2+3x-10)^2 - (x^2-3x-10)^2 = 0$

> **Tip**
> Try using a single letter to represent $x+y$ and another single letter to represent $p-q$.

17 ★★★

$f(x) = x^2 - 7x + 12$

The equation $f(x) = b$ has exactly one solution. Find the value of b.

> **Tip**
> You might find it helpful to work out what the graph with equation $y = x^2 - 7x + 12$ looks like. It is often helpful to think about the symmetry of quadratic graphs.

Chapter 5
Consider different cases

For problems that seem abstract, or which have large or clumsy numbers, it is useful to consider a specific example, or case, of the problem. To decide what strategy to use, it is helpful to start by considering small cases, special cases and extremes.

Small cases are useful when you are dealing with a large number range. If you were asked to find the sum of the first 500 numbers, you could start by finding the sum of the first five then the first ten numbers to see if you can find a pattern that leads to the solution. Similarly, if are asked to work with a value such as $n = 1000$, you might decide to substitute smaller values to find a useful pattern or starting point.

When you use a smaller value, you are more likely to find a solution if you choose a small value that shares properties with the larger value. For example, if your larger value is a multiple of 5 or 10, choose a smaller case that meets those conditions. So for 1000 you might choose 10 or for 625 you might choose 25 as it is also a square number that is a multiple of 5. Consider whether the number is prime, cubed, decimal or irrational and choose smaller values accordingly. For problems involving number theory or algebra it might help to do some specific case calculations using numbers (in place of variables).

Special cases are useful in spatial, algebraic and numerical problems. In spatial problems you might consider what happens if the angles are right-angled or equal, or you may use a unit diameter, radius or other value (for example, use a diameter of 1 in a formula to explore the area of a sphere). In algebra it often helps to consider what happens when $x = 1$ or $x = 0$. Both 1 and 0 have particular properties and substituting those variables might help you find a solution. For numerical problems, special cases might involve odd or even numbers, squares, cubes, primes and so on.

The third case involves extremes of the situation. You can think of this as considering the limits. This could be as simple as considering the largest or smallest possible values in a context, the closest point or vertex in a figure or an 'impossible' scenario (such as a circle with a diameter of 0) or the three vertices of a triangle being on the same line.

The examples below show you how this strategy can be useful in both numerical and geometrical problems.

Problem 5.1: Maria knows she will have to write six tests this year. Each test is marked out of 100. Maria wants to get a mean result of at least 85 for the year. What is the lowest possible mark out of 100 that she can score on a test?

Tip

The problem asks for the lowest possible mark. This suggests that extremes or limits might be useful in the solution.

Start by considering the lower extreme, a mean result of 85.

To get a mean result of 85 Maria would need to get a sum of 510 marks for the six tests.

$$\frac{\text{(sum of 6 tests)}}{\text{number of tests}} = 85$$

So, 85 × 6 = sum of 6 tests.

Now consider the other extreme.

What if she gets 100/100 for five of the tests?

That would give her 500 marks.

She could then get 10 marks for the sixth test and still get a mean mark of 85.

The lowest possible mark she can get is 10/100.

> **Problem 5.2:** In the diagram on the right, AB is the diameter of the circle, C lies on the circumference and O is the centre of the circle.
>
> What is the relationship between the areas of triangle OAC and triangle OBC? Explain your answer.

Tip

The question asks 'What is the relationship?' so it is reasonable to assume that there is a relationship. Consider cases such as: the areas are equal, one area is double the other, or the areas are proportional in some way.

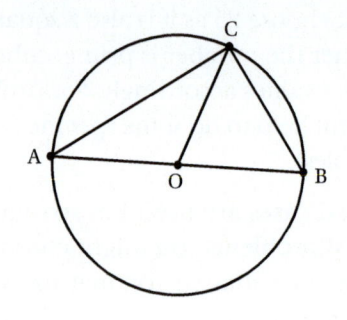

In the diagram it looks as if the areas might be the same. Can you provide evidence to convince yourself that this is the case?

When you consider different cases, you have to keep in mind the key elements of the original problem. These are:

- there is a circle
- AB is the diameter of the circle
- O is the centre of the circle
- points A, B and C are on the circumference of circle.

All of these statements must stay true. You might be able to move some of the points so the answer is obvious. There doesn't seem to be anything special about the placing of point C, so it might be acceptable for you to move the points around. It wouldn't be acceptable to move C so that it is no longer on the circumference of the circle, though, because that would change the scenario.

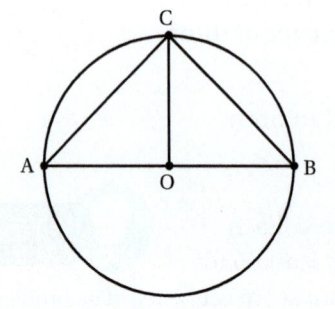

This diagram shows one case. C has moved so that it is halfway between A and B but still on the circle. There is now a line of symmetry in the diagram and the two triangles are clearly equal.

Here is another case.

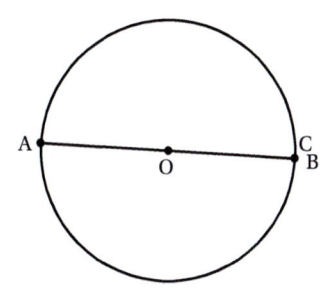

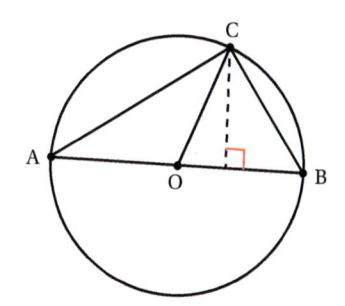

C has moved so that it is on top of point B. This time the two triangles both have zero area, so they are the same.

The idea that the two areas are the same is looking plausible.

The area of a triangle is half of the base multiplied by the perpendicular height.

In the right-hand triangle, the area is the radius of the circle (OB) multiplied by the dotted line (the perpendicular height), divided by two.

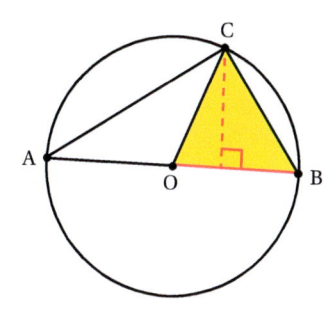

In the left-hand triangle, the area is the radius of the circle (AO) multiplied by the perpendicular height, divided by two. But what is the perpendicular height for the left-hand triangle? It is actually the dotted line.

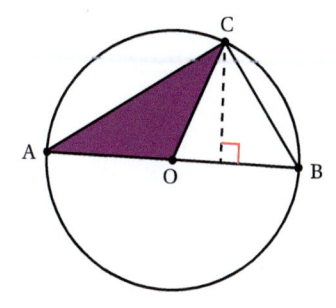

So they do have the same area and you can explain why.

In this problem you have looked at different cases, but you have also drawn diagrams (see Chapter 1) and changed your point of view (Chapter 3).

To consider different cases in geometrical problems the following changes can be useful:

- Moving points around (but preserving the initial scenario).
- Trying to make a special situation (for example, a line of symmetry).
- Moving points to extreme positions.

The following problems may be solved using more than one method; however, the worked solutions provided at the back of this book are based on the method introduced above.

1 ★☆☆

In a restaurant, chairs can be arranged around square tables, as shown in the diagram. The restaurant owner has a total of 55 chairs.

a How many chairs are needed if five tables are arranged in this way?

b Find the rule for the number of chairs needed for n tables.

c Is it possible to use all 55 chairs with tables arranged like this? Explain your answer.

The restaurant needs to be set up for 32 guests at a function. The party leader wants the guests to be split into two equal groups, so they will sit at two large tables.

d How many small square tables are to be used to make each of these large table settings?

2 ★☆☆

Alina is asked to choose five different common fractions and to write them down in ascending order.

She thinks carefully and then writes:

$$\frac{1}{6} \quad \frac{1}{5} \quad \frac{1}{4} \quad \frac{1}{3} \quad \frac{1}{2}$$

a Suggest another set of fractions that she could have written.

b Suggest another set of fractions where none has a numerator of 1.

c Suggest another set of fractions, all of which have their numerator greater than their denominator.

> **Tip**
> There are lots of ways to do this. One way is to change the original set of fractions.

3 ★☆☆

Which is greater in each pair?

a 400 g and 400 mg   or   0.5 kg and 90 g

b 0.1 km and 150 cm   or   110 m and 900 cm

c 0.75 hours and 600 seconds   or   50 minutes and 0.1 hours

4 ★☆☆

Elliott has a bag of coloured balls. Each ball is either red, green or yellow.

The probability of picking a red ball at random is $\frac{3}{7}$.

The probability of picking a yellow ball at random is the same as picking a green ball.

a There are nine red balls. How many balls are there in total?

Elliot adds more red and yellow balls to the bag. The probability of picking a green ball at random is now $\frac{3}{25}$.

b What is the total number of balls in Elliott's bag now?

5 ★☆☆

On average there are over 100 000 strands of hair on a child's head. Blondes average about 140 000 strands, brunettes average 108 000 strands and redheads average 90 000 strands. Hair grows at a rate of about 150 mm a year. The average person loses roughly 0.25 per cent of their hair strands each year.

If the hair does not grow back:

a Roughly what percentage of their hair strands would redheads lose after 82 years?

b How many years would it take for an average blonde to lose one tenth of their hair strands?

6 ★☆☆

23.64 × 805 = 1903.02

How can you tell that this statement is incorrect?

7 ★★☆

I choose three consecutive integers and add them together.

5 + 6 + 7 = 18

I notice that 18 is also the result of 6 × 3. I select another set of three numbers and add them together.

2 + 3 + 4 = 9

I notice that 9 is also the result of 3 × 3.

It looks like the sum of three consecutive numbers is the same as the middle number multiplied by three.

a Is this always true?

b Can you find a rule for adding four consecutive integers?

c How might you extend your rule to add five or more consecutive integers?

8 ★★☆

Four snails have a race.

Assuming that the snails move at a constant speed (as shown in the diagram) to the finish line, which one will get there first?

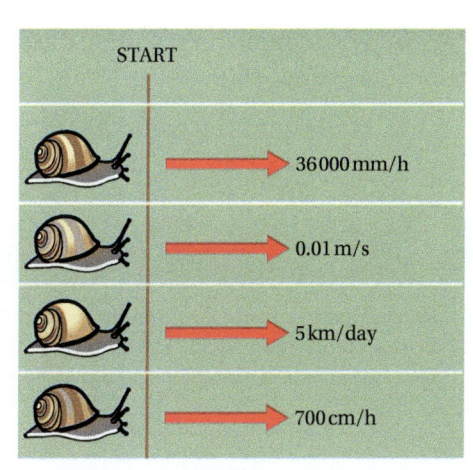

- 36 000 mm/h
- 0.01 m/s
- 5 km/day
- 700 cm/h

Cambridge IGCSE Mathematics Extended Problem-solving Book

9

Animals in zoos are normally kept behind double fences for safety.

This style of circular pen is used for the chipmunks and rats. It has a diameter of 20 m. It is surrounded by a double fence with a gap of 2 m between the fences.

a   How much longer is the outside fence than the inner fence?

b   Suppose the gap was changed to 3 m. What would the difference be then in the length of the fences?

c   What is the general rule?

d   What happens if the pens are square or rectangular in shape?

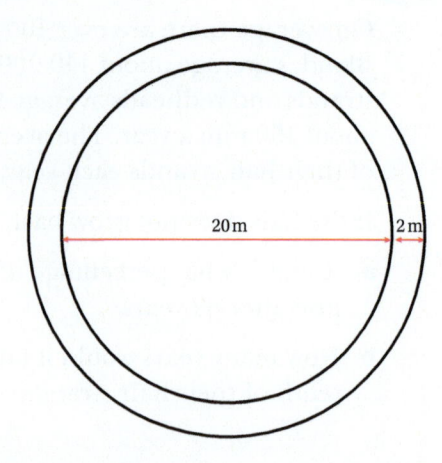

10

Delia draws a shape on a coordinate grid as shown below:

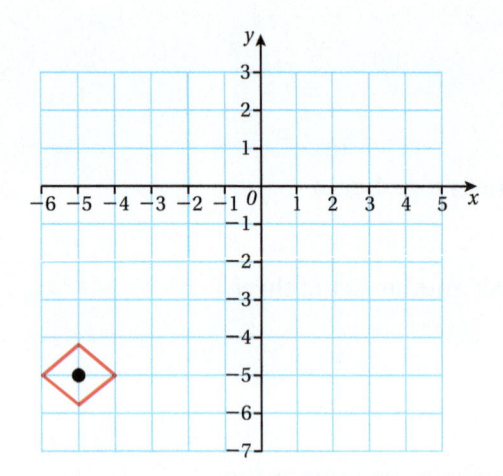

She notices that the centre of her shape (marked with the black dot on the diagram) lies on the line $x = -5$.

a   How could Delia translate her shape so that its centre remains on the line $x = -5$?

Daisy's shape also lies on the line $y = x$.

b   How could you translate the shape so that its centre remains on the line $y = x$?

c   How could you translate the shape so that its centre lies on the line $y = x + 3$?

Tip

Remember to use vector notation to describe a particular translation.
Is there more than one solution to each part of this question? If so, can you write your answers in a more general way (using words or mathematical notation)?

Chapter 5: Consider different cases

11 ★★☆

The diagram shows two cereal boxes.

Choc Flakes: 28 cm × 17 cm × 5 cm
BioWheat: 21 cm × 15 cm × 9 cm

Kiefer says, "I think the Choc Flakes box has the greater volume."

Arpad says, "I think the BioWheat box has the greater surface area."

Raymon says, "Only one of you can be correct. Whichever box has the greater volume must also have the greater surface area."

Who is correct? Justify your answer.

> **Tip**
> There are several steps to this problem. You could start by calculating the volume and surface area of each box.

12 ★★☆

Micah is asked to investigate what happens when a shape is reflected in two perpendicular mirror lines in turn.

He draws the following picture and makes the observation, "Ah! The result is the same as a translation of the original shape."

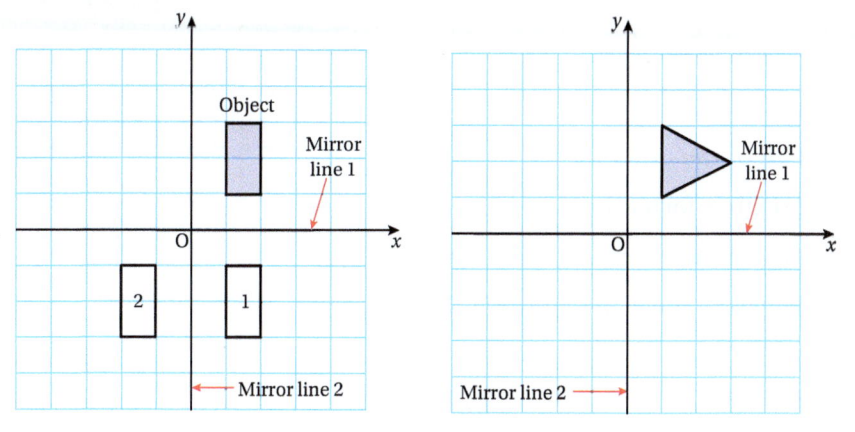

Micah's teacher looks at his work and asks, "Are you sure?"

a Suggest what Micah could do next in his investigation to address this.

b By considering the starting point shown in the diagram above, decide whether or not you agree with Micah's first idea.

> **Tip**
> 'Perpendicular mirror lines' means that the mirror lines are at right angles (90°) to each other.
> Why did Micah choose his pair of mirror lines to be the x and y axes? Are there other pairs that he could have chosen?

59

13 ★★☆

Melissa has designed this logo for her new business. It is based on an isosceles triangle with a semicircle on each side.

Calculate the perimeter of Melissa's logo. Give your answer correct to 2 d.p.

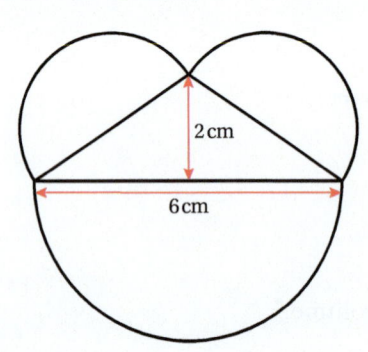

Diagram not to scale

2 cm

6 cm

Tip

Remember: you can use Pythagoras' theorem to calculate missing lengths in right-angled triangles.

14 ★★☆

Calculate the mean of the following three numbers:

$\sqrt{24}$ $\sqrt{54}$ $\sqrt{96}$

Tip

What change will you need to make before you can add the three numbers?

15 ★★★

Each of the seven small triangles in the diagram is an isosceles triangle. The large outer triangle is also isosceles.

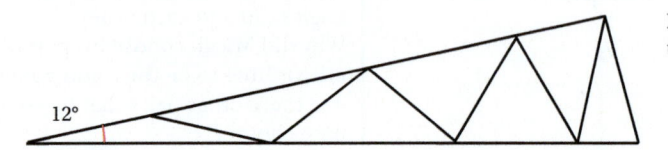

Diagram not to scale

12°

Tip

Read the question carefully. What information can you use? Can you label anything on the diagram?

Given one angle, can you work out all of the others?

Ingrid says, "No. You don't have enough information."

Helen says, "Yes. You can work out all of the other angles."

Pete says, "I wonder what would happen to the other angles if the first one was 10° instead of 12°."

a   Decide whether Ingrid or Helen is correct. Make sure you justify your answer.

b   Try out Pete's idea. What would happen if he started with an angle of 10°?

c   Is there a different starting angle for which this *will* work?

Chapter 5: Consider different cases

16 ★★★

a What's the same and what's different about the following fractions and their decimal equivalents?

$$\frac{1}{9}, \frac{1}{99}, \frac{1}{999}, \frac{1}{9999}, \frac{1}{99999}, \frac{1}{999999}$$

b Explain how you can use your findings to work out the equivalent fraction to each of these recurring decimals. Do this part without a calculator.

  i $0.\dot{7}$

  ii $5.\dot{3}$

  iii $0.1\dot{4}$

  iv $2.5\dot{0}000\dot{9}$

> **Tip**
> You know about 0.1111... What will 0.2222... be?
> How can this help?
> Remember to consider the equivalent decimal number to each fraction.

17 ★★★

Jack holds out a coin and tries to cover up the Moon. He can't make it fit exactly – the coin is too big. He gets a friend to hold the coin steady and moves backwards until the coin is a good fit over the Moon. He finds that he has had to walk approximately 2.5 m away from the coin.

Given that the Moon has a diameter of 3474.8 km, and the coin has a diameter of 22.5 mm, use Jack's findings to estimate the distance of the Moon from the Earth.

> **Tip**
> Try to draw a diagram showing Jack, the coin and the Moon. Label the lengths that you know and the distance that you want to find. Remember to make some conversions!

18 ★★★

Solve the equation

$$(2^x)^2 - 20(2^x) + 64 = 0$$

19 ★★★

9, 17, 27, 39, 53, ..., ...

Find the nth term of this sequence, by comparing the terms to those in the sequence

1, 4, 9, 16, 25, ..., ...

Chapter 6
Make connections

Problem-solving is central to learning mathematics at all levels. By this stage in your mathematical career, you will have developed, selected, applied and compared many different strategies.

The strategy (or strategies) that you choose and use to solve a problem often depends on whether or not the problem is similar to those you've worked on before.

Making connections as a strategy involves thinking about how you have previously solved similar problems as well as considering which strand of mathematics you are dealing with. If a problem involves unknown quantities or requires a justification or proof, it makes sense to think about algebra and to see whether you can make an equation (or expression or inequality) using variables to justify your thinking and prove that your solution works for all cases. If a problem involves shape and space, it makes sense to consider a diagram and whether or not you can add lines or try out specific cases.

When you are deciding which strategy to use, it might help to ask yourself the following questions:

- What do I need to do?
- How is this problem similar to ones I have solved before?
- What is the connection between the problem and the maths I already know?
- How will I tackle this problem?

Problem 6.1: Multiply two consecutive even numbers.

Do you always get a multiple of 8? Justify/explain your answer.

How could you approach this problem? Think of maths topics that might be relevant.

You could start by trying a few specific cases using simple numbers to see if it appears to be true (but this won't justify or prove it if you think it is the case):

$2 \times 4 = 8$　　　　　$6 \times 8 = 48$

$4 \times 6 = 24$　　　　　$10 \times 12 = 120$

All of these are multiples of 8. It is looking good so far (but you haven't justified it).

You need a proof, so try writing an algebraic expression for the problem. What can you use for the two numbers? If you call them a and b then that doesn't include the idea that they are **even** numbers. You could call them $2a$ and $2b$. You need a and b to be consecutive whole numbers. This tells us that either a or b is even. If you do $2a \times 2b$ you get $4ab$ but one of a and b is even so the whole thing must be a multiple of 8.

Here is a slightly more formal way to do the same thing, using just a single letter. If the first even number is $2a$ then you can call the next one $2a + 2$. When you multiply these you get $2a(2a + 2)$. This is equal to $4a^2 + 4a$, which is $4a(a + 1)$.

Let's look at $4a(a + 1)$.

If a is odd then $a + 1$ is even and we have $4 \times$ odd $\times$ even, which is a multiple of 8 (because 4 multiplied by an even number is a multiple of 8). If $a + 1$ is odd then a is even and we have $4 \times$ even $\times$ odd, which is a multiple of 8. So the whole thing is a multiple of 8.

> **Problem 6.2:** Choose any three consecutive positive integers. Add them together.
>
> Is the answer always a multiple of 3? Is the answer always a multiple of 6? Explain your answer.

Tip

Most problems won't be identical to ones you've already solved, but similar problems can usually be solved using the same approach and strategy. The key is to recognise and understand the problem.

This problem is similar to the previous one, so you could use some similar techniques.

First, try a few specific cases using simple numbers just to get a feel for what is going on. Then use some algebra and try to create an expression to describe what is happening.

$1 + 2 + 3 = 6$ (this is a multiple of 3 and also a multiple of 6)

$2 + 3 + 4 = 9$ (this is a multiple of 3 but is not a multiple of 6)

You have already shown that the answer is **not** always a multiple of 6 because you have found one that doesn't work.

Using algebra, you could call the first number a. The next number will therefore be $a + 1$ and the one after that will be $a + 2$. This is similar to what we did in the previous example so you are using the experience you gained doing that question.

When you add these together you get $a + a + 1 + a + 2$, which equals $3a + 3$. To show that this is clearly divisible by 3 you could factorise: $3(a + 1)$, to show that you have an integer $(a + 1)$ multiplied by 3.

If you call the middle number n then it happens to be even easier. The three numbers are: $n - 1$, n, $n + 1$, and adding these gives $3n$. Note that you didn't use three different letters to describe the numbers. This is often useful.

You can use some similar techniques to help you work on this next problem.

> **Problem 6.3:** Think of a number (a positive integer), square it and subtract the number you first thought of.
>
> When is the answer a prime number? Explain your answer.

$1^2 - 1 = 0$ $4^2 - 4 = 12$

$2^2 - 2 = 2$ $5^2 - 5 = 20$

$3^2 - 3 = 6$ $6^2 - 6 = 30$

So far this looks interesting. You always seem to get an even number as the answer. Does that seem sensible? Will that ever change?

Only one of the answers is a prime number: $2^2 - 2 = 2$

There are several ways you could continue here, but one is to use some algebra like you did in problems 1 and 2.

Call the number you thought of n. Then you get $n^2 - n$.

This can be factorised to give $n(n - 1)$. But a prime number has exactly two factors, so if this is going to be prime then one of the numbers n and $n - 1$ has got to be equal to 1.

If $n = 1$ then you get $1^2 - 1 = 0$, which doesn't work (because 0 is not a prime number).

If $n - 1 = 1$ then $n = 2$ and you get the answer you know about already: $2^2 - 2 = 2$

All of the others will have extra factors, so they cannot be prime numbers.

For example:

$7^2 - 7 = 7 \times 6$

The answer is a prime number only when the number first thought of is 2.

The following problems may be solved using more than one method; however, the worked solutions provided at the back of this book are based on the method introduced above.

Nick has a funny poster on the wall in his office. Bernard has a poster with a similar joke.

ALWAYS GIVE 100% AT WORK
12% MONDAY
23% TUESDAY
40% WEDNESDAY
20% THURSDAY
5% FRIDAY

Nick's poster

ALWAYS GIVE 100% AT WORK
14% MONDAY
18% TUESDAY
29% WEDNESDAY
36% THURSDAY
3% FRIDAY

Bernard's poster

Assuming that this poster refers to time, rather than effort, answer the following questions.

a If Nick actually worked in this way, for how long would he work on a Friday?

b How much longer would Nick work for on a Wednesday compared to a Monday?

c Why can't you tell for certain who works for longer on a Tuesday?

Tip

You will need to decide how long a working day is. What is its usual length?

2

Suggested cooking times for poultry are 50 minutes per kilogram plus an additional 30 minutes.

A caterer needs to cook a 3 kg chicken and a 7.5 kg turkey for an event.

He wants both birds to be ready at the same time and he needs 20 minutes to carve and prepare them, once they are taken out of the oven. He wants to serve lunch at 1.00 p.m.

a How long will the turkey be in the oven by itself before being joined by the chicken?

b Find a formula to find the time taken, t minutes, to cook a chicken weighing m kg.

For a different event, the caterer plans to cook a goose. This goose will take 5 hours and 5 minutes to cook.

c How much does the goose weigh?

d If the caterer plans to have a late lunch at 2.30 p.m. at the second event, what is the latest time he can put the goose in the oven?

3

Prices for laying lawns are directly proportional to the area of the lawn needed.

For a lawn measuring 8 m by 10 m, there is a charge of $320.

For a lawn measuring 12 m by 12 m, there is a charge of $576.

a How much will it cost to lay a lawn measuring 12 m by 8 m?

b To lay a different lawn costs $560. If the measurements are in whole metres, what could the dimensions of the lawn be?

4

Jyoti told her teacher that $y = x$ and $y = -x$ can be drawn as two straight lines that are perpendicular to each other.

The teacher asked Jyoti what the gradient of each graph is.

a Complete Jyoti's responses:

The gradient of $y = x$ is … .

The gradient of $y = -x$ is … .

The teacher asked Jyoti to write down the equation of the line that has the same y-intercept as the graph $y = 2x - 3$, but which is perpendicular to it.

b Write the equation for the perpendicular line.

Cambridge IGCSE Mathematics Extended Problem-solving Book

The teacher asked Jyoti to write a statement on the board using the correct terminology to describe perpendicular lines, but to make it simple for the other students to remember.

c Write a suitable statement for the class.

5

The probability of pop star Karri K releasing a song on a Thursday is 0.62.

If her song is released on a Thursday, the probability of this song becoming a number one single in the charts is 0.48.

If her song is released on any other day, the probability of it becoming a number one single is only 0.18.

What is the probability that Karri K will have a number one hit with the next song she releases?

> **Tip**
> What kind of diagram would be useful here?

6

A farmer has started making chips to sell at the weekly farmers' market. She does not want to buy expensive packing equipment, so she asks her family to pack the chips for her each week. They must make each packet a similar weight.

At certain times the farmer does a random test to check the mass of some packets.

These were the results one day:

Sample 1: 57.8 g, 61.1 g, 62.3 g, 58.9 g, 59.5 g, 60.6 g, 60.1 g, 58.8 g, 58.5 g, 61.3 g, 59.5 g

Sample 2: 58.1 g, 58.7 g, 59.3 g, 58.9 g, 59.3 g, 58.8 g, 60.4 g, 59.1 g, 59.4 g, 58.9 g, 60.2 g

The packets need to be labelled with the mass. The farmer plans to label them as being 60 g. Is she right to do this?

Give your reasons.

7

Ondine and Elizabeth live in Sampit and Rengat, respectively, two villages that are 18 km apart.

The girls plan to meet up on Saturday at Elizabeth's house.

Ondine plans to hike to Rengat, leaving home at 9:10. She can walk at a steady speed of 5 km per hour.

Elizabeth's brother will be cycling to Sampit and should pass Ondine on the way.

Elizabeth's brother plans to leave Rengat at 9:40. For the first 16 km, he will be travelling at 24 km/h, but the remainder of the route is very steep and he estimates that he will only arrive in Sampit at 10:40.

a   When will Ondine meet Elizabeth's brother?

b   How far will Ondine be from her house when they meet?

c   How far will Elizabeth's brother have travelled?

d   What time is Ondine expecting to arrive at Elizabeth's house?

e   At what speed did Elizabeth's brother cycle up the steep hill?

f   What distance apart are they at 10:20?

8

The graph shows the journey of a car and a scooter.

The scooter rider travelled from Hanoi to Viet Tri.

The car driver took the same route to Viet Tri but returned to Hanoi.

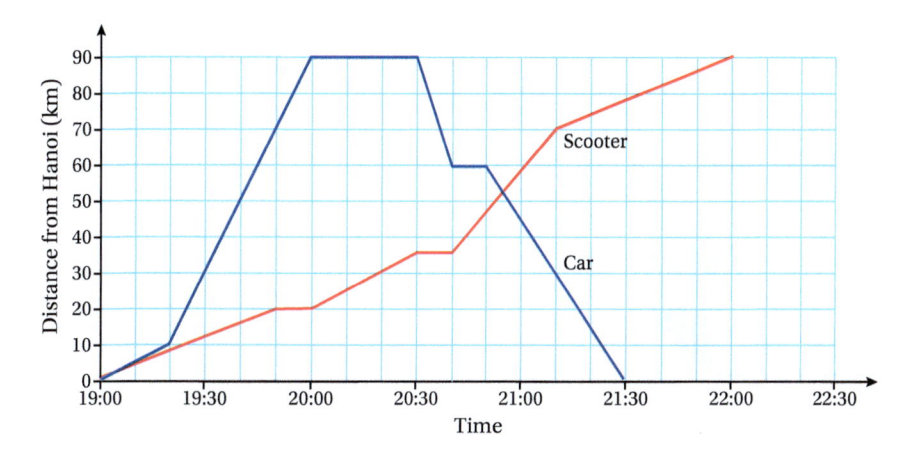

a How far did the scooter rider travel in the first 25 minutes?

b How long did it take the car to travel the first 10 km?

c How many stops did the scooter rider make and what was the total time she spent resting?

d What was the fastest stage of the journey for the car driver?

e What was the driver's speed at this fast stage?

f At approximately what time did the car and the scooter pass each other?

g Roughly how far did the scooter rider still have to go when she met the car driver?

h What was the average speed for the whole journey for the scooter rider?

i What was the average speed for the return journey for the car driver?

9

Johan says if you transform the graph $y = 2x + 4$ by the transformation $y + 7$, the intercept on the y-axis will become $(0, 11)$.

Is he correct?

Explain your answer.

10

This sequence is generated by adding 2, then 4, then 6,… (the next even number each time).

0, 2, 6, 12, 20, 30 …

a Write down the next three terms.

b Find the nth term for the sequence.

c How does the algebra tell you that every term in the sequence must be even?

11

Two spiders are in a room which is 4.5 m long, 3 m wide and 2 m high.

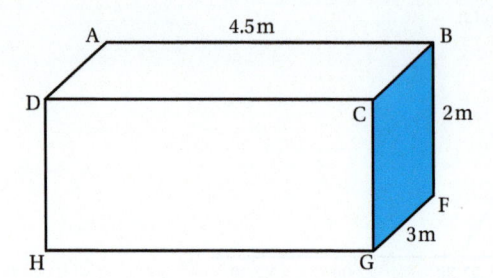

The male spider is at vertex A and the female spider is at vertex G.

a How far must the male spider crawl to get to the female if it only crawls along the edges of the room?

b If instead the male stays at A and the female spider travels along the diagonal of the face GCDH, then along edge DA to get to the male, how much shorter will her journey be?

12

Raj draws a square of length 7.0 cm correct to the nearest millimetre. He then draws a circle that he intends to fit exactly inside the square, but which might not fit because of the accuracy of his drawing.

Calculate the maximum difference between the area of the circle and the area of the square.

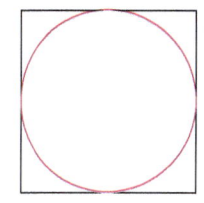

13

Li keeps rabbits in his yard. They drink from two cylindrical water bottles, one small and one large.

The smaller bottle has a diameter of 8.5 cm and a height of 23 cm.

The larger bottle has a radius of 5.5 cm and a height of 25 cm.

How much **more** water does the larger bottle hold? Give your answer to the nearest millilitre (ml).

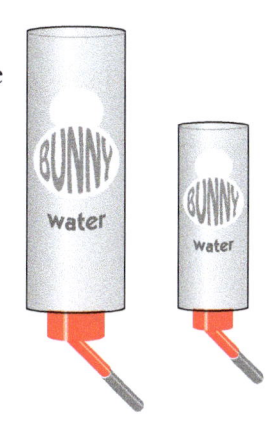

> **Tip**
>
> Can you work out the volume of a cylinder? What is the link between cubic centimetres (cm^3) and millilitres?

14

The following question is posed to a class:

Find an equivalent expression to $10 \times \sqrt{15}$.

The teacher takes the answers suggested by the first four students:

A: $\sqrt{150}$ B: $\sqrt{1500}$ C: 40   D: 35

Which, if any, of their values are correct? Explain your answer.

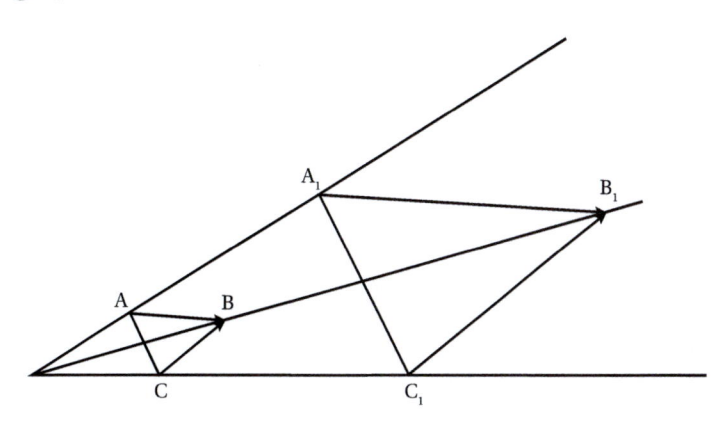

15

In the diagram of two similar triangles above,
$\overrightarrow{AB} = 2\mathbf{a} - \mathbf{b}$, $\overrightarrow{CB} = \mathbf{a} + 2\mathbf{b}$ and $\overrightarrow{C_1B_1} = 3\mathbf{a} + 6\mathbf{b}$

a Express $\overrightarrow{AC}$ in terms of **a** and **b**.

b Express $\overrightarrow{A_1B_1}$ in terms of **a** and **b**.

16

All standard television screens are mathematically similar. The size of a TV screen is advertised as the diagonal length, in inches.

Carlos owns a 36.7-inch wide-screen TV and measures its actual width as 32 inches.

a What is the aspect ratio (ratio of width to height) for a wide-screen TV?

Eddie is buying a 42-inch wide-screen TV (where 42 inches is the length of the diagonal).

b Work out the length and width of his new TV.

17

A square-based pyramid is made so all of its edges are 2 m long.

a How high is the pyramid?

b Suppose the edges were all 3 m long. How high would it be now?

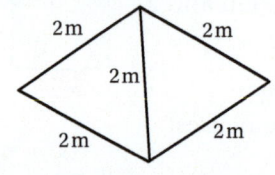

c What is the general rule for a pyramid of side length a metres?

> **Tip**
> How can you make right-angled triangles? How could this help?

18

A pair of tongs has arms 25 cm long. When not in use, the angle between the two arms is 60°.

Aliyah uses the tongs to pick up a round sweet 5 cm in diameter.

By how much will the angle between the two arms be reduced?

> **Tip**
> Draw a diagram to help you see what is happening. Which topic will you need to use?

19 ★★☆

a Would you expect there to be any correlation between the average number of hours a secondary school student sleeps each night and the year group they are in?

b Write a hypothesis about this.

c Design a questionnaire to test your hypothesis.

d What type of diagram might be a useful way to display the data?

20 ★★☆

Mr Robert is teaching his maths class about linear programming. He has a problem for them to solve, using small interconnecting bricks.

He gives each student eight red bricks and six yellow bricks and tells them to model a problem based on how many chairs and tables a company could make with a limited supply of materials.

Each table requires two red bricks and two yellow bricks. Each chair requires two red bricks and one yellow brick.

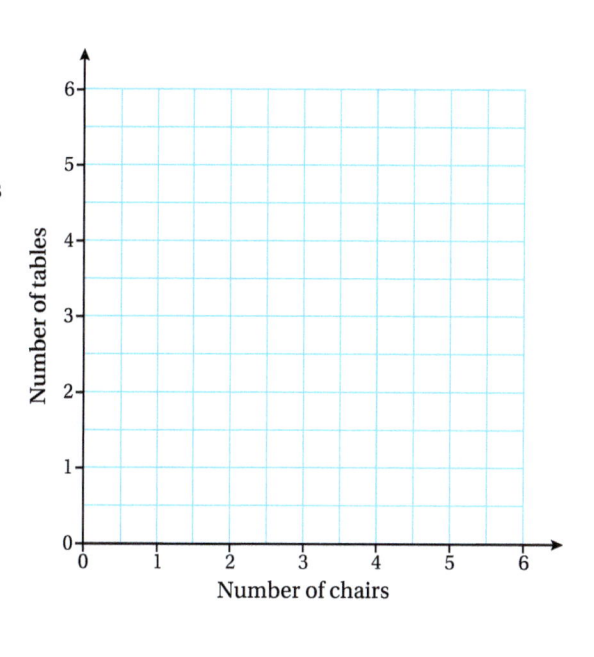

a Write an inequality to show the number of tables and chairs that could be made with the red bricks.

b Write an inequality to show the number of chairs and tables that could be made with the yellow bricks.

c Show these inequalities on the axes given. At what point do the graphs cross?

Cambridge IGCSE Mathematics Extended Problem-solving Book

21 ★★★

Everything in Shop A is being sold at the same percentage discount. Shop B is also selling all of its stock at a discount but it is not cutting its prices by as much.

A jacket now costs $209 in Shop A but $259 in Shop B. The original price (RRP) for the jacket was $310.

a What percentage discount from the RRP is being offered in each shop?

b A pair of trainers is priced at $62 in Shop A. How much will they cost in Shop B?

22 ★★★

The dial on a washing machine has a radius of 3.2 cm. It can be turned so that the arrow points to each of five equally spaced settings.

The dial is turned clockwise from 0 through a curved arc of length 121 mm. Which setting has been chosen?

> **Tip**
> Think carefully about the sort of maths methods you need to use.

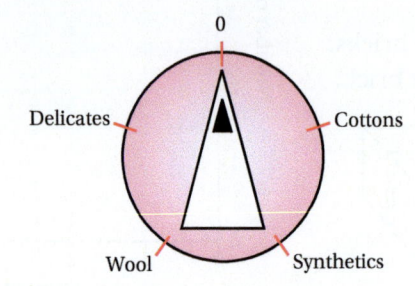

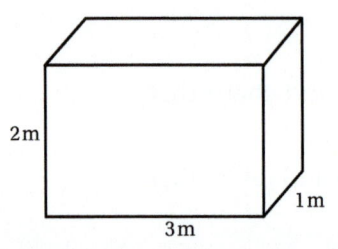

23 ★★★

By how much could the volume of this cuboid vary if its side lengths were measured correct to:

a the nearest metre

b 3 s.f.

c the nearest millimetre

24 ★★★

Consider each pair of expressions and decide which expression is the larger.

a $\dfrac{3}{\sqrt{5}}$ or $\dfrac{5}{2\sqrt{5}}$

b $\dfrac{4}{\sqrt{8}}$ or $\dfrac{25}{\sqrt{50}}$

c $\dfrac{10}{\sqrt{7}+3}$ or $\dfrac{6}{\sqrt{7}-3}$

> **Tip**
> How do you compare fractions? Can you apply the same technique here?

25 ★★★

Anjali takes counters from a bag containing only blue counters and red counters. There are 120 counters in the bag, with more red counters than blue counters. Each time she takes a counter Anjali records its colour and then returns it to the bag. The probability that Anjali has drawn exactly one red counter after two draws is 0.42. Assuming that each counter is equally likely to be chosen find the number of red counters in the bag.

> **Tip**
> Some questions will appear to give you more than one possible answer. Is there a clue in the question that will help you decide which answer is the right one?

26 ★★★

a   Find the nth term for each of the sequences

   i   5, 8, 11, 14, 17, . . .

   ii   3, 5, 7, 9, 11, . . .

b   Use your answers to **a i** and **a ii** to find the 10th term of the sequence

   15, 40, 77, 126, . . .

c   Show that 15 960 is not in the sequence

   15, 40, 77, 126, . . .

27 ★★★

Two numbers, x and y, are given in standard form:

$x = a \times 10^n$ $5 < a < 10$

$y = b \times 10^n$ $5 < b < 10$

Write the number $x + y$ in standard form.

> **Tip**
> Remind yourself of the rules of standard form and work from there.

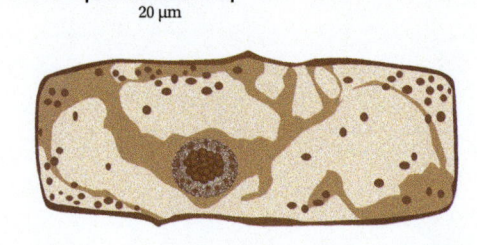

Chapter 7
Use logical reasoning

In some problems you have to consider many different pieces of information, decide how to organise them and then work through the problem in a series of steps. Working logically and applying mathematical reasoning is a useful approach for these kinds of problems.

Logical reasoning often means that you will apply one of the other strategies (diagrams, lists, tables, equations, estimation, trial and improvement) as you work. You can think about logical reasoning as a broad approach that allows you to:

- read and understand the problem and identify any assumptions you can make
- work out what is mathematically true, what could be true based on that, and what cannot possibly be true
- think about the things that could be true and use mathematical reasoning to work out whether they are true or not
- break a problem into smaller steps to see whether these lead you to the solution
- keep track of your work so that you can use what is true to justify your solution.

Logical reasoning is useful for problems in which information for one case is given and you are asked to consider a different case, where there is a condition attached (for example, if . . . then . . . statements) or where you have to make a decision based on evidence. In reality, you use some degree of logical reasoning to solve all problems.

Estimation and common sense are useful when you apply this strategy, particularly when you have to decide whether something is true or not.

In Biology you can calculate the actual size of something that has been viewed through a microscope using the given scale.

Problem 7.1: The diagram below shows a magnified cell. Four students have worked out the actual length of the longest side of the cell, but some of them have got the wrong answer.

Which of the answers is correct?

a 5.6 µm   b 56 µm   c 560 µm   d 5600 µm

Chapter 7: Use logical reasoning

Logical reasoning is useful for visual problems too. Use rounding to estimate the length of the cell. The scale line on the diagram is 20 µm long and the cell is about three times as long as that line, so it must be about 60 µm. The answer must therefore be **b** = 56 µm.

Problem 7.2: Here are six views of the same cube.

Which symbol is opposite the red cross?

One way to answer this question is to draw a diagram showing the faces.

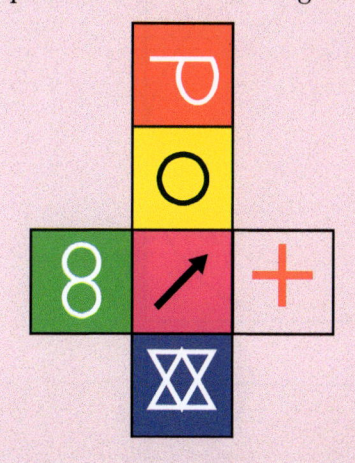

> **Tip**
>
> Imagine holding the cube in different positions. Try to work out which faces are opposite each other.

Another is to spot that the cross appears on the same picture in the question as the P, the O, the arrow and the crossed triangles.

The red cross must be opposite the number 8.

The following example shows how you can apply some of the other strategies as part of the logical reasoning process.

Problem 7.3: The diagram below shows a red square with a purple circle drawn through its vertices and a blue square drawn so it touches the purple circle on all sides.

What is the relationship between the area of the red square and the area of the blue square? Explain how you know.

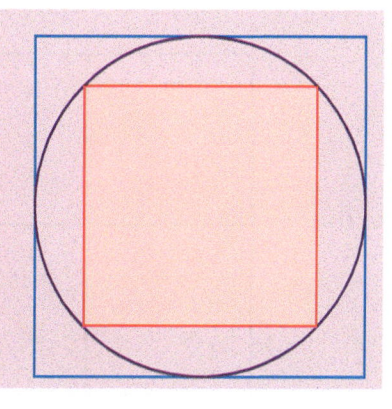

> **Tip**
>
> If you can't do it please don't worry. This is a mathematical problem that is supposed to be difficult. Remember, if you can just 'see' the answer then it wouldn't be a mathematical 'problem'.

Before you read the next page, have a go at the question.

What ideas have you got? Here are some things you can try.

- Get a rough idea of what the answer will be; you know that the blue square is bigger than the red square, but it is certainly less than, say, four times the area. This is not the way to work out the final answer, not least because you can't provide an explanation, but it will help you decide if your answer seems reasonable later.
- You don't know any measurements, so do you need to provide some?
- Will it help to call the side length of the red square x? Or the radius of the circle could be r. Maybe this will be useful and maybe it won't.
- Try putting on some extra lines. Will they help?

> **Tip**
>
> The extra lines are helpful after you've rotated the red square.

Did you manage to answer the problem?

If not, here's one way that you could have solved it by changing the way you look at the diagram.

If you rotate the red square nothing vital changes.

The area of the red square is still the same and the purple and blue shapes are unaffected.

Does this help you to see the relationship between the red square and the blue square?

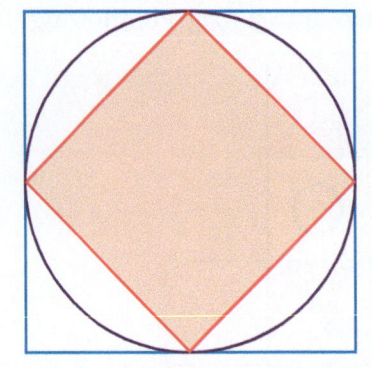

To make this very clear you can remove the circle.

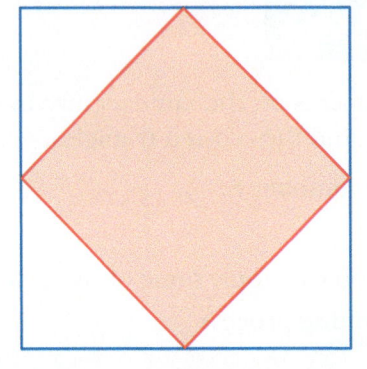

Then you can divide the shape up like this.

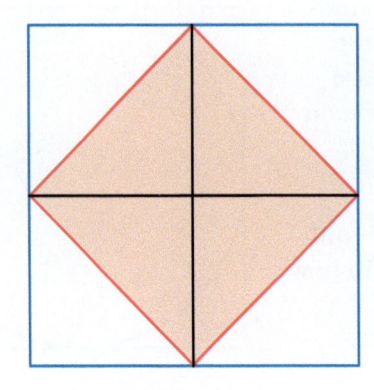

Chapter 7: Use logical reasoning

Now you can explain that the area of the red square is half the area of the blue square.

Here is an example of a full answer.

if you rotate the red square so the vertices of the red square meet the middle of the sides of the blue square you do not change its area.

The two extra lines I have added join the vertices of the red square, cutting it into quarters that are right-angled triangles. These lines also join the middle of the sides of the blue square, cutting it into quarters that are squares.

The total area of the red right-angled triangles is half the area of the blue square.

So the area of the red square is half the area of the blue square.

> **Tip**
>
> You had a rough idea that the area of the blue square is between one and four times the area of the red square, and it is. Estimating the answer can be a useful check that your final answer is sensible.

1

Running tracks come in two standard lengths. Indoor tracks are 200 m long and outdoor tracks are 400 m long.

a Mikhail's event is the 1500 m.

How many laps of each track will Mikhail run in his race?

b Kenji will be running both the 5 km and 10 km races.

How many laps of each track will he run in each race?

2

The rule for calculating how long to cook a joint of meat is '40 minutes per kilo and an additional 25 minutes, at 180° C'.

a Create a formula to calculate the cooking time for meat of any size cooked this way.

Jose wants to serve Sunday lunch at 12.30. The meat weighs 3.75 kg and it must stand for 10 minutes after it is taken out of the oven.

b Jose thinks he needs to put the meat in the oven at 9 am. Is he correct?

3

The ingredients for a recipe for a chocolate cake that serves eight people is shown below.

Cake	Icing
150 g dark chocolate	120 g dark chocolate
6 eggs	100 g hazelnuts
125 g unsalted butter	125 ml double cream
400 g chocolate spread	
100 g ground hazelnuts	

Nadira is having a dinner party and has invited 20 guests. She wants to have enough cake for each guest to have one slice.

a How much dark chocolate should she buy?

b The dark chocolate is available in 200 g bars. How many bars will she need?

c Express the amount of chocolate used to chocolate left over as a ratio in its simplest form.

d On another occasion, Nadira reduces the recipe to serve six people. How much chocolate spread does she need?

4

Halah does some form of exercise each day.

Each day she decides at random to do one of the following: swim 40 lengths, jog 10 km or complete a two-hour cycle ride.

a Draw a sample space diagram showing all the possibilities of the exercise Halah could do on two consecutive days.

b What is the probability that she swims on both days?

c What is the probability that she does not do the same exercise on both days?

5

Five cleaners can clean an office building in two hours and 45 minutes.

a How long should it take three cleaners working at the same rate to clean the building? Give your answer correct to the nearest minute.

b Each cleaner is paid the same hourly rate, and their time is rounded up to the next whole hour. Does reducing the number of cleaners from five to three reduce the amount paid in wages?

6

Two school basketball coaches want to do a study of each of their teams and need the average height of all the team members including the reserves.

Coach McKay used the data in the table on the right to find the mean height for his team.

a Work out the mean height for the McKay team.

Team McKay	
Height (cm)	Frequency
$145 \leqslant h < 155$	1
$155 \leqslant h < 165$	2
$165 \leqslant h < 175$	2
$175 \leqslant h < 185$	8
$185 \leqslant h < 195$	3
$195 \leqslant h < 225$	4

Coach Cooksey used the data from the last health check on each member of his team to find the mean height. The data were as follows:

150 cm, 156 cm, 187 cm, 199 cm, 203 cm, 178 cm, 194 cm, 188 cm, 167 cm, 194 cm, 152 cm, 226 cm, 225 cm, 199 cm, 188 cm, 221 cm, 178 cm, 143 cm, 142 cm, 170 cm.

b Which coach will have the more accurate mean height for his team? Explain your answer.

7

Valerie told Fritz that the expression for the area of this rectangle was $x^2 - 7x + 6$.

Fritz said she was wrong. He told Valerie that the expression for the area was $2(2x - 7)$.

a Who was correct? Justify your answer.

Fritz also (correctly) told Valerie that the area was numerically 2 more than the perimeter. He explained as an example that if the perimeter was 12 cm, then the area would be 14 cm².

b What were the dimensions of the rectangle?

Valerie did her calculations and told Fritz that x could have two values. She said x could equal 2 cm or 9 cm. Fritz laughed and told her to use logic to work out why this was not true.

c Explain why Fritz found Valerie's statement funny.

8

Two glasses that are the same size contain orange drinks, made from squash and water.

The first glass is $\frac{1}{4}$ squash and $\frac{3}{4}$ water.
The second glass is $\frac{1}{6}$ squash and $\frac{5}{6}$ water.

The two glasses are poured into a large drinks bottle.

a What fraction of the resulting drink is squash?

Amit is serving drinks at a party. He has two large jugs of fruit punch. The jugs are identical in size, but one contains punch that is $\frac{2}{5}$ apple juice and the other contains punch that is $\frac{3}{10}$ apple juice.

b Amit wonders how the drink will change if he pours some from both jugs into a glass.

Is it possible for Amit to create a drink that is exactly $\frac{1}{2}$ apple juice?

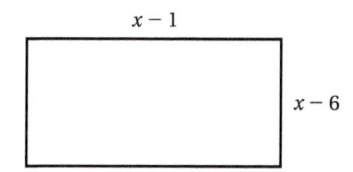

9 ⭐⭐☆

Yasmin is given a set of instructions to create an image:

> Mark a point on your page and label it 'O'.
>
> Draw a 1 cm square with its bottom left-hand corner 1 cm to the right of O.
>
> Enlarge this square by a scale factor of 2 about O.
>
> Translate the smaller square 1 cm to the left.
>
> Rotate the two smaller squares 90° clockwise about the centre of the larger square.
>
> Rotate the whole diagram (up to and including the fifth step) 180° about the centre of the larger square.

a What should Yasmin's completed image look like?

b How many lines of symmetry does the resulting image have?

c What order of rotational symmetry does the resulting image have?

d Design a set of instructions to create the image below.

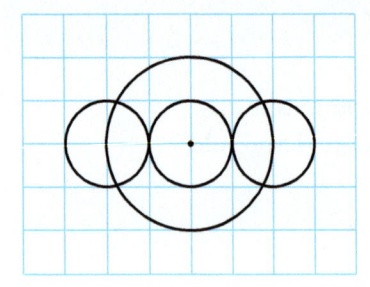

10 ⭐⭐☆

Meg has 105 chocolate buttons. Grace has 95 chocolate buttons.

By what percentage will each girl need to change their number of chocolate buttons so that they have exactly 100 each?

11 ⭐⭐☆

Mr Cheung has a box of board markers. It contains six blue markers, five black markers, seven green markers and two red markers. When he needs a marker, he picks one from the box at random, uses it and then places it back in the box.

On Monday Mr Cheung needed a marker on two occasions.

a What is the probability that he randomly picked the same colour both times?

b What is the probability that he randomly picked a different colour the second time?

c If Mr Cheung forgets to put the first marker back in the box, what is the probability now of taking the same colour of marker both times?

d Is the probability, when he forgets to put it back in, higher or lower than when he does put it back?

12 ⭐⭐☆

Peter is 2.03 m tall. He and his three shorter friends are planning on going camping. They will be using a traditional tent in the shape of a triangular prism.

What dimensions must their tent be if Peter is to be able to comfortably stand upright and lie flat to sleep alongside his three friends?

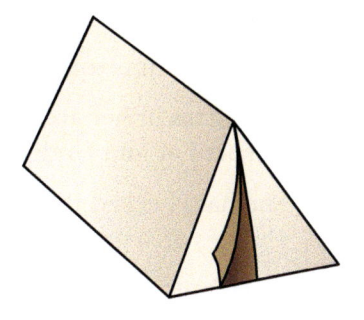

> **Tip**
>
> You will need to make some assumptions to answer this question. You know how tall Peter is but how much space will he need from side to side?

13 ⭐⭐☆

The cost of an extension to a house is directly proportional to the floor area of the extension. The floor area of an extension was 4 m by 5 m and its cost was $15 000.

a What would be the largest floor area possible for $23 000 if the dimensions must be in complete metres?

The extension could be completed in four weeks if the builder had three labourers working five-day weeks from 8 am until 5 pm with him.

b How many labourers are needed to finish the work within three weeks?

c With the builder and this number of labourers, exactly when after their start day should the job be completed?

The labourers are paid a daily rate, and the builder has decided that the jobs left on the last day are best done by him on his own.

d How many extra hours work would the builder be doing without the other labourers, and will the entire job still be completed within three weeks?

The labourers are paid a flat rate of $100 per day and the total price charged by the builder covers labour, materials and profit in the ratio $26:39:25$.

e What percentage of the price charged is profit?

14 ⭐⭐☆

The table shows the number of students in each year group at a new school.

It has been decided there should be a student council of 20 students.

The head teacher wants to take a stratified sample of 20 students to be on this student council.

> **Tip**
>
> What would be the problem with each method?

The deputy head wants to have four students from each year group on the student council.

Year 7	243
Year 8	176
Year 9	162
Year 10	88
Year 11	51

a If the head uses her method, how many of each year group will be on the council?

b Give your opinion on the method you think is best.

15

Susanne wants some carpet fitted in her flat.

Two firms in her area specialise in floorings: Carpet Lay and Underfoot.

She has checked their websites and plotted their charges on a graph to compare their prices.

a How much does each company charge to lay 5 m² of carpet?

b Which company is the cheaper to fit 7.5 m² of carpet?

c What is the largest whole number of square metres that Carpet Lay would lay at a lower price than Underfoot?

Susanne needs a total of 9 m² of carpet laid.

d Which company should Susanne use?

e How much will this cost her?

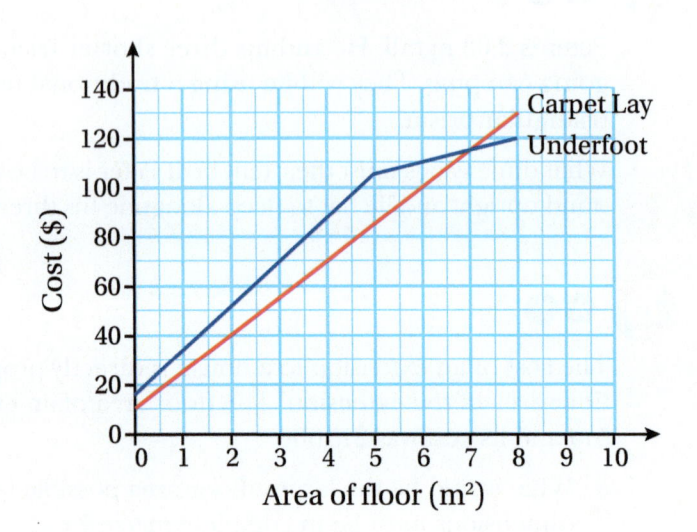

16

The depth of water in a harbour depends on the time of day and the tides.

Time (hours am)	0	1	2	3	4	5	6	7	8	9	10	11	12
Depth (metres)	7.0	10.7	12.0	12.1	10.5	7.5	4.6	2.6	1.5	1.2	1.9	4.1	8.0

a Copy the axes, plot the points and join them up with a smooth curve.

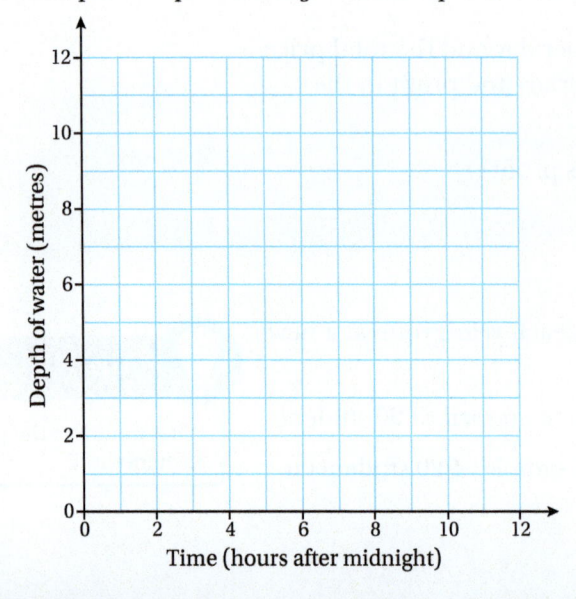

The local ferry needs at least 4 metres of water to stay afloat.

b Between what times should it not attempt to dock?

c Is there going to be another period of 'danger' time within a 24-hour day?

17

The data in the table shows the number of microbes present in a petri dish after certain periods of time.

Number of microbes	63	90	123	258	315	378	447	690	1215
Number of minutes	4	5	6	9	10	11	12	15	20

a Estimate how many microbes were present after eight minutes.

b Is it possible to predict how many microbes might be present after 50 minutes? Explain your answer.

18

In how many ways can you get from flag A to flag B:

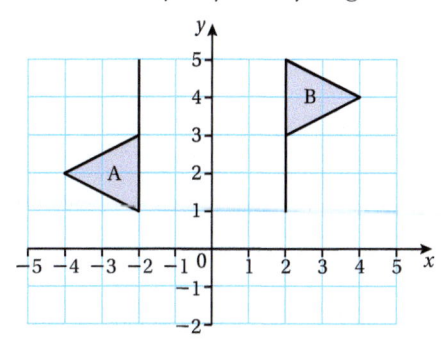

a using a single transformation?

b using exactly two transformations?

> **Tip**
> Remember to provide all of the information necessary to fully describe each transformation.

19

Mrs Grant decided to do a survey with her Year 7 class to find out how much time they spend playing games on their phones.

She recorded the amount of time the students spent playing games on the previous day.

a Copy and complete the histogram below.

b Complete the frequency table.

Time (minutes)	Frequency
$10 \leqslant t < 20$	5
$20 \leqslant t < 60$	4
$60 \leqslant t < 120$	
$120 \leqslant t < 150$	3

Mrs Grant told the class that in her opinion anyone who spent more than 100 minutes per day playing the games probably wasn't spending enough time on their homework.

c How many students were not doing enough homework?

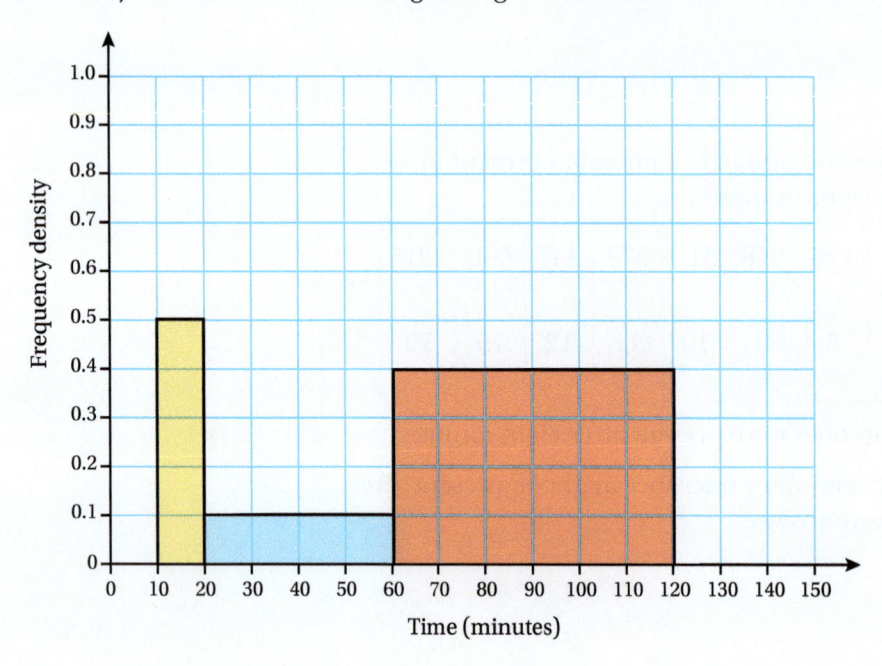

Chapter 8
Use equations, formulae or ratios

Algebra is a very powerful tool in problem-solving because it allows you change long wordy problems into short, clear mathematical statements.

To use this strategy, you have to analyse the written problem, translate it into an equation (or expression) and then solve it to find the answer.

When you analyse the problem, you have to consider which operations are needed as well as what you know and what the unknowns are. You might also need to use a known formula in your solution.

The following steps are useful for this strategy:

- Read the problem carefully. Work out what you need to find and what information is already given.
- Assign a letter (variable) to any unknown quantities you need to find.
- State what each variable represents. For example, let the length be x and the width be y.
- Connect the given and unknown quantities using an equation, formula or ratio.
- Find the solution.
- Answer the original question.

Let's look again at Problem 3 from Chapter 7 to see how using letters to represent unknown lengths and a known formula can provide an efficient solution.

> **Tip**
>
> Finding the solution to an equation does not necessarily mean you have solved the problem. You might need to use one or more values from the equation and do another calculation to make sure you answer the original question.

Problem 8.1: The diagram below shows a red square with a purple circle drawn through its vertices and a blue square drawn so it touches the purple circle on all sides. What is the relationship between the area of the red square and the area of the blue square? Explain how you know.

> **Tip**
>
> You need to apply logic to make sure your answer is sensible. For example, if you are asked for the area of a figure you cannot have a negative value in the answer.

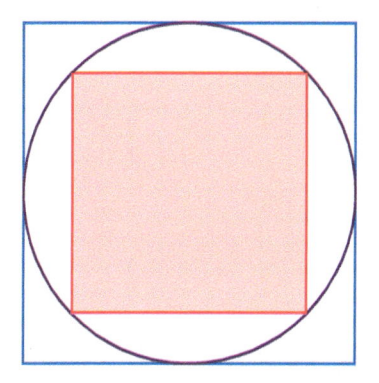

The area of the blue square can be found using the formula $A = s^2$, where s is the length of the side of the square.

Each side of the blue square is equal to the diameter of the circle.

So, let the side of the blue square be d.

Therefore, the area, $A = d^2$

You cannot immediately find the length of a side of the red square, but you can determine that each diagonal is equal to the diameter of the circle (d).

You also know that the diagonals of a square bisect each other at right angles.

Add the diagonals to the diagram and label them.

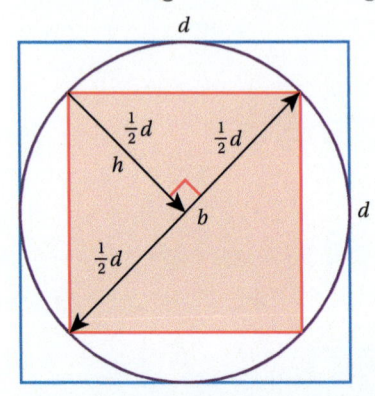

The area of the red square can be found using the formula for triangles.

Area of a triangle is $A = \frac{1}{2}bh$

Area of red square = $2\left(\frac{1}{2}bh\right)$ (twice the area of the triangle forming half the square)

So, area of the red square = bh

base $b = d$ (each diagonal is d)

height $h = \frac{1}{2}d$ (diagonals bisect each other)

So, area of the red square = $d\left(\frac{1}{2}d\right)$

$= \frac{1}{2}d^2$

This shows that the area of the red square $\left(\frac{1}{2}d^2\right)$ is half the area of the blue square (d^2).

Here is another problem that can be solved algebraically.

> **Tip**
>
> Use the diagonal of the red square as the base of the triangle.

Problem 8.2: The formula for a triangular number is $T = \frac{1}{2}n(n+1)$.

Prove that $8T + 1$ is always a square number.

You need to show that it will work for all triangular numbers.

This can be done algebraically:

$8T + 1 = 8 \times \frac{1}{2}n(n+1) + 1$

$= 4n^2 + 4n + 1$

This factorises to give $(2n + 1)^2$, which is square.

Chapter 8: Use equations, formulae or ratios

1

A positive number is four more than five times its reciprocal.

a What is the number?

Another positive number is five more than six times its reciprocal.

b What is this number?

c What is $(n-1)$ more than n times its reciprocal? Explain how you know.

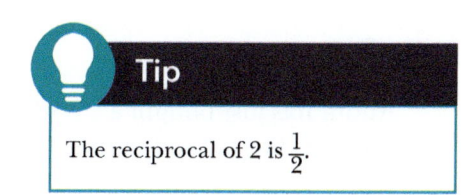

> **Tip**
>
> The reciprocal of 2 is $\frac{1}{2}$.

2

Sections of decorative fencing are made with metal and wooden rods.

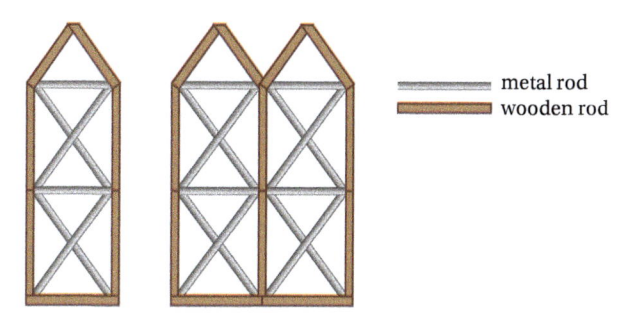

— metal rod
— wooden rod

a How many metal rods will be needed in the next pattern?

b How many wooden rods are needed for the fourth pattern?

c Find the number of metal rods needed for the nth pattern.

The metal rods cost $2 each and the wooden rods cost $2.50 each.

d Sue needs a fence consisting of 12 sections. How much will this cost?

3

Which is greater?

a 80% of $10 or 75% of $12?

b 50% of one chocolate cake or 25% of two chocolate cakes?

c the cost of a CD bought in store for $12.99 or one bought online with a 5% discount code but a delivery charge of $1.99?

> **Tip**
>
> You have probably assumed that all the cakes are identical. Consider how your answer would change if you did not make this assumption.

4

Sygny is y years old. Mark is z years old.

Together their ages total 20 years.

Sygny is 8 years older than Mark.

How old are Sygny and Mark?

Cambridge IGCSE Mathematics Extended Problem-solving Book

5 ★☆☆

Abdul has just bought a circular dining table of diameter 240 cm. It comes flat-packed to make it easier to transport. His front door is a rectangle, 2.1 m tall and 1.05 m wide. Will he be able to fit the table top through the door?

> **Tip**
>
> Can you see that the circular table is not going to fit through the door if held vertically or horizontally? Abdul will need to tilt it to try to get it inside.

6 ★☆☆

The number of living bacteria cells on the petri dish in the science lab is inversely proportional to the number of hours it remains in the refrigerator.

The number of living bacteria cells on a petri dish that has been in the refrigerator for four hours is 20 000.

Jamila thinks that the longer the time in the refrigerator, the fewer number of bacteria cells. She worked out the number of bacteria cells she thought would be on the dish.

a Find a formula Jamila could use.

b What number of bacteria cells would Jamila's formula give for a dish that has been in the refrigerator for eight hours?

c What problems are there with Jamila's formula?

7 ★☆☆

Melvin is a landscape gardener and he needs to hire a small digger for his next job.

The cost of hiring a digger from JCEs is shown as a straight-line graph.

Move It Builders also hire out diggers but they have a basic fixed charge in addition to their daily charge. Their charges are also shown as a straight-line graph.

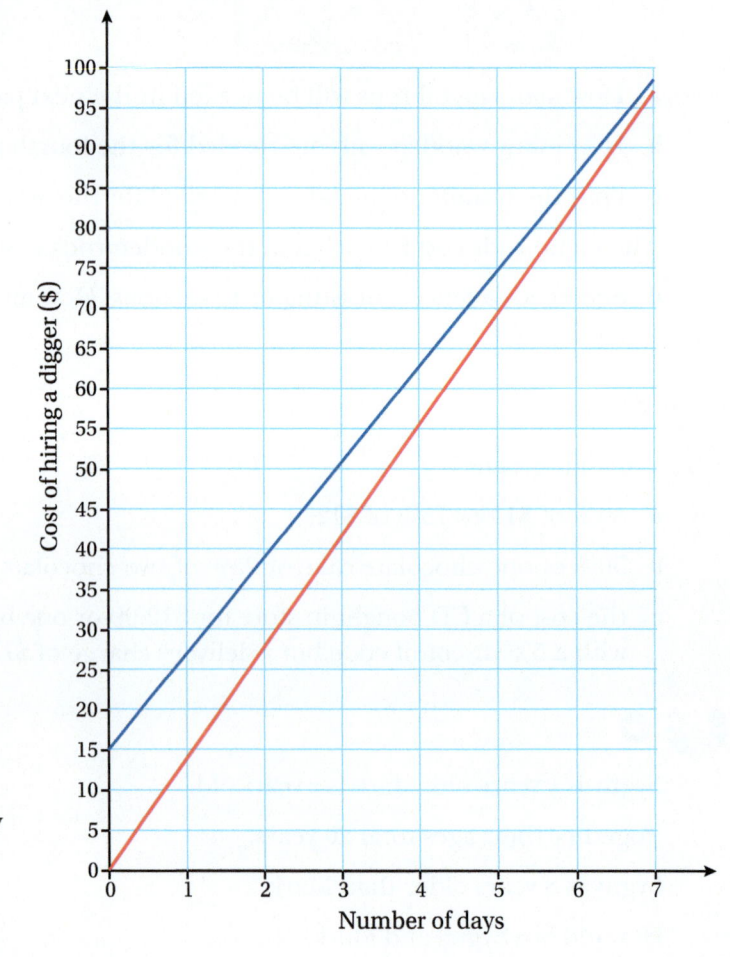

a Which line refers to the charges for each of the companies?
b What is the basic fixed charge made by one of the companies?
c How much per day does JCEs charge?
d Is Move It Builders' daily charge more or less than what JCEs charge? By how much?
e What would be the charge if Melvin hired the digger from Move It Builders for 5 days?
f What would be the total cost if Melvin needed the digger for two weeks and he hired it from Move It Builders?
g If Melvin needed the digger for two weeks, would it be cheaper from Move It Builders or JCEs?
h For the two-week period, how much less would it cost to hire from the cheaper company?

8

Sarah draws the graph of $y = (x - 2)(x + 2)$.

She decided that if she made the transformation $y + 4$ on her graph she would be sketching the graph of $y = x^2$.

Is she correct?

Explain your answer.

9

Xola is reorganising the chickens in his shed.

If he puts three in each cage, there is one chicken left with no cage to go into.

If he puts four in each cage, one cage is left empty.

a How many chickens does Xola have?
b How many cages does he have?

10

a Find three consecutive even numbers that add up to 228.
b Find three consecutive odd numbers that add up to 291.
c The sum of the squares of two consecutive numbers is 1301. Find the numbers.
d The difference between two numbers is 6. The sum of the two numbers is 80. Find the numbers.

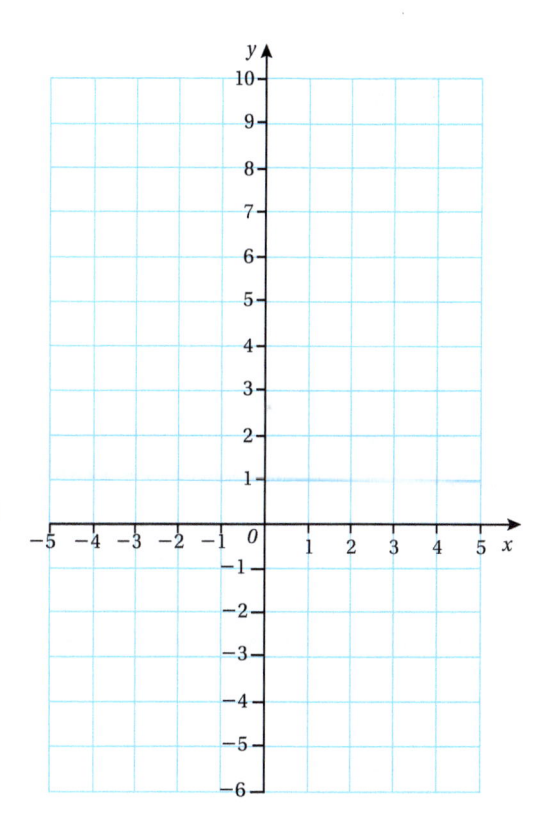

11

The sequence 2, 10, 24, 44, 70, … can be written as
$(1 \times 2), (2 \times 5), (3 \times 8), (4 \times 11), (5 \times 14), …$.

a Write an expression for the nth term of the sequence.

One of the terms in the sequence is 234.

b Write this term in the form $(a \times b)$, where a and b are values to be determined.

12

The area of a square is given as $4x^2 - 12x + 9$.

Find an expression for the perimeter of the square.

13

a Create a formula, in terms of x, to calculate the area of the shaded border.

b The area of the border is 204 cm². What are the dimensions of the outer rectangle?

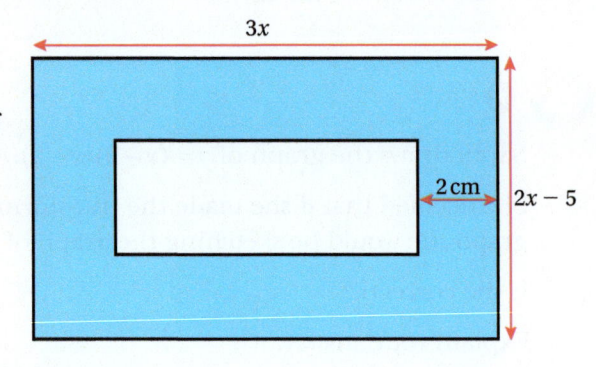

(Outer rectangle: $3x$ by $2x - 5$; inner border offset 2 cm)

14

Aaron went to the local fruit market and bought four apples and five bananas for $2.05.

Brahm went to the same fruit market and bought three apples and seven bananas for $2.35.

Aaron and Brahm asked their maths teacher for an easy method to find the price of an apple and the price of a banana.

She told them they could create an equation for the cost of the fruit each of them bought and solve them simultaneously.

a Write the two equations.

b What is the cost of an apple?

c What is the price of a banana?

d Can you show this same information as straight-line graphs? How would you use your graphs to find the price of the apple and the banana?

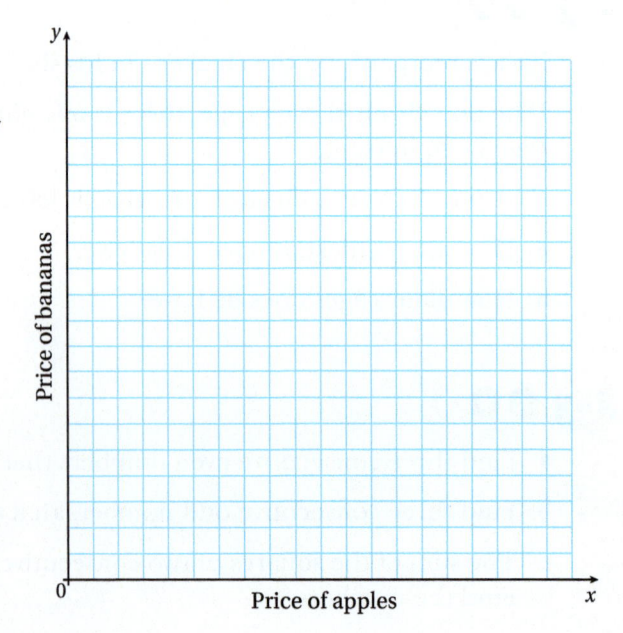

15

100 people were asked to complete a questionnaire about their pets.

Out of the 100 people, 17 had both a cat and a bird. A total of 54 had either a cat or a bird, but not both. 30 people owned a bird.

a If one person was chosen at random, what is the probability they had neither a cat nor a bird?

b If one person was chosen at random, what is the probability they only owned a cat?

16 ★★☆

What conditions are there on the values of x and y if a can be anything and each equation is always correct?

a $(a^x)^y = 1$

b $(a^x)^y = a$

c $(a^x)^y = \sqrt{a}$ $(a \geq 0)$

17 ★★☆

The planet Mars takes 24.6 hours to rotate on its axis. The Earth takes 24 hours to rotate on its axis.

a Express these times in hours as ratios in their simplest form Mars : Earth, in integer form.

b Express these times in minutes as ratios in their simplest form.

The mass of Mars is 6.4×10^{23} kg. The mass of Earth is 6.0×10^{24} kg.

c Express the masses as ratios.

The highest mountain in the solar system is Olympus Mons, measuring approximately 27 km. Olympus Mons is on Mars.

The highest mountain on Earth, Mount Everest, is 8848 metres.

d Using a suitable degree of accuracy, express the heights as ratios:

Olympus Mons : Mount Everest

18 ★★☆

Triangles ABC and XYZ are similar.

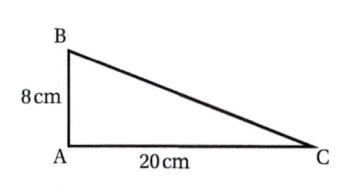

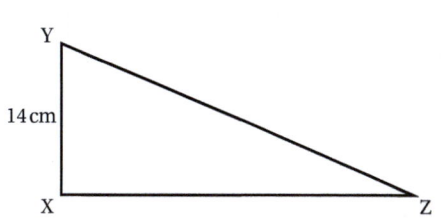

In triangle ABC, length AB is 8 cm and AC is 20 cm.

In triangle XYZ, length XY is 14 cm.

a Work out the area of triangle XYZ.

b Express area of triangle ABC : area of triangle XYZ in its simplest form.

c What type of numbers are in the ratio? Explain why this is so.

19 ★★★

a Complete the table of values for the graph $y = x^2 - 6x - 5$.

x	-2	-1	0	1	2	3	4	5	6
y									

b Write down the coordinates of the turning point of the graph.

c Write down the exact values of the roots of the equation.

d Write down the coordinates of the turning point of the graph of $-y$.

e Write down the exact values of the roots of the equation $-y = x^2 - 6x - 5$

20 ★★★

Zain wanted to transform the graph of $y = x^3$ to the graph of $y = (x - 8)^3$ He wrongly used the translation vector $\begin{pmatrix} 0 \\ -8 \end{pmatrix}$.

a Explain why this is wrong.

b Starting from Zain's new, incorrect version, what translation vector should he use to get to the correct answer?

21 ★★★

Brandon is learning about the sine and cosine graphs.

His teacher asked Brandon to sketch both the sine and cosine graphs, showing all coordinates of the points where the graphs cross the axes.

a Sketch the sine graph and the cosine graph on the same set of axes.

His teacher then asked Brandon to describe the sine graph in terms of a transformation of the graph of $y = \cos(x)$.

b Write down this transformation.

The teacher then asked Brandon to change it around and to describe the cosine graph in terms of a transformation on the sine graph.

c Write down this transformation.

d Would you describe these transformations as reflections or translations?

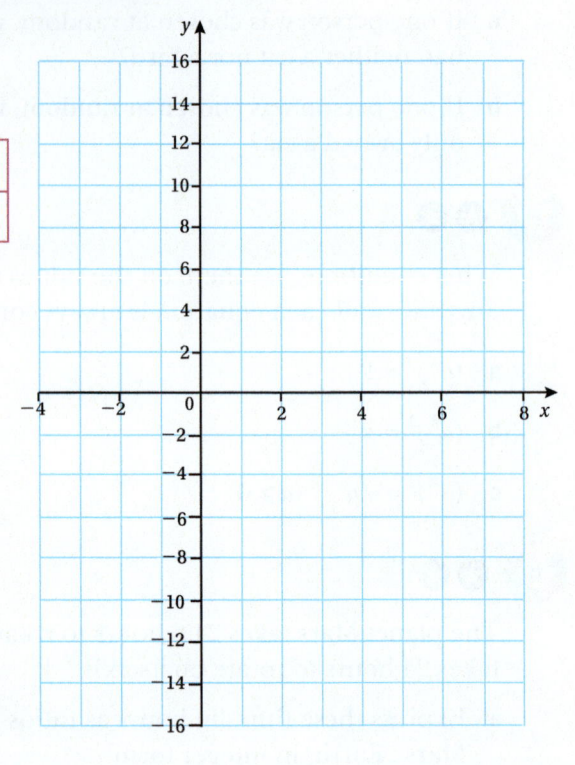

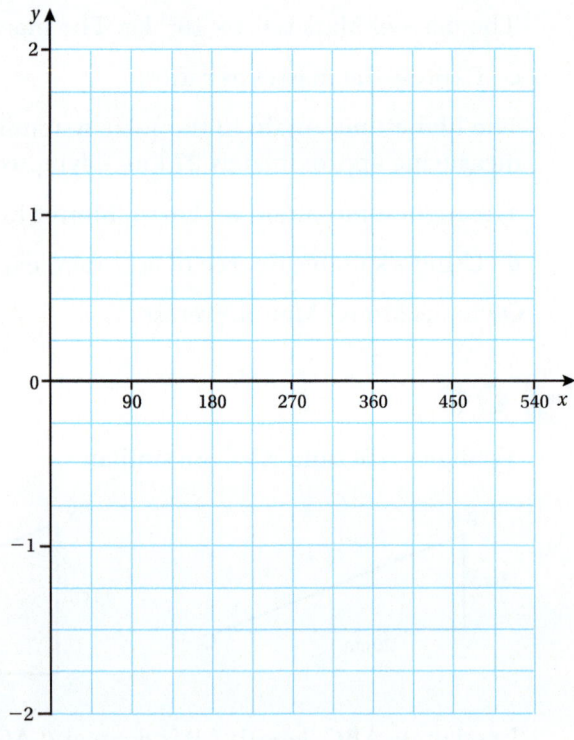

Chapter 8: Use equations, formulae or ratios

22 ★★★

A square is surrounded by four identical rectangular tiles, as shown.

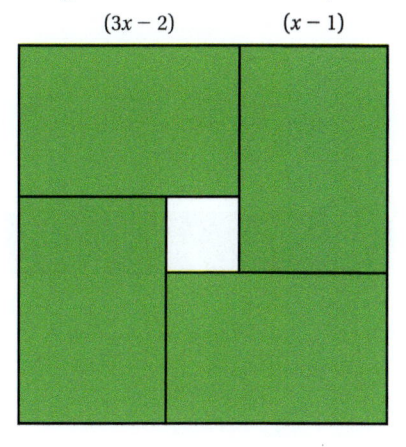

$(3x - 2)$ $(x - 1)$

a Find an expression for the total area of the four identical tiles.

b Find an expression for the area of the large square.

c What is the area of the unshaded square?

23 ★★★

In a test, students are asked to calculate the area of the shape shown below. They are instructed to give their answer correct to 1 d.p.

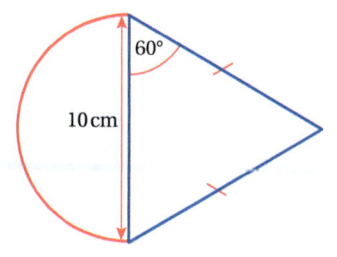

60°
10 cm

A student's answer is shown here:

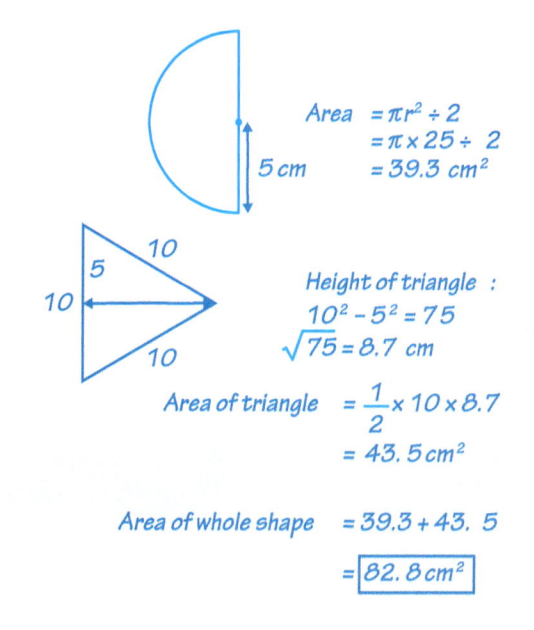

5 cm

Area $= \pi r^2 \div 2$
$= \pi \times 25 \div 2$
$= 39.3 \ cm^2$

10
5
10
10

Height of triangle :
$10^2 - 5^2 = 75$
$\sqrt{75} = 8.7 \ cm$

Area of triangle $= \dfrac{1}{2} \times 10 \times 8.7$
$= 43.5 \ cm^2$

Area of whole shape $= 39.3 + 43.5$
$= \boxed{82.8 \ cm^2}$

Tip
The student's answer is very close. Why is it not exact?

The teacher marks the answer as incorrect, although he awards some marks for the method.

a What is the problem with the answer?

b What is the answer that the teacher was looking for?

24 ✪✪✪

A square piece of paper, of side length 8 cm, is folded so that the bottom right-hand corner, C, meets the midpoint of the top edge AB.

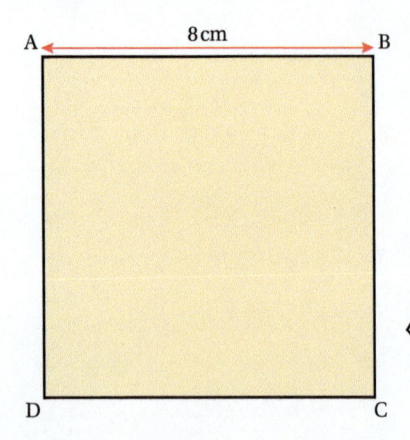

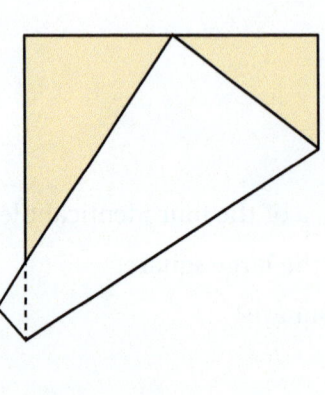

> **Tip**
>
> Remember that for similar triangles you only need to consider the angles.

a Show that the three triangles created are mathematically similar.

b Show that the lengths of the sides of the smallest triangle are exactly a quarter the size of the largest triangle.

25 ✪✪✪

a Use the diagram of an equilateral triangle to find the exact value of:

   i $\tan 60°$ **ii** $\sin 60°$ **iii** $\cos 60°$.

> **Tip**
>
> What do you know about the properties of an equilateral triangle?
> Why is the triangle divided in half?

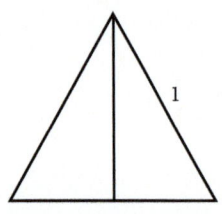

b How does this diagram show that $\sin 60° = \cos 30°$ and that $\sin 30° = \cos 60°$?

26 ✪✪✪

The diagram shows a hexagon ABCDEF.

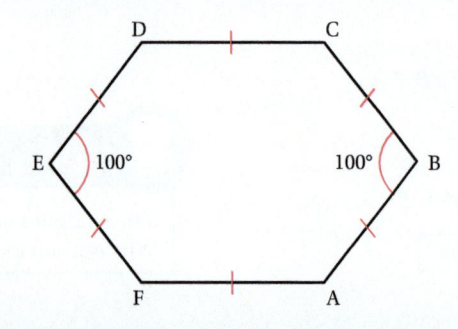

> **Tip**
>
> Can you add some lines to produce useful triangles?

All 6 sides of the hexagon have length 6 cm, but the shape is not regular. Angles ABC and DEF are both 100°. Find the area of hexagon ABCDEF.

27 ★★★

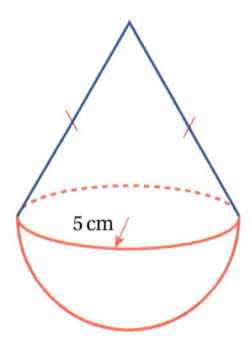

The diagram shows a toy made from a hemisphere with radius 5 cm attached to a right cone with base radius 5 cm. The volume of the hemisphere and the cone are exactly the same.

Calculate, in terms of π, the total surface area of the toy.

> **Tip**
> You don't know the height or the slant height of the cone. Add lines to the diagram to help you find them.

28 ★★★

The diagram shows trapezium ABCD. Angle ADC is 90°.

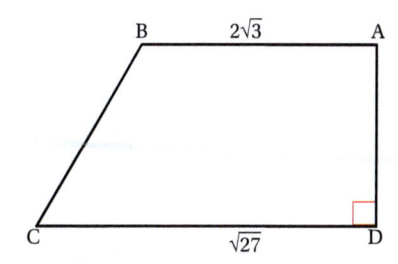

AB = $2\sqrt{3}$ cm and CD = $\sqrt{27}$ cm. The area of ABCD is $\sqrt{75}$ cm².

Calculate the exact perimeter of ABCD.

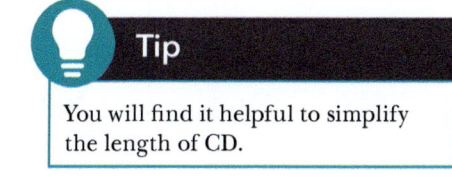

> **Tip**
> You will find it helpful to simplify the length of CD.

Chapter 9
Organise data and work systematically

In problems where you have to consider many possibilities, it is useful to work systematically and find suitable ways of organising your work.

Lists, tables, charts, Venn diagrams, probability spaces and tree diagrams can all help you organise and keep track of your thinking as you work through a problem.

When you record your working and ideas systematically, in an organised way, you can easily review what you have already done. Systematic recording allows you to keep track of data, easily spot missing (or duplicate) values or data points and work out what else you need to complete a pattern and find a solution. You have already seen that the solution to many different problems can lie in recognising patterns. Systematic recording allows you to see patterns more easily and extend them if necessary.

Problem 9.1: This is the flag of South Korea.

Around the edge of the central circle there are four 'trigrams'. These are made up of three lines. The one on the right has three solid lines.

And this one has a broken line at the bottom and the top, with a solid line in the middle.

If you just use solid lines and broken lines, what fraction of all the possible trigrams (made using three lines) appear on the South Korean flag?

First of all, do you understand the problem? There are other trigrams that haven't yet been drawn, such as the one on the right.

It looks as if you will need to work out how many possibilities there are. If you just start writing them down (which is a reasonable starting point) there is a risk that you will miss some of them, or maybe write the same one twice.

These are the ones you have got so far.

A better way to solve this problem would be to work systematically. You could start with three solid lines and no broken lines. That is easy because there is only one of them, as shown on the right.

Next you could have two solid lines and one broken line.

This example is systematic in the way the broken line has moved downwards. Can you finish off the rest of the trigrams?

The final list that you get is as follows.

There are eight of them and you can be confident that because you have worked systematically you haven't missed any out, or got any of them twice. Go back to the original question: **what fraction of all the possible trigrams (made using three lines) appear on the South Korean flag?**

There are four of them on the flag and you know there are eight altogether, so $\frac{1}{2}$ of the trigrams appear on the flag. If you want to test out your ability to work systematically you could try to find all of the ways to make a diagram that uses four lines.

Organising your work can save you time. This example shows how using a table can help you be systematic and efficient.

> **Problem 9.2:** The postman knew it was Mrs Garcia's birthday because of the large number of cards and packages he had to deliver. When he asked Mrs Garcia how old she was, she told him that yesterday her age was a square number, but today it is a prime number.
>
> Can the postman work out how old Mrs Garcia is?

You need to find two consecutive numbers where the first one is a square number (yesterday's age) and the next number is a prime number (Mrs Garcia's age today, on her birthday).

Guessing numbers at random doesn't seem sensible. You could either list the prime numbers and find out whether the number before each one is a square number, or you could do it the other way round and list all of the square numbers and see whether the number after each one is prime.

Both methods will work, but the second one is a more sensible choice because working out some square numbers is much easier than listing prime numbers.

You might have realised that you don't need to bother trying the odd square numbers from now on (so the rows 7 and 9 in the table below have been shaded out), because when you add 1 it will be even and can't be prime.

Which numbers work? Mrs Garcia could be 2, 5, 17, 37 or 101 years old. She is an adult, so that means she is either 37 or 101. Hopefully it would

n	Square number (n^2)	Add one to this	Is it prime?
1	1	2	Yes
2	4	5	Yes
3	9	10	No
4	16	17	Yes
5	25	26	No
6	36	37	Yes
7	49		
8	64	65	No
9	81		
10	100	101	Yes

be obvious from Mrs Garcia's appearance whether she is 37 or 101, so it is likely that the postman **can** work out how old she is.

The following problems may be solved using more than one method; however, the worked solutions provided at the back of this book are based on the method introduced above.

1

The first two questions on a worksheet are:

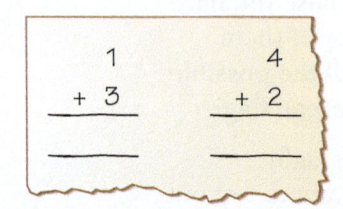

$$1 + 3 \qquad 4 + 2$$

a Using positive integers less than 10, how many different addition questions could be on the rest of the worksheet? (Note the order in addition is not important, so $1 + 3$ is the same as $3 + 1$, therefore these do not count as different questions.)

b If the worksheet includes negative integers greater than $^-10$, how many different answers to addition calculations could there be?

2

Insert the operators: $+$, $-$ and $\times$ into the three boxes below. You should use all of them once each.

$5 \square 2 \square 10 \square -3$

In how many ways can you get a negative result?

3

$a + b = 1$

How many different pairs of values of a and b will satisfy this equation if:

a a and b are non-negative integers

b a and b are positive decimal numbers with 1 d.p.

c a and b are positive decimal numbers with 2 d.p.?

d How would your answer to part **a** change if a and b were allowed to take negative values?

> **Tip**
> How could you write out the answers in a systematic way?

Chapter 9: Organise data and work systematically

4

Tomasz helps himself to sandwiches from a buffet lunch. He notices that the sandwiches have all been cut into identical triangles.

> **Tip**
>
> Think of a logical way of trying out all of the possible arrangements of the sandwiches.
> You also need to decide on a sensible way to record your findings so that you can be sure you have found all of the possible polygons.

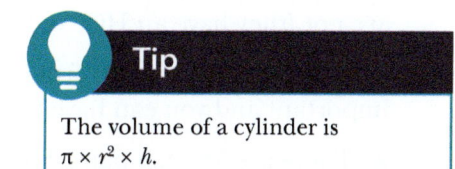

Tomasz places his sandwiches so that they fit together to create a square. He wonders how many different polygons he can create by arranging two or more sandwiches on his plate.

a Assuming that Tomasz matches the edges of the sandwiches, how many different polygons can he create, using:

   i   exactly two sandwiches

   ii exactly three sandwiches

   iii all four sandwiches?

b Is it possible for Tomasz to create all of the special types of quadrilateral, using two or more sandwiches from his plate?

5

Using the fractions $\frac{2}{3}$ and $\frac{1}{5}$ and combining them using any of $+, -, \times$ and $\div$:

a What is the biggest answer you can get?

b What is the smallest possible answer?

6

A factory makes packing boxes for cylinders.

Each box is a cuboid measuring 40 cm × 40 cm with a height of 15 cm.

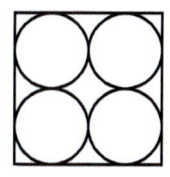

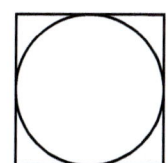

> **Tip**
>
> The volume of a cylinder is $\pi \times r^2 \times h$.

a What are the maximum dimensions (radius and height) of the cylinders that can fit into each box?

b Make a guess as to which box has the most unused space.

c Use calculations to check your guess. What did you find?

7 ⭐☆☆

Ntombi has five cards from a pack of playing cards: two jacks, a queen, a king and an ace. She shuffles the cards and picks two at random.

a Make a list of all the possible pairs of cards she could pick.

b What is the probability she picks the two jacks?

c What is the probability she does not pick any jacks?

8 ⭐☆☆

For a set of ten numbers the following information is known:

mode = 3, range = 10, median = 3, mean = 6.

The numbers are all integers and there are only three different integers involved.

a Can you find the ten numbers?

For another set of four odd numbers the mean is 20, the mode is 3 and the median is 3.

b What are the numbers?

In this second set of four numbers, some changes are made. The numbers are still all odd, the mode is still 3 but the median is now 5.

c What numbers are now in this set?

The numbers are changed again, so the four odd numbers have a mode of 3 and a median of 10.

d What are the numbers in this set now?

e What happens if the mode of four odd numbers is 3 and the median is 15?

f Investigate all possible sets of four odd numbers with a mode of 3 and mean of 20.

> **Tip**
>
> Working systematically can help you spot a pattern here. Remember: in this question the median must always remain an integer.

9 ⭐⭐☆

🖩 Two numbers are called co-prime if their highest common factor (HCF) is 1. For example, 9 and 10 are co-prime, but 10 and 14 are not (they have an HCF of 2).

You choose two numbers from 1 to 12 where the order is not important and you can have the same number twice.

a There are 78 such pairs. Show how you know this is correct.

b What fraction of the integer pairs from 1 to 12 are co-prime?

Chapter 9: Organise data and work systematically

10 ★★☆

Jeff draws a heptagon and numbers the vertices in order. He then draws a diagonal on the shape and adds the numbers at the ends of the diagonal. He then repeats the process with another diagonal. So far Jeff has a total of 21 (5 + 10 + 6).

Jeff draws all of the possible diagonals and adds the numbers on.

a What is his final total?

Phil does the same thing with a hexagon.

Ali does the same thing with a pentagon.

b If Phil and Ali add their totals together, will they have a bigger number than Jeff?

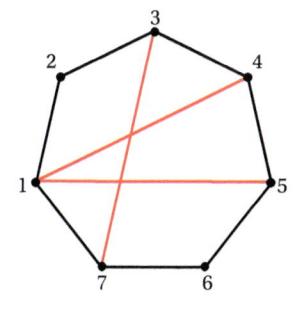

> **Tip**
>
> A diagonal of a shape joins two vertices that are not next to each other.

11 ★★☆

A splash pool is to be made by digging a hole in the shape of two overlapping circles, each of diameter 4 m.

The centres of the circles are 2 m apart.

The cost of the pool is broken down into the base (which is $800 per square metre) and the sides ($225 per metre of edge).

Work out the cost of the pool.

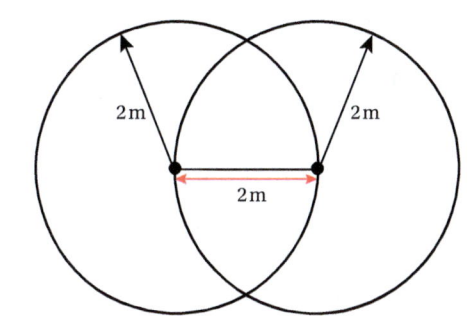

12 ★★☆

Find values for *a*, *b* and *c* that make this equation true:

$245 = 1^a + 2^b + 3^c$

13 ★★☆

Calculate the missing length in the diagram below.

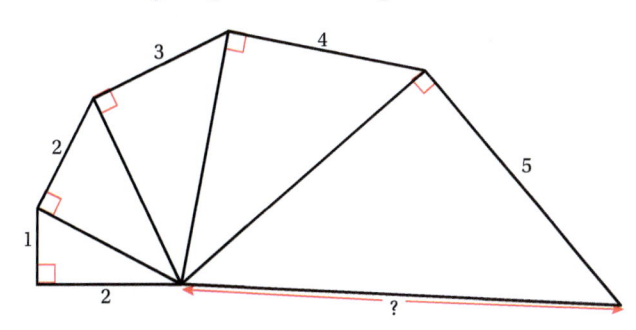

> **Tip**
>
> Work with one triangle at a time. Why is the working easier if you leave your calculations in surd form?

14 ★★★

To make an ordinary cake you mix the ingredients together and then bake the mixture.

A friendship cake mixture is different. You add a little extra milk each day and only bake some of the mixture.

Mai starts a new friendship cake mixture.

After a week, Mai divides her mixture into four, keeps one portion for herself and gives the other three portions to friends.

Her friends then keep their mixture for a week, adding milk and stirring it each day.

After a week, everyone divides their mixture into four portions, keeps one of them and gives the other three portions to other friends.

This process can continue for weeks.

After one week, Mai has given some of the original mixture away, so four people have got some mixture.

a How many people have the mixture after four weeks?

b How many will have the mixture after six weeks?

c Given that the population of a country is about 66 million, how many weeks would it take until everyone could have received Mai's friendship cake mixture?

d Why is it unlikely that everyone would receive it?

15 ★★★

The equivalent decimal of every fraction is either terminating (it stops) or is recurring (it repeats forever).

Where N can take the value of any positive integer from 1 to 10, how many of the fractions $\frac{1}{N}$ are recurring when you find their decimal equivalents?

> **Tip**
>
> Remember that a fraction represents a division calculation. You could use short division or another written method to turn each fraction into a decimal. Make sure you continue for long enough to decide whether the fraction represents a terminating or recurring decimal.

16 ✪✪✪

Three triangles are drawn as shown in the diagram below.

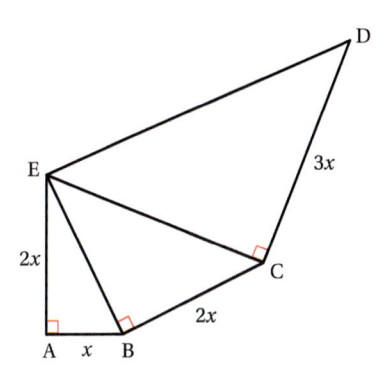

> **Tip**
>
> Draw each triangle separately, starting with ABE and apply Pythagoras' theorem carefully, once for each triangle. After each calculation transfer everything that you have learned to the next triangle.

Find the length ED, giving your answer as an exact multiple of x

17 ✪✪✪

a Find the coordinates of the points where the graph with equation $y = x^2 - 4x + 3$ meets the graph with equation $y = 2x + 3$.

b Sketch both graphs on the same pair of axes, labelling the coordinates of all points of intersection between the graphs (and with axes)

18 ✪✪✪

If $f(x) = \dfrac{1-x}{1+x}$

show that $ff(x) = x$.

Guess, test and improve

When you are faced with a problem that you cannot see immediately how to solve, it can be helpful to play around with the given information as a starting point.

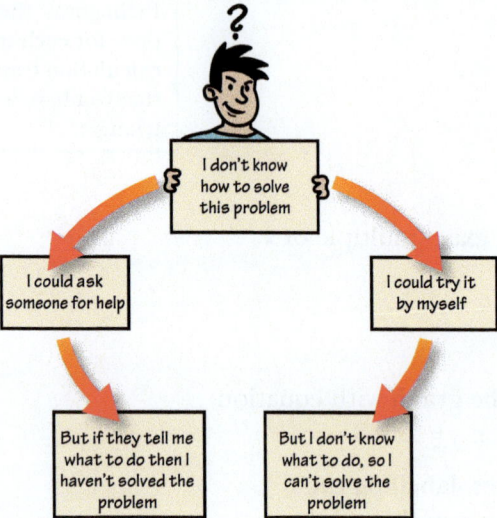

```
            I don't know
           how to solve
           this problem
           ↙         ↘
    I could ask      I could try it
   someone for help   by myself
        ↓                 ↓
   But if they tell me   But I don't know
   what to do then I     what to do, so I
   haven't solved the    can't solve the
   problem               problem
```

This strategy involves guessing what you could possibly do and trying it out. The key to this strategy is to apply the other strategies you know to get a better understanding the problem. If what you try doesn't seem to work, then you try a different approach to improve your chances of finding a solution. This is not the same as a trial and error approach. It involves thinking about the problem logically and linking it to the areas of mathematics, the processes you've learned, and strategies that might help to solve the problem.

The process here involves devising a plan, then carrying it out and evaluating as you go to see whether it is moving you towards a solution or not.

You might find it helpful to write down the things you do know (for example, the key ideas from the question) and which areas of mathematics these relate to.

> **Problem 10.1:** Ben bought a bag of rice at the supermarket. He wonders how many grains of rice there are in the bag.
>
> Can you help him?

There are all sorts of things that seem to make this question impossible to answer.

- Not every bag of rice has exactly the same number of grains of rice in it.
- Different varieties of rice are different sizes (for example long grain rice is longer than risotto rice).
- Individual grains vary in size.
- You don't know how big the bag is. If he has bought a 1 kg bag then there will be approximately twice as many grains as there will be in a 500 g bag.

You will have realised by now that there isn't going to be an exact answer, so you need to work out a rough answer. It is often useful to work out a ball-park figure, and as long as it is of the right order of magnitude (which means it has roughly the correct number of digits) then that will be reasonable.

If you decide a problem is difficult and do nothing then it won't get solved! You could start to try some things that might be useful.

Option 1: Count every grain of rice in a bag.

This is not sensible in reality as you haven't got a bag of rice and the answer is probably rather big, so it will take a long time and that involves counting rather than doing maths, so try something else.

Option 2: Weigh a single grain and then work out how many grains there will be in 1 kg.

The problem here is that a single grain of rice will be extremely light, and certainly less than 1 g. Your scales aren't accurate enough to do this though (and you don't have any rice to weigh anyway).

Option 3: Find out how many grains are in 1 g and then multiply by 1000.

This is an improvement on the previous option because it uses the fact that 1000 g = 1 kg. But you still don't have any rice to weigh.

Option 4: Find out how big a grain of rice is.

Can you draw a picture of an uncooked grain of rice? (Uncooked rice is smaller than the fluffy, cooked rice). One grain is about half a cm long and maybe 2 mm high.

What shape is a grain of rice?

It's a bit like a cylinder but with sloping ends. In fact, it is roughly a cuboid! You could work out the rough volume of the grain of rice by assuming it is a cuboid that is $\frac{1}{2}$ cm by 2 mm by 2 mm.

Work out the volume of a bag of rice and compare this to the volume of a grain of rice. In the kitchen cupboard at home you are probably used to seeing 1 kg bags of food (sugar, flour, pasta, rice, and so on). You can get a mental image of a 1 kg bag of sugar, using your ruler to help, visualise the size that is about 10 cm by 15 cm by 8 cm.

But the units are all different. That is awkward, so you could work in mm.

The volume of a single grain of rice is about 5 mm × 2 mm × 2 mm. This is 20 mm³.

The volume of the bag is about 100 mm × 150 mm × 80 mm. This is 1 200 000 mm³.

1 200 000 ÷ 20 = 60 000, so you could estimate there are roughly 60 000 grains in a bag.

Ask yourself, does this seem reasonable?

If 60 000 grains of rice weigh 1 kg then about 60 of them would weigh 1 g. So this does seem possible. The errors in your estimate of the sizes are likely to be outweighed by the fact that rice grains are not cuboids, but they also don't fit together perfectly in the bag.

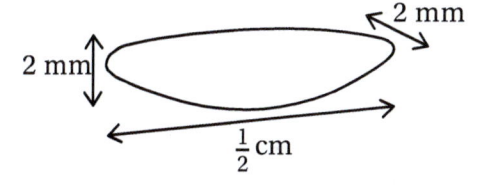

This example shows how you can start with no idea of how to get to a solution and move closer towards one by making intelligent guesses and improving on those that don't work to move towards a better option.

The following problems may be solved using more than one method; however, the worked solutions provided at the back of this book are based on the method introduced above.

1

Jyoti and Indira are making towers with cubes.

Between them they have 12 cubes, each of different sizes.

There is a 1 cm cube, a 2 cm cube, a 3 cm cube, a 4 cm cube and so on up to the biggest cube, which measures 12 cm along each edge.

For the first towers they make, Jyoti uses the six smallest cubes and Indira uses the six largest.

a How much taller was Indira's tower compared to Jyoti's?

The girls then decide to make two towers of the same height using six cubes each.

b Work out a combination of cubes that each girl could have.

2

Which of the statements about the number 12 345 678 912 are true?

i It is odd.

ii It is a multiple of 3.

iii It is a prime number.

iv Dividing the number by 5 leaves a remainder of 2.

v It is a multiple of 4.

3

A grandfather is twice as old as his son Dimitri. Dimitri was 29 years old when his own son Paolo was born.

The total of the ages of the three family members is 131 years.

Find the ages of the grandfather, Dimitri and Paolo.

4

The sum of the ages of three family members is 134 years.

Raj is five times as old as his daughter Savita.

His wife Lata is nine years Raj's junior.

How old is Lata?

Chapter 10: Guess, test and improve

5

For every eight students going on a school trip there must be an accompanying teacher. The school hired some 42-seater buses to transport everyone on the trip. Each bus has one adult driver.

a There is a school trip planned for 140 students. How many teachers will need to be on this trip?

b Some extra teachers have decided they want to join the trip. There are now 21 teachers available. How many extra students could go on the trip?

c It was too late to take extra students, so the original 140 students went with the extra teachers. What is the new ratio of students to teachers?

d Including the bus drivers, what is the ratio of students to adults?

e What fraction of the group are now adults?

6

Two identical triangles are drawn using two diameters and two vertical lines, inside a circle of radius 7 cm.

If this diagram is placed on a 1 cm coordinate grid, so that the centre of the circle is located at the origin, what will be the coordinates of points A and B?

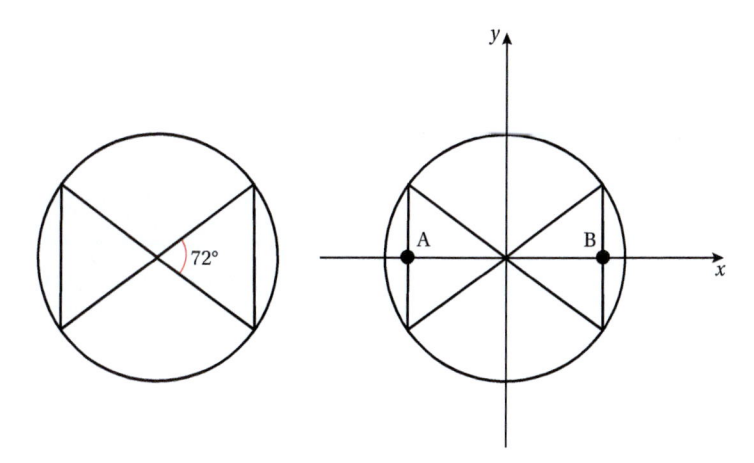

7

For a set of eight integers the following information is known:

the biggest number is 16.

Mean = 7.5. Mode = 3 and 5. Range = 15.

a Can you find the other numbers in the set?

b How many different solutions are there?

> **Tip**
>
> You know how many numbers there are: draw boxes for them and then write in what you know.

Cambridge IGCSE Mathematics Extended Problem-solving Book

8

In a set of five positive integers the range is 15, the mode is 2 and the median is 5.

a If the mean is 7, what are the numbers?

b If the range, mode and median stay the same, what is the biggest possible mean value if this is an integer value?

c If the range, mode and median stay the same, what is the smallest possible mean value?

9

$3 = \dfrac{a}{b} + c$

a, b and c are integers.

a Suggest values of a, b and c that will make the calculation correct.

b Suggest values of a, b and c that will make the calculation correct where $b > 1$.

c Suggest values of a, b and c that will make the calculation correct where $b < 0$.

10

A magic square has numbers in each row, column and diagonal that add up to the same thing (the 'magic number').

For the magic square below, the magic number is 2.1.

0.74		
$\dfrac{129}{150}$		
		$\dfrac{33}{50}$

> **Tip**
> Copy the diagram and fill in the cells as you work them out.

Complete the magic square.

11

Alesha has a pack of playing cards. She picks one card at random, puts it on the table and then picks a second card.

Is it more likely that Alesha will get two aces, or two red kings?

How much more likely?

> **Tip**
> Would a diagram help? What about simplifying the problem, so she picks just one card?

12 ★★☆

Adam has two pairs of grey socks, three pairs of brown socks, a blue pair and a stripey pair. He also has four ties. His ties are pink, blue, purple and grey.

Adam takes a pair of socks and a tie at random each morning.

What is the probability that:

  a He takes a pair of grey socks and the pink tie?

  b He takes the stripey socks and the purple tie?

  c He takes grey socks and a matching tie?

  d He takes socks and a tie of the same colour?

  e He takes socks and a tie of different colours?

> **Tip**
>
> What sort of diagram might be helpful here?

13 ★★☆

Rabbits can have from 4 to 8 kits (baby rabbits) in each litter.

The probability of how many kits any female rabbit might have in a litter is given in the table.

Number of kits per litter	4	5	6	7	8
Probability	0.1	0.2	0.3	0.3	x

What is the probability that two randomly picked female rabbits have a total of ten kits in one breeding season?

14 ★★☆

There are approximately 5×10^9 red blood cells per millilitre of blood. James' blood volume is approximately nine pints.

One pint is equal to 568 ml.

If James donates 10 percent of his blood, how many red blood cells has he still got?

Cambridge IGCSE Mathematics Extended Problem-solving Book

15 ★★★☆

Joe carried out a combination of transformations on a starting shape on a centimetre-square grid:

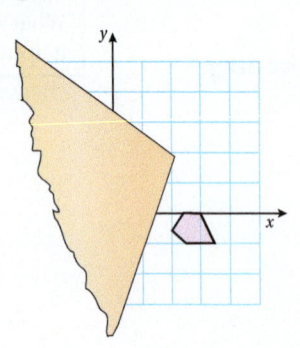

Tip

How can you work backwards through this problem? What are the 'inverse' transformations that need to be applied?

Translate by the vector $\begin{pmatrix} 2 \\ -1 \end{pmatrix}$.

Rotate 90° clockwise about (1, 0).

All but Joe's final image is hidden under a piece of paper.

What will the diagram look like when the paper is lifted?

16 ★★★☆

a Explain how the pair of triangles shown below could be used to show that $\sqrt{8} = 2 \times$ square root of 2.

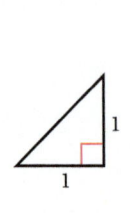

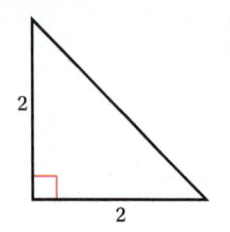

Diagrams not to scale

Tip

What can you work out?

Tip

Why is it useful that the two triangles are right-angled? The two triangles are mathematically similar. What does this mean and how can it help you?

b Draw a pair of triangles to demonstrate that:

$\sqrt{18} = 3 \times$ square root of 2

17 ★★★☆

A field is 80 m long by 70 m wide. A goat is tethered to a pole in the centre of the field by a rope 15 m long.

A farmer plants wheat across the width of the field for 30 m from one end. The goat eats all the wheat it can reach.

It costs $65 to plant a 1 m strip of wheat the width of the field, and the farmer is paid $4.50 per square metre harvested. The farmer plants strips the complete width of the field but he does not move the goat.

The farmer still makes a profit. How much profit?

18 ★★☆

The manager of the local cinema did not want to give his employees a pay raise. He said on average they were earning more than the weekly national average wage of $130 per week.

Weekly wages in $	Frequency
61 – 80	2
81 – 100	5
101 – 150	9
151 – 200	2
201 – 250	1
251 – 300	1

a Why would finding the median wage not be helpful for the manager?

Feeling under pressure, the manager decided to increase the weekly wages of his two lowest paid employees to put them in the $81–100 wage bracket.

b How have these pay rises affected the average wage of the employees? What has happened?

19 ★★☆

Angelo is inviting some friends for afternoon tea. He wants to make chocolate brownies and lemonade.

In the cupboard there is 350 g of sugar. Each glass of lemonade needs 30 g of sugar and each brownie requires 20 g of sugar.

Let x represent the number of glasses of lemonade and y represent the number of brownies.

a Write an inequality to show how much lemonade and how many brownies Angelo could make.

Angelo expects his friends will each have one glass of lemonade and at least one brownie.

b Write an inequality to show the number of friends Angelo could invite.

20 ★★★

The formula for the kinetic energy (in joules, J) of an object of mass m (in kg), travelling at a speed v (in m/s), is:

$$KE = \frac{1}{2}mv^2$$

Two students calculate the kinetic energy of a tennis ball of mass 56 g after it is served at a speed of 120 miles per hour.

Their answers are shown below:

Student 1:

$KE = \frac{1}{2}mv^2 = \frac{1}{2} \times 56 \times 120^2 = 403\,200$ J

Student 2:

The mass of the tennis ball needs to be changed into kg.

56 g = 0.056 kg

The speed of the tennis ball needs to be changed into metres per second (m/s).
Using the conversion 5 miles = 8 km:

$\frac{120}{5} = 24$

24 × 8 = 192 so 120 mph = 192 km/h

192 km/h = 192 000 m/h

There are 60 × 60 = 3600 seconds in one hour.

$\frac{192\,000}{3600} = 53.3333...$ m/s

KE = 0.5 mv^2

0.5 × 0.056 × 53.3 = 1.4924

1.4924² = 2.227...

So the KE = 2.2 J.

Both students have done some things correctly in their calculations but they have both have ended up with the wrong answer.

Explain how each student should alter their method to achieve the correct result of 79.6 joules.

21 ✪✪✪

A piece of paper is folded to make a kite as shown in the diagram.

The side lengths of the original piece of paper are in the ratio 1 : √2.

Calculate the perimeter of the kite.

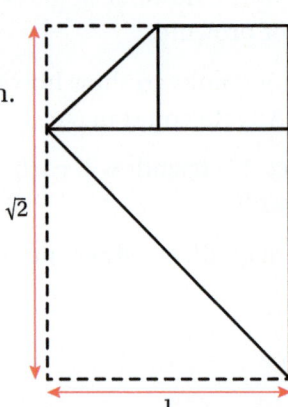

Diagram not to scale

22 ✪✪✪

The functions $f(x)$ and $g(x)$ are given by

$f(x) = x^2 - 7x + 12$

$g(x) = 2x^2 - x - 15$

Find the value of x such that the ratio

$f(x) : g(x)$ is 3 : 4

23

A bunch of keys is thrown from a window, so that they follow the path shown in the diagram. The keys are thrown from 4 metres above the ground.

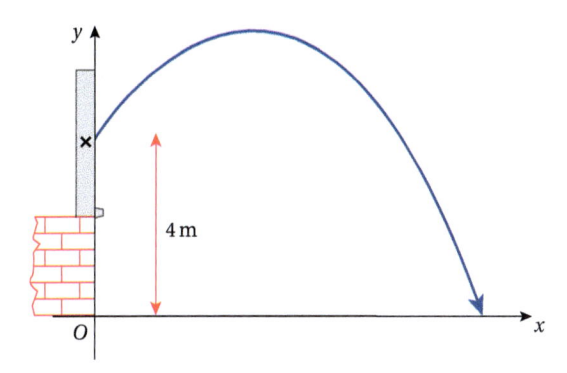

If the ground is considered to be the x-axis, and the wall and window the y-axis, with the wall and ground meeting at (0, 0), then the x and y-coordinates of the bunch of keys after t seconds are given by:

$$x = t$$
$$y = t - 5t^2 + 4$$

a How far above the ground is the bunch of keys after 0.2 seconds?

b How far from (0, 0) is the bunch of keys after 0.8 seconds?

c After how long will the keys strike the ground?

24

The diagram shows a *Golden Rectangle* ABCD.

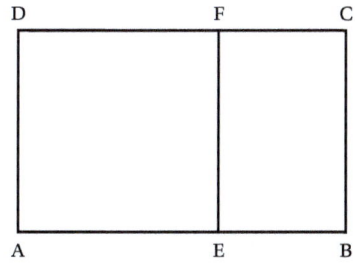

The rectangle is divided into a square and a smaller rectangle by adding the line EF. Given that the rectangle ABCD is similar to the rectangle BCFE find the value of $\frac{AB}{BC}$.

Chapter 11
Put it together

We often need to use more than one problem-solving technique in the same question. Combinations of adding lines, simplifying problems, looking at problems from a different point of view and so on are often needed to complete solutions. The key is to stand back and try to work out which topics are involved and which techniques are usually used when dealing with those topics. New questions will not be exactly like problems that you have solved before but you should think about the processes that you used when working on the same topics in the past. Good problem solvers will make mistakes, learn from following the wrong ideas, and gain useful experience along the way. To develop your skills, try to solve the problem yourself first, before you look at the hints.

When you work through this example, consider how the techniques from Chapters 1 to 10 have been used. Think about your own problem-solving experience and ask yourself basic questions about what you are doing.

> Three identical circles each have radius $\frac{\sqrt{3}}{2}$ cm and centres A, B and C. The three circles are drawn so that they all touch each other once. Find the area of triangle ABC.

Tip

The first thing to note here is that the question is about shapes, but there are no shapes to be seen. When this happens you must always draw a diagram.

Begin by drawing a diagram, of course! (See Chapter 1: Draw a diagram)

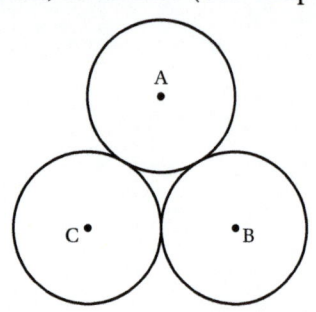

It is sensible to draw the triangle described in the question (see Chapter 3: Change your point of view). The question is really only about triangle ABC and doesn't relate to the circles at all. Draw the triangle separately so that you can work on a less cluttered version (see Chapter 5: Consider different cases). Notice that the length of each side of the triangle ($\sqrt{3}$) is twice the radius of each circle $\left(\frac{\sqrt{3}}{2}\right)$.

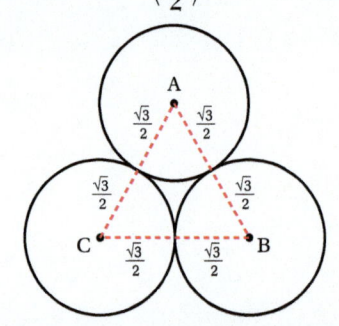

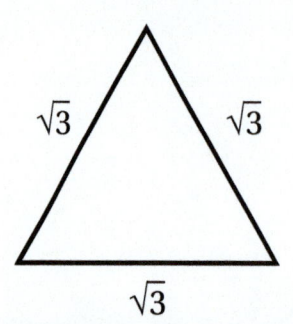

Tip

What do you know about circles? The triangle is drawn so that its edges join the centres of touching circles. How does the radius relate to the lengths of the edges of the triangle?

Chapter 11: Put it together

What do you need to know when finding the area of a triangle? You could think about the angles in this equilateral triangle and use the formula $A = \frac{1}{2}ab\sin C$ (Option 1 below) or you could find the height of the triangle using Pythagoras' theorem and then use the formula $A = \frac{1}{2} \times \text{base} \times \text{height}$ (Option 2 below). Either way this is now a recognisable problem (see Chapter 6: Make connections). Both methods will give the correct answer.

Tip

Always remind yourself what the question asked you to find. It is about the area of a triangle. Think about the basics of finding the area of a triangle and see how they could be applied to this problem

Option 1

The triangle is equilateral, so you will now know that the three angles are each 60°. You could then redraw the triangle:

$A = \frac{1}{2}ab\sin C$

$= \frac{1}{2} \times \sqrt{3} \times \sqrt{3} \times \sin 60$

$= \frac{3\sqrt{3}}{4}$ cm²

Tip

Remember to think about what kind of triangle you have. Is it right-angled? Isosceles? Equilateral? What are the properties of these triangles and how could they help?

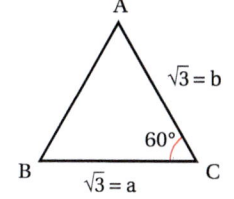

Option 2

Alternatively you could re-draw the diagram in this way:

By Pythagoras' theorem

$h^2 = (\sqrt{3})^2 - \left(\frac{\sqrt{3}}{2}\right)^2$

$= 3 - \frac{3}{4}$

$= \frac{9}{4}$

$h = \frac{3}{2}$

So

area $= \frac{1}{2} \times \text{base} \times \text{height}$

$= \frac{1}{2} \times \sqrt{3} \times \frac{3}{2}$

$= \frac{3\sqrt{3}}{4}$ cm²

Tip

Another way to calculate the area of a triangle involves the height. If you need to find the height then draw it on your diagram. What shapes have you now formed and how will these help?

Tip

Take care when handling the surds and fractions. You are making use of techniques from several topics at once here.

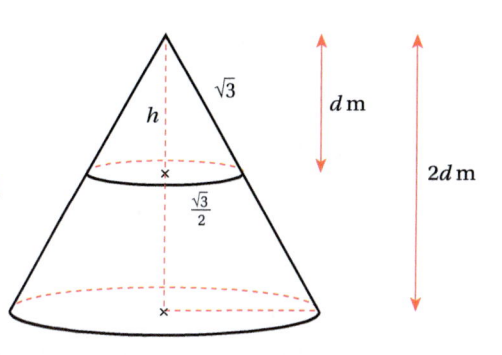

1 ★★★

The diagram shows a right circular cone with height $2d$ metres. The base of the cone also has radius $2d$ metres.

The cone is cut along a plane that is parallel to the base and d metres from the base (i.e. half way up) to form a smaller cone and a frustum. Find the ratio.

{curved surface area of small cone : curved surface area of the frustum}

2 ★★★

a Show that $\frac{x+1}{x-1} = 1 + \frac{2}{x-1}$

b If $4 \leqslant x \leqslant 10$ what is the largest possible value of $\frac{x+1}{x-1}$?

3 ★★★

If $a \oplus b = ab - \dfrac{a}{b^2}$

a show that
$a \oplus b = b \oplus a$ only if $a = b$

b solve the equation
$\dfrac{3}{c} \oplus c = \dfrac{21}{8}$

4 ★★★

Find the area of regular pentagon with side 5 cm.

5 ★★★

The geometric mean of three numbers x, y and z is given by $\sqrt[3]{xyz}$. Find three different numbers with geometric mean 6 and sum 25.

6 ★★★

The matrix **A** is given by $\mathbf{A} = \begin{pmatrix} 1 & 4 \\ 2 & 3 \end{pmatrix}$.

The matrix **A** has an *eigenvalue* k and an *eigenvector* **v** if $\mathbf{Av} = k\mathbf{v}$

For example, 5 is an eigenvalue of **A** and the vector $\begin{pmatrix} 1 \\ 1 \end{pmatrix}$ is an eigenvector of **A** because $\begin{pmatrix} 1 & 4 \\ 2 & 3 \end{pmatrix} \begin{pmatrix} 1 \\ 1 \end{pmatrix} = \begin{pmatrix} 5 \\ 5 \end{pmatrix} = 5 \begin{pmatrix} 1 \\ 1 \end{pmatrix}$.

Show that -1 is another eigenvalue of **A** and find the associated eigenvector.

> **Tip**
>
> If we transform a vector **v** and it maps to a multiple of **v**, say $x\mathbf{v}$, then **v** is called an *eigenvector* of the transformation and x is an *eigenvalue*.

7 ★★★

a Solve the pair of simultaneous equations:

$ax + 3y = 5$

$3x + 4y = 8$

b If the solution of the simultaneous equations in part **a** is $x = b$, $y = b$, find the value of a and the value of b.

8 ★★★

Make x the subject of the formula
$y = \dfrac{x+1}{x-1}$

9 ★★★

a On the same pair of axes sketch the lines with equations

$y = 2x + 1$

$y = 4x - 7$

b Find the area of the quadrilateral enclosed by the two lines in part **a** and the *positive* co-ordinate axes.

10 ★★★

If $x^2 - y^2 = 65$ and $x - y = 5$ find the value of $x^2 + y^2$

1 Draw a diagram

1 **a** 4 metres

    b 8 bricks

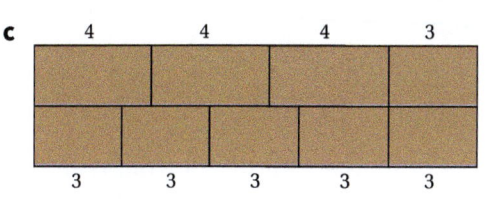

    c

        4 m + 4 m + 4 m + 3 m

        3 m + 3 m + 3 m + 3 m + 3 m

    d 19 bricks

        20 bricks

> One less than five bricks = 4
>
> Length + 1 = number of bricks
>
> Any combination of 4 and 3 to total 15.
>
> 4 m + 4 m + 4 m + 3 m would need:
> 5 + 5 + 5 + 4 bricks (for each plank there is one more brick than its length, in metres)
>
> or
>
> 3 m + 3 m + 3 m + 3 m + 3 m would need:
> 4 + 4 + 4 + 4 + 4 bricks

2 The area into which the fruit can fall has a diameter of 3 m and therefore a radius of 1.5 m. This means the tree can be planted anywhere 1.5 m away from the edge of the lawn.

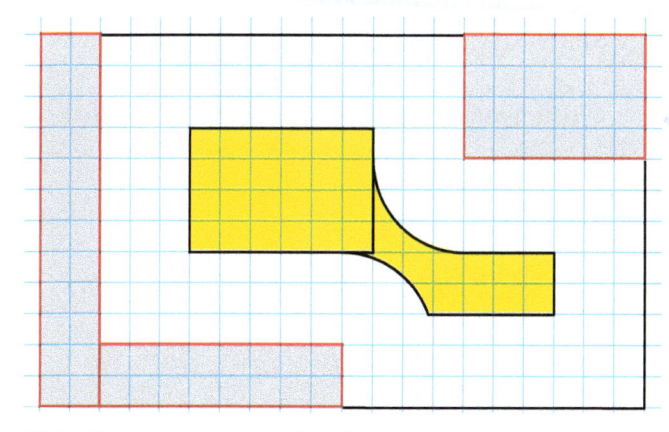

This diagram has a scale of two squares to 1 m. The yellow shaded area is where the cherry tree can be planted.

> You can choose any scale you like.
>
> To show where the cherry tree can go there are straight lines 1.5 m away from the edge of the lawn and arcs (parts of circles) at the corners of the flower bed and the vegetable patch.

3 The helicopters cover 25 km from each town, so two circles are needed. The fire brigade covers the section closer to B than A, so we need the locus of points equidistant from both towns.

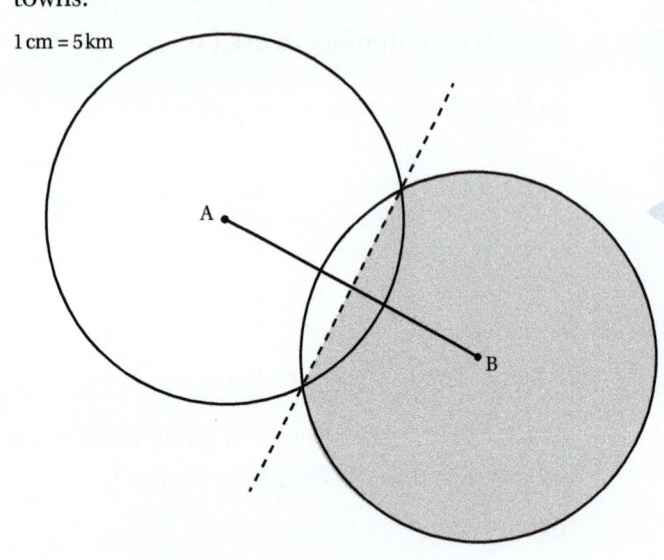

1 cm = 5 km

Here the scale is 1 cm = 5 km (you might have chosen a different scale).

Start with a line of 8 cm (to represent the 40 km distance between the towns).

With compasses draw a circle centre B and radius 5 cm.

With compasses draw a circle centre A and radius 5 cm.

The locus of points equidistant from B and A is the perpendicular bisector of line AB.

Shade the region that is closer to B than A and covered by the helicopter.

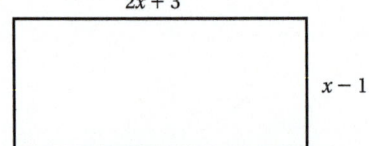

---

4 a

$2x + 3$ by $x - 1$ rectangle

An expression for the perimeter is $6x + 4$

To work out the perimeter of a rectangle, you need to add up the sides. To work out the area you multiply the two sides.

A diagram will help.

b An expression for the area is $(2x + 3)(x - 1)$, which can be expanded and simplified to give $2x^2 + x - 3$.

Make an equation and expand and simplify it.

c $2x^2 + x - 253 = 0$, which can be factorised to give $(2x + 23)(x - 11) = 0$

You need to solve $2x^2 + x - 3 = 250$.

$x = {}^-11.5$, or $x = 11$

x cannot be negative (because that would mean at least one of the sides of the rectangle would be negative), so $x = 11$ and the two sides are 25 cm and 10 cm.

The longest side is therefore 25 cm.

d The perimeter is 70 cm.

Worked solutions: 1 Draw a diagram

5

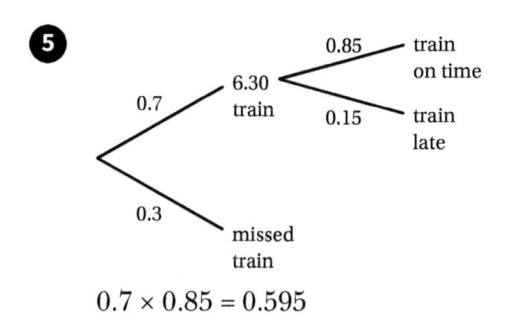

```
           0.85  train
      6.30 ─────  on time
  0.7 ─ train
 ╱         0.15  train
╱               late
╲
  0.3
      missed
      train
```

$0.7 \times 0.85 = 0.595$

A tree diagram might be useful here.

6 a

+	1	2	3	4	5
1	2	3	4	5	6
2	3	4	5	6	7
3	4	5	6	7	8
4	5	6	7	8	9
5	6	7	8	9	10

b 10

c $\dfrac{3}{25}$

Here is a diagram that will work well.

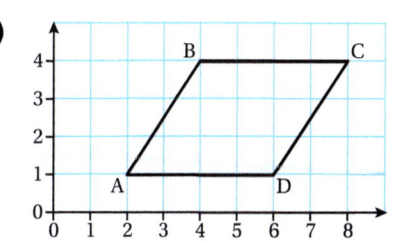

7

[Grid showing parallelogram with vertices A(2,1), B(3,4), C(7,4), D(6,1)]

a $\overrightarrow{CD} = \begin{pmatrix} -2 \\ -3 \end{pmatrix}$

b $\overrightarrow{AB} = \begin{pmatrix} 2 \\ 3 \end{pmatrix}$

The length AB is the same as the length CD but the vectors are in opposite directions.

c ABCD is a parallelogram – a four-sided shape with two sets of parallel sides.

A diagram of the situation helps you see what is going on.

BC is $\begin{pmatrix} 4 \\ 0 \end{pmatrix}$ and AD is $\begin{pmatrix} 4 \\ 0 \end{pmatrix}$ so BC is parallel to AD

AB is $\begin{pmatrix} 2 \\ 3 \end{pmatrix}$ and DC is $\begin{pmatrix} 2 \\ 3 \end{pmatrix}$ so AB is parallel to DC

Cambridge IGCSE Mathematics Extended Problem-solving Book

8

[Diagram: triangle with 20 cm height at 1 metre from apex, and 150 cm height at far end]

A good diagram shows that this is a question about similar triangles.

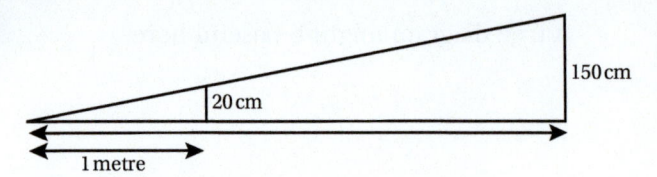

The scale factor of the enlargement is
150 cm ÷ 20 cm = 7.5

1 m × 7.5 = 7.5 m

The projector needs to be 7.5 m away for the image to fill the screen. So, it has to be moved back another 6.5 m.

9

	Hot chocolate	Tea	Coffee	Total
Women	8	9	**12**	29
Men	8	**7**	**10**	**25**
Total	16	**16**	22	**54**

A diagram like this 2-way table will help here.

The bold numbers are given in the question and the rest can be worked out.

Of the 54 workers surveyed, 22 preferred coffee, 16 preferred tea and 16 preferred hot chocolate.

Tea is not the most popular drink. Coffee is the most popular hot drink among the workers and hot chocolate is equally as popular as tea.

10 The shortest distance (d) is the hypotenuse of a right-angled triangle.

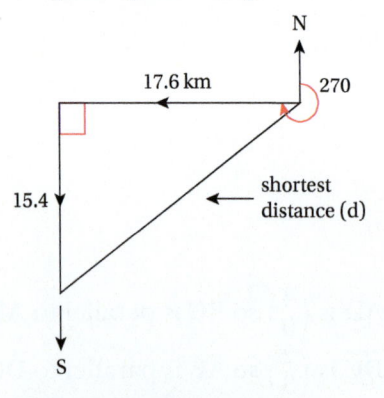

[Diagram: right-angled triangle with horizontal side 17.6 km pointing west from a point with bearing 270°, vertical side 15.4 going south, and hypotenuse labelled "shortest distance (d)"]

Draw a sketch showing the route.

A bearing of 270° is due west.

The sketch shows that the route forms a right angle, so you can use Pythagoras' theorem to find the distance needed.

$(17.6)^2 + (15.4)^2 = d^2$

$309.76 + 237.16 = 546.92$

$d = \sqrt{546.92}$

$d = 23.39$ km (correct to 2 d.p.)

11 a

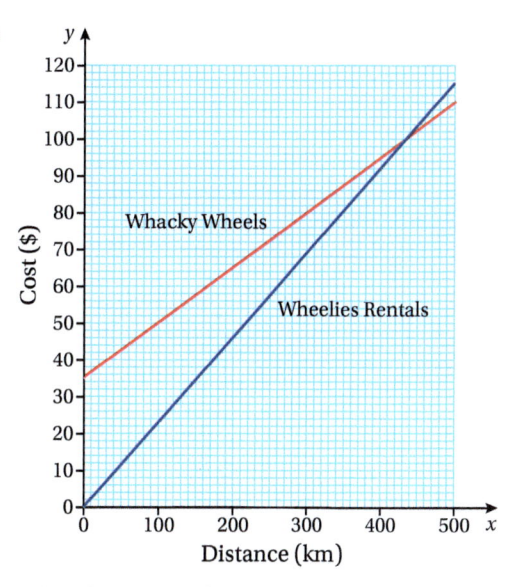

[Graph showing Cost ($) vs Distance (km) with two lines: Whacky Wheels and Wheelies Rentals]

The graph is helpful in answering the rest of this question.

b Wheelies Rentals

c $5

Whacky Wheels: $35 + $75 = $110

Wheelies Rentals: 5 × $23 = $115

12

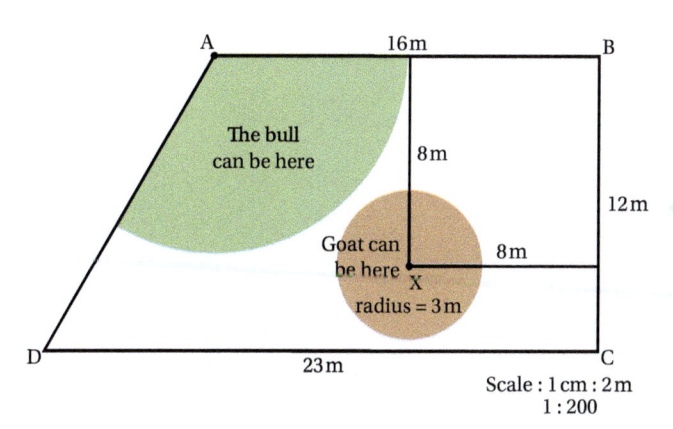

[Scale diagram showing quadrilateral ABCD with bull's roaming area (shaded) near A and goat's circular area around X. AB = 16m, BC = 12m, DC = 23m, distances 8m and 8m from B, goat radius = 3m. Scale: 1cm : 2m, 1 : 200]

A good way to solve this is to draw a scale diagram. You could use a scale of 1 cm to 2 m.

On the scale diagram, construct:

- A circle of radius 1.5 cm about X to show where the goat can go.
- A locus of radius 4 cm about A between the fence lines AD and AB where the bull can roam.

Any path between D and B that does not enter either of the shaded areas would be safe to use.

13 a

[Diagram: Row 1 shows rectangles with width $x+3$ and length $2x-3$, with 25 patches across. Row 2 shows rectangles with width $2x-3$ and length $x+3$.]

25 patches

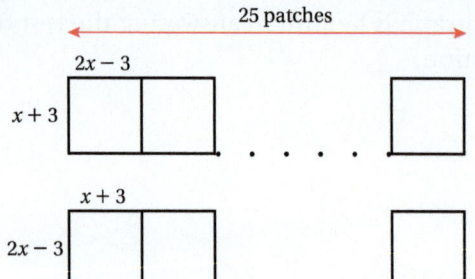

There are 25 patches in each row.

The width could be $25(x+3) = 25x + 75$

or it could be $25(2x-3) = 50x - 75$

b $64x - 96$ or $32x + 96$

$32(2x-3)$ or it could be $32(x+3)$

c The two possible expressions for the area are $(25x+75)(64x-96)$ and $(50x-75)(32x+96)$.

These are equal because they are both equivalent to working out $25(x+3) \times 32(2x-3)$.

This is $800(2x^2 + 3x - 9)$.

d $2.8\,m^2$ is the same as $2.8 \times 100\,cm \times 100\,cm = 28000\,cm^2$.

The equation is therefore:
$800(2x^2 + 3x - 9) = 28000$

Dividing through by 800 gives:
$2x^2 + 3x - 9 = 35$

$2x^2 + 3x - 44 = 0$ can be factorised to give $(2x+11)(x-4) = 0$, so $x = {}^-5.5$ (which isn't possible for this scenario) or $x = 4$.

The dimensions of the patches are: $2x-3$ by $x+3$ and when $x=4$ this gives 5cm by 7cm.

14 a

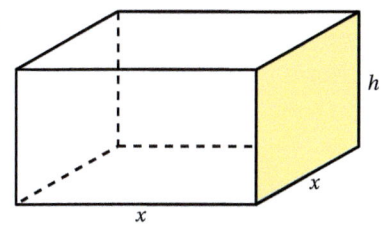

The volume is $x^2 \times h$. This equals 1440, so:
$x^2 h = 1440$, which means $h = \dfrac{1440}{x^2}$

It's useful to draw a diagram of the container.

b The base has area x^2.
Each of the side walls (shown in yellow on the diagram) has area hx, which is $x \times \dfrac{1440}{x^2}$, which simplifies to give $\dfrac{1440}{x}$.
There are four of these, so the total area of paper is $x^2 + \dfrac{5760}{x}$

c Area = 144 cm²

$1440 = x^2 \times 10$

So $144 = x^2$

$x = 12$

d 624 cm²

15

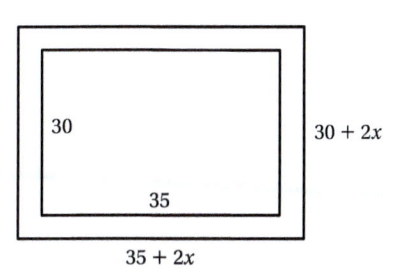

The diagram shows the top view of the pool and the path.

a $(35 + 2x)(30 + 2x) - 35 \times 30 = 130x + 4x^2$

You could work out the area of the outer rectangle and then subtract the area of the inner rectangle.

b $3196.80 \div 30 = 106.56$

Square metres of border.

$4x^2 + 130x = 106.56$

Solve this equation.

$x = 0.8$ m

16

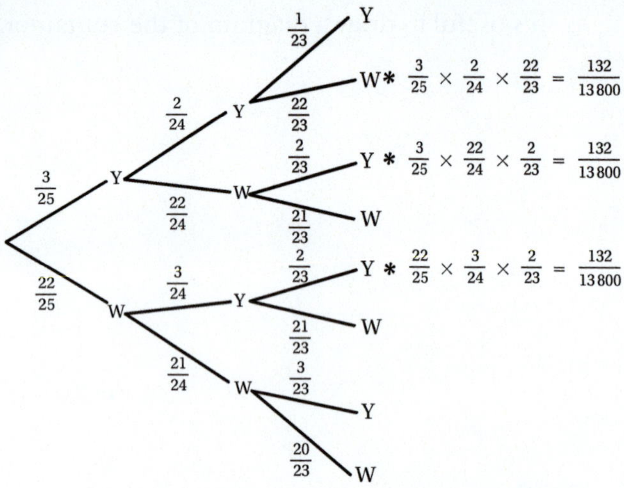

[Tree diagram showing branches with probabilities:
- From start: 3/25 to Y, 22/25 to W
- From Y: 2/24 to Y, 22/24 to W
- From W: 3/24 to Y, 21/24 to W
- Further branches with 1/23, 22/23, 2/23, 21/23, 3/23, 20/23 leading to Y or W
- Routes marked with *:
  - W*: 3/25 × 2/24 × 22/23 = 132/13800
  - Y*: 3/25 × 22/24 × 2/23 = 132/13800
  - Y*: 22/25 × 3/24 × 2/23 = 132/13800]

> A probability tree diagram is probably the most useful diagram here.

a P (3 yellow) = $\frac{3}{25} \times \frac{2}{24} \times \frac{1}{23} = \frac{6}{13800} = \frac{1}{2300}$

b P (3 white) = $\frac{22}{25} \times \frac{21}{24} \times \frac{20}{23} = \frac{9240}{13800} = \frac{77}{115}$

c $\frac{132}{13800} + \frac{132}{13800} + \frac{132}{13800} = \frac{396}{13800} = \frac{33}{1150}$

> The three routes labelled on the diagram all work, so you need to add them.

17

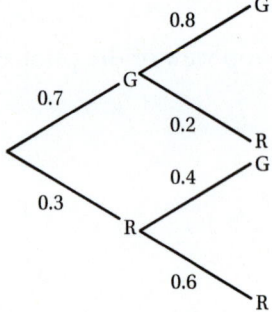

[Tree diagram:
- 0.7 to G, 0.3 to R
- From G: 0.8 to G, 0.2 to R
- From R: 0.4 to G, 0.6 to R]

> A tree diagram might help.

a 0.7 × 0.8 = 0.56

b (0.7 × 0.2) + (0.3 × 0.4) = 0.26

> Two outcomes: green then red (GR) and red then green (RG).

18

```
            badminton      squash
                        0.35 ─ K wins        K wins both: 0.85 × 0.35
              0.85 ─ K wins
                        0.65 ─ J wins        K wins badminton,
                                             J wins squash: 0.85 × 0.65
              0.15 ─ J wins
                        0.35 ─ K wins        J wins badminton,
                                             K wins squash: 0.15 × 0.35
                        0.65 ─ J wins        J wins both: 0.15 × 0.65
```

Here is the tree diagram.

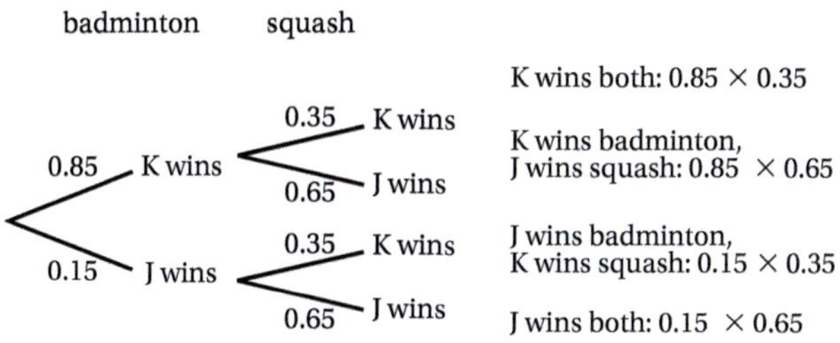

a $0.85 \times 0.35 = 0.2975$

b $0.15 \times 0.35 = 0.0525$

c $0.85 \times 0.65 + 0.15 \times 0.35 = 0.605$

19

```
                      1/200 ─ chance of getting malaria     7/10 × 1/200 = 7/2000
         7/10 ─ got tablets
                      199/200 ─ chance of not getting malaria

                      1/50 ─ chance of getting malaria      3/10 × 1/50 = 3/500
         3/10 ─ no tablets
                      49/50 ─ chance of not getting malaria
```

A tree diagram can be helpful.

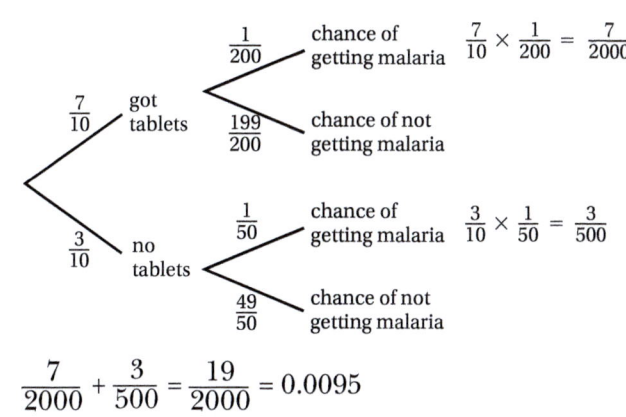

$$\frac{7}{2000} + \frac{3}{500} = \frac{19}{2000} = 0.0095$$

---

20 a

[Venn diagram with three circles P, C, M: P only = 29, C only = 43, M only = 17, P∩C only = 11, P∩M only = 19, C∩M only = 23, all three = 15, outside = 43]

A Venn diagram is likely to be useful here.

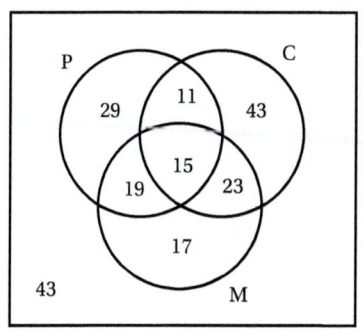

53 study two subjects – so 11 study Physics and Chemistry but not Maths.

74 study Physics, so 15 study all three.

92 study Chemistry, so 43 study only Chemistry.

There are 200 students so 17 study only Maths.

b $\frac{17}{200}$

c $\frac{68}{200}$

11 studied Chemistry and Physics, 19 studied Physics and Maths, 23 studied Chemistry and Maths, 15 studied all three.

Total: 68 of 200 students.

21 a

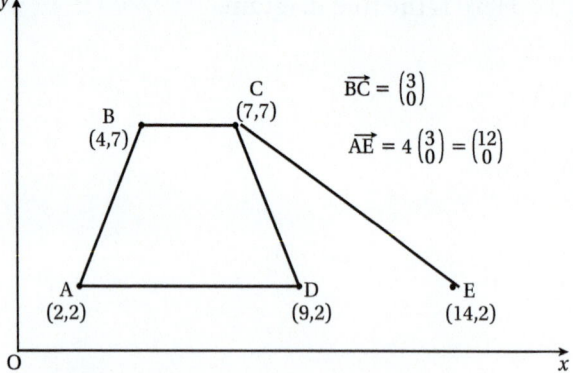

An isosceles trapezium has one line of symmetry, so D could be (9, 2) as C to D will be 2 units to the right and 5 units downwards.

b $\overrightarrow{AC} = \begin{pmatrix} 5 \\ 5 \end{pmatrix}$

c E (14, 2)

d $\overrightarrow{BE} = \begin{pmatrix} 10 \\ -5 \end{pmatrix}$

---

22 a i, ii

> There are three possible triangles that fit Amira's description.

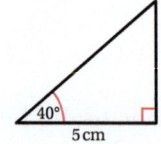

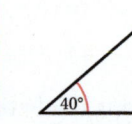

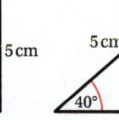

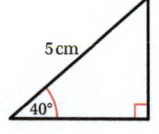

iii She could say that the hypotenuse is 5 cm.

Other answers are possible too.

> For only one triangle to be possible, Amira must make sure that her conditions follow one of the conditions of congruence:
>
> SSS, SAS, ASA, AAS or RHS

b i

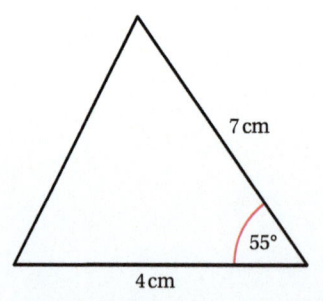

There is only one triangle that satisfies Janet's conditions because she has given SAS.

ii $a^2 = b^2 + c^2 - 2bc \cos A$

$a^2 = 7^2 + 4^2 - 2 \times 7 \times 4 \times \cos 55°$

$a = 5.734...$

> A scale drawing will enable you to measure the length of the third side: 5.7 cm to the nearest mm.

> A more accurate method to find the length of the third side is to use the cosine rule.

23

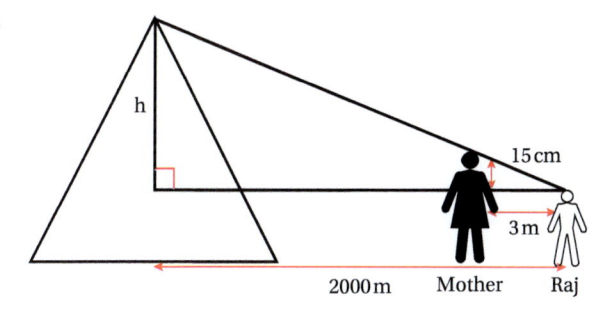

The ratio of height : distance is the same for both Raj's mother and the hill.

0.15 : 3

h : 2000

$0.15 \div 3 \times 2000 = 100$ m

This is a complicated scenario. A diagram can help you see what is going on.

Divide by 3 and multiply by 2000.

The hill is about 100 m tall.

---

24 **a** width : length

40 : 55

8 : 11

$112 \div 8 = 14$

$11 \times 14 = 154$ cm

You might want to draw diagrams to show what is going on.

This is the length.

b $148.5 \div 11 = 13.5$

$13.5 \times 8 = 108$ cm

This is the width.

c Width of photo = area ÷ length

= 127.5 ÷ 15

= 8.5 cm

Factor of enlargement

= new width ÷ original width

= 25.5 ÷ 8.5

= 3

First work out the width of the original photo using the length and area given in the question.

Then work out the scale factor of the enlargement by comparing the two widths.

The area will increase by a factor of $3^2 = 9$.

Area of poster = (127.5×9) cm²

= 1147.5 cm²

25

This is the sort of question where a graph can really help.

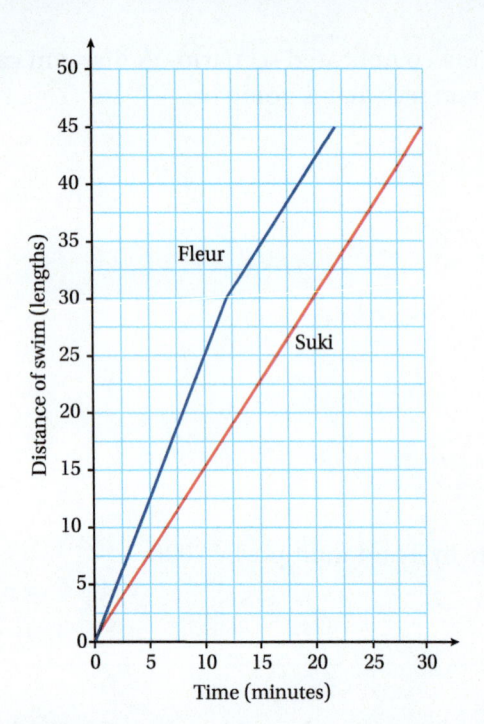

a 15

b 10 minutes

c 45 ÷ 30 = 1.5 lengths per minute

d 8 minutes

e About 2 lengths per minute

f 15 more lengths, which is 60 in total, but she might get tired and start to slow down.

26 a

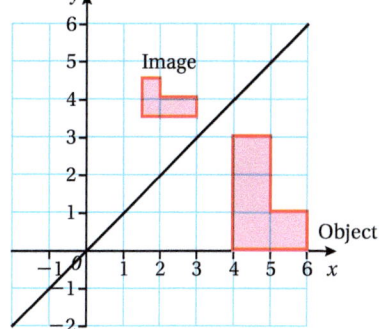

[Graph showing object at approximately (4,0)-(6,1)-(6,3)-(5,3)-(5,1)-(4,1) and image reflected across y=x line, labeled "Image" at upper left around (2,4)-(3,5) and "Object" at lower right]

Choose a shape without any symmetry to easily see what is going on.

Here is an example.

b

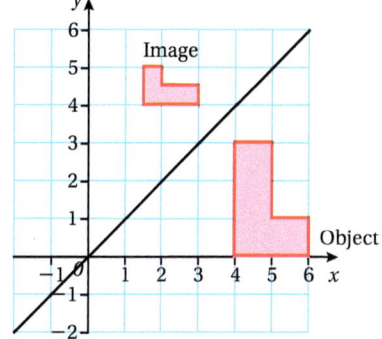

[Similar graph with object and image in slightly different positions]

The orientation and size of the final image are the same when the transformations are carried out in a different order, but it ends up in a different place.

c 1, 2, 3

1, 3, 2

2, 1, 3

(2, 3, 1)

3, 1, 2

3, 2, 1

There are five different final images.

Consider all the possible arrangements of the three transformations.

You have already drawn the first and last one.

The others result in an image that is the same size and same way around, but which is in a different place, except for order 2, 3, 1 which has an image in the same place as order 1, 2, 3.

27 a

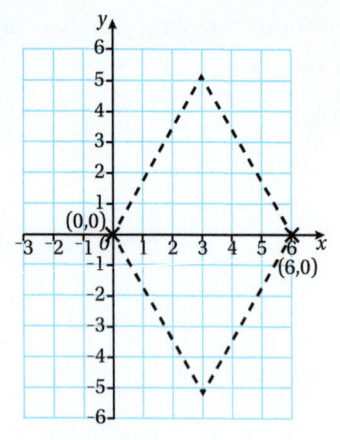

$a^2 + b^2 = c^2$

$3^2 + b^2 = 6^2$

$9 + b^2 = 36$

$b^2 = 27$

$b = \sqrt{27}\ (= 5.196...)$

$(3, \sqrt{27})$ or $(3, -\sqrt{27})$

> There are two possible locations for the third vertex.
>
> The x-coordinate is 3.
>
> Use Pythagoras' theorem to calculate the vertical height of the equilateral triangle.

b

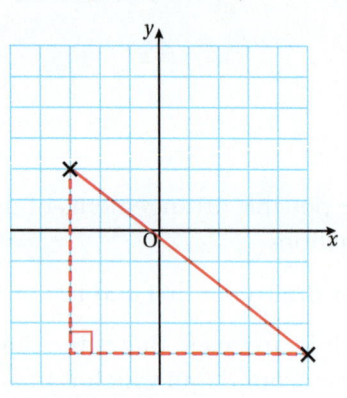

$6^2 + 8^2 = c^2$

$c^2 = 100$

$c = \sqrt{100} = 10$

$5^2 + b^2 = 10^2$

$25 + b^2 = 100$

$b^2 = 75$

$b = \sqrt{75}\ (= 8.660...)$

Area $= \frac{1}{2} \times 10 \times \sqrt{75}$

Area $= 43.301...$

43.3 square units

> Here is a diagram showing the two points.
>
> This time you only need to know the length of the sides. Pythagoras tells you the side has a length of 10.
>
> Now, if you have an equilateral triangle of side 10 you can do this.
>
> Calculate the area of the equilateral triangle $\left(\frac{1}{2} \times \text{base} \times \text{height}\right)$

28

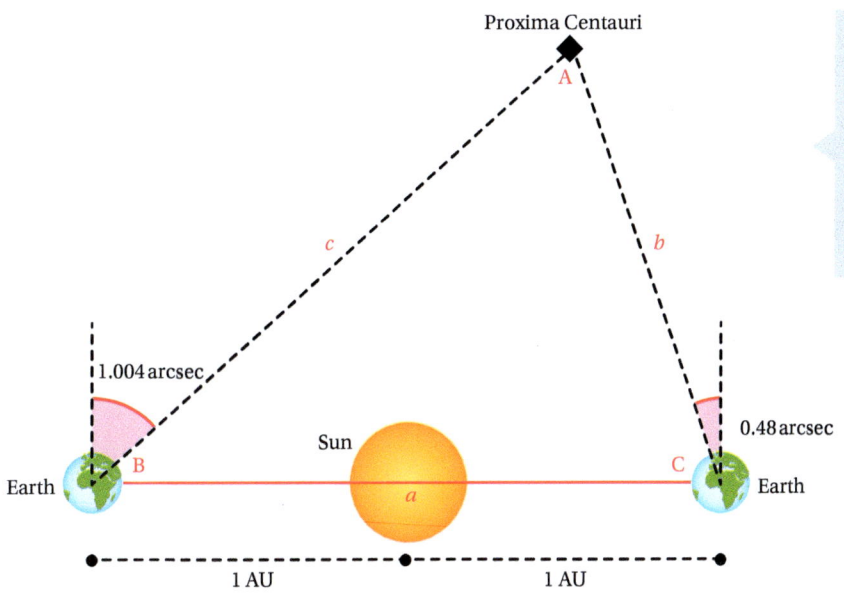

[Diagram: Triangle with Proxima Centauri at vertex A (top), Earth at vertex B (left) with angle 1.004 arcsec, Earth at vertex C (right) with angle 0.48 arcsec. The Sun lies on segment BC (labeled a), with 1 AU on each side. Sides b and c are dashed lines from the Earths to Proxima Centauri.]

> There are lots of aspects of this question that aren't particularly clear, so you will need to make some assumptions (which is fine as long as you explain them) and a good diagram will be a very important starting point.

It looks as if the angles are measured perpendicularly from the line through the Sun, so:

angle B is $90° - 1.004$ arcsec

angle $C = 90° - 0.48$ arcsec

angle A is $1.004 + 0.48 = 1.484$ arcsec

$$\frac{a}{\sin A} = \frac{b}{\sin B} = \frac{c}{\sin C}$$

$b = \dfrac{2\text{AU}}{\sin(1.484\,\text{arcsec})} \times \sin(90° - 1.004\,\text{arcsec})$

This gives $b = 4.169\,773\,711 \times 10^{13}$ km

$c = \dfrac{2\text{AU}}{\sin(1.484\,\text{arcsec})} \times \sin(90° - 0.48\,\text{arcsec})$

This gives $c = 4.169\,773\,711 \times 10^{13}$

The distance is therefore about 4.2×10^{13} km

> It is not obvious which distance is being asked for – so let's work out lengths b and c.
>
> These answers are the same for the first 10 significant figures (which makes sense because Proxima Centauri is very, very far away compared to the diameter of the orbit of the Earth).

29 For $3x + 2y = 15$

$x = 0 \Rightarrow 2y = 15$ so $y = \dfrac{15}{2}$

$y = 0 \Rightarrow 3x = 15$ so $x = 5$

For $y - 2x = 4$

$x = 0 \Rightarrow y = 4$

$y = 0 \Rightarrow -2x = 4$ so $x = -2$

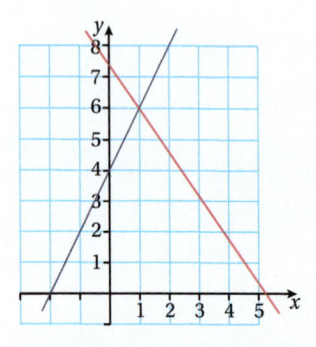

> Find the coordinates of the points where each line crosses the axes. This will help you to draw the lines.

> Now draw a diagram using this information.

$3x + 2y = 15 \Rightarrow 6x + 4y = 30$

$y - 2x = 4 \Rightarrow -6x + 3y = 12$

Adding: $7y = 42 \Rightarrow y = 6$

Triangle height = 6

Base length = $5 - -2 = 7$

Area of triangle = $\dfrac{1}{2} \times 7 \times 6 = 21$

> The y-coordinate of the point at which the lines meet will be the same as the height of the triangle. Use simultaneous equations to work out this y-coordinate. You will need to eliminate x or find x and use that to find y. Here we eliminate x.

> Note that the points at which the lines crossed the x-axis have been found, so you can find the length of the triangle's base.

> Use the standard formula for the area of a triangle.

30

```
D      F        A
┌──────┬────────┐
│      │        │
│      │        │ 1
│      │        │
└──────┴────────┘
C   1   E  k-1   B
◄─────── k ───────►
```

Draw the rectangle first, marking the length k cm and the width 1 cm. Add the line that creates the square and smaller rectangle (EF in the diagram).

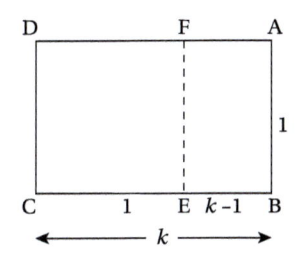

You can see that the square must be 1 cm by 1 cm, so the distance BE must be $(k-1)$ cm.

$$\frac{AD}{AB} = \frac{EF}{BE}$$

Now use the fact that the rectangles are similar.

So

$$\frac{k}{1} = \frac{1}{k-1}$$

Multiply both sides by $(k-1)$, then expand and solve.

$k(k-1) = 1$

$k^2 - k = 1$

$k^2 - k - 1 = 0$

$$k = \frac{-(-1) \pm \sqrt{(-1)^2 - 4(1)(-1)}}{2}$$

$$k = \frac{1 \pm \sqrt{5}}{2}$$

But

$\frac{1-\sqrt{5}}{2} < 0$ and k is a length, so cannot be negative.

So

$$k = \frac{1+\sqrt{5}}{2}$$

For interest, this number is called the *Golden Ratio* or *Golden Section*.

31

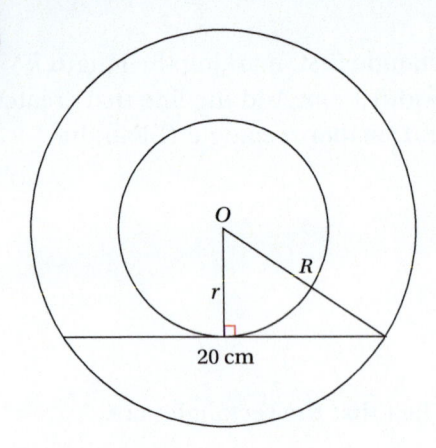

$r^2 + 10^2 = R^2$ [1]

Area of ring $= \pi R^2 - \pi r^2$

$\phantom{\text{Area of ring }} = \pi(R^2 - r^2)$

But equation [1] tells us that
$R^2 - r^2 = 10^2 = 100$

So area of ring $= \pi(100)$

$\phantom{\text{So area of ring }} = 100\pi \text{ cm}^2$

> We need to think about the radius of each circle if we are going to find an area, but we don't need to find the actual value of either radius.

> The triangle is right-angled because a radius and a tangent will always meet at a right angle. Use Pythagoras.

> What did the original question ask you for? Use this and the diagram as a guide.

> It is always worth reminding yourself what the original question was asking you to do.

2 Work back from what you know

1 $\sqrt{64} = 8$ and $\sqrt{81} = 9$, so $8 < \sqrt{70} < 9$

> You don't know how big $\sqrt{70}$ is, but you might know some other square root values..

Looking at the statement in the question:

$10\sqrt{70} > 8 \times 10$ so the statement is incorrect.

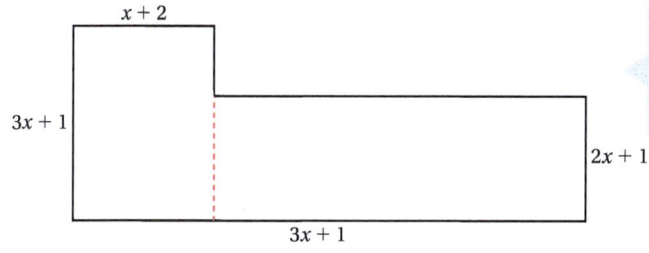

2 a

[Diagram: L-shaped figure with dimensions $x+2$ (top), $3x+1$ (left), $2x+1$ (right), $3x+1$ (bottom)]

> First, divide the area into 2 rectangles.
> Work out the area of each rectangle and add them to find the total area.

$$\begin{aligned}\text{Area} &= (3x+1)(x+2) + (3x+1)(2x+1) \\ &= (3x+1)(3x+3) \\ &= 9x^2 + 12x + 3\end{aligned}$$

b $3x + 1 = 16\,\text{m}$, so $3x + 3 = 18\,\text{m}$

> Use the factorised form of the area.

Area $= 16 \times 18 = 288\,\text{m}^2$

c 78 posts

> Work out the perimeter.

d $78 \times 3 = 234\,\text{m}$ of wire

e $(78 \times 18.50) + (234 \times 2.30) = \$1981.20$

3

> You might not be able to answer this immediately, but you can make some simultaneous equations and solve them.

6 mangoes and 4 pawpaws cost $5.80.

> Use the first sentence and double the amounts.

5 mangoes and 4 pawpaws cost $5.50, so the extra mango must cost 30¢.

> Use the second sentence.

The price of a pawpaw is $1.

4 $835 \div 16.5 = 50.61$

> If the figures were exact then you would work out $840 \div 16$. Here, to be safe, you need to assume the van can only cope with 835 kg and that the stones weigh 16.5 kg

He can transport 50 stones.

5 a

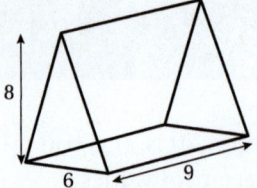

The area of the triangular cross-section is
$\frac{1}{2} \times 6 \times 8 = 24 \, cm^2$

The volume of the prism is $24 \times 9 = 216 \, cm^3$

b The volume of the pentagonal prism is
$36 \times L = 216$

$L = 216 \div 36 = 6 \, cm$

> Label a copy of the diagram.

6

Volume of cylinder $= \pi \times 3^2 \times 11 = 311.01767... \, cm^3$

$311 \, cm^3 = 311 \, ml$

$500 \, ml - 311.01767 \, ml = 189 \, ml$ (3 s.f.)

> You could start by working out the volume of a cylinder of water that is 11 cm high.

> Volume of water (a cylinder) = area of circular base × height

> Volume of water (in ml)

> Volume of water left in bottle

7 a 3 : 5 gives 8 parts.

$32 \div 8 = 4$

$3 \times 4 = 12$ non-calculator questions on each test and 20 calculator questions.

b 15 tests × 20 = 300 calculator questions.

c 15 × 32 = 480 questions, so each teacher will write 240 questions.

For Miss Choudhury, 60 of those are calculator questions and 180 are non-calculator.

$\frac{60}{240} = \frac{1}{4}$

> Start by working out the number of parts in the ratio.

> This is complicated, so let's find out how many questions there are altogether.

8 a p(green ball) = 0.64, so p(not a green ball) = 0.36.

The probability of getting a white ball is the same as that of getting a yellow ball, so they must each be $0.36 \div 2 = 0.18$.

b 9 yellow balls out of the total number = 0.18

$0.18 = \frac{18}{100} = \frac{9}{50}$ so there are 50 balls in total.

> You can't solve this immediately, but you do know this.

9 The probability that Mie or Frances finish first is
0.23 + 0.15 = 0.38

> You don't need to work out the probability that Anisha finishes first.

So the probability Sue or Anisha finish first is
1 – 0.38 = 0.62

---

10 12 × 5 = 60

> This is a challenging problem.
>
> If the mean of 5 numbers is 12, what do you know? When you work out the mean of five numbers you add them up and divide by 5, so before the sum was divided by 5 it must have totalled 60 (because 60 ÷ 5 = 12).

60 ÷ 15 = 4

> You also know that there are 15 parts in the ratio.

4 : 4 : 12 : 16 : 24

The largest number is 24

> Multiplying the numbers in the ratio by 4 gives these figures, and the largest one is 24.

11

Student	Number of sixes in 10 rolls	Relative frequency
A	7. Total number of sixes is 7.	0.7
B	4. Total number of sixes is 11.	0.55
C	3. Total number of sixes is 14.	0.47
D	6. Total number of sixes is 20.	0.5
E	4. Total number of sixes is 24.	0.48

> It probably makes sense to start working out the probability after each student has had a go.
>
> Now you might want to skip a few. After 10 students have done their throws, there are 44 sixes and the relative frequency is 0.44.
>
> After 15 students have done their throws, there are 68 sixes and the relative frequency is 0.45.
>
> After 20 students have done their throws, there are 83 sixes and the relative frequency is 0.415.
>
> The relative frequency is going up and down, but it looks as if it is settling somewhere close to 0.4.
>
> When more trials happen the relative frequency is generally closer to the actual value.

The actual value of the probability is probably about 0.4, which means that the dice is a biased one.

12

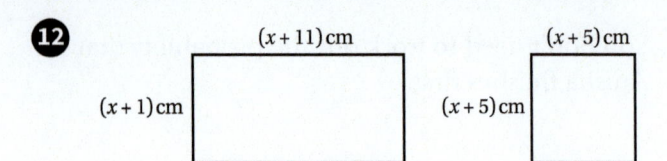

The area of the rectangle is
$(x+1)(x+11) = x^2 + 12x + 11$

The area of the square is $(x+5)^2 = x^2 + 10x + 25$

These are equal, so $x^2 + 12x + 11 = x^2 + 10x + 25$

This simplifies to give $2x = 14$, so $x = 7$

The dimensions of the rectangle are therefore 8 cm by 18 cm.

$18 \times 8 = 144 \text{ cm}^2$

> You can't immediately work out the size (using numbers) of the sides of the rectangle, but you know that the area of the rectangle is the same as the area of the square, so start by working those out.

13

a The big square has area $5x \times 5x = 25x^2$

Subtract the area of the small square (x^2) to leave $24x^2$

b $24x^2 = 1944$, so $x^2 = 81$, which means that here $x = 9$

The perimeter of the shape is $20x$, which equals 180 cm.

> You can't immediately see what the perimeter will be, so start by working out the value of x.

14

a The angles in a regular hexagon are 120°, and those in a regular pentagon are 108°.

> In a regular shape all the angles must be the same so working these out might be a good starting point.

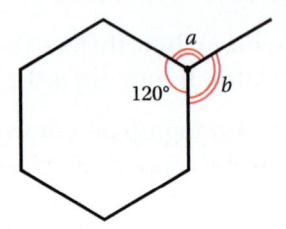

The angles around a point should add up to 360°, but here they make 336°, so they don't fit the pattern of the quilt.

b 3 × 120° = 360°, so regular hexagons will fit around the edge. Equilateral triangles would also fit:

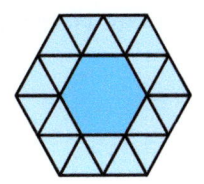

> The interior angle of a regular pentagon is 108°.

> This means the other angle is 144°.
>
> You now have to identify the regular polygon that has an interior angle of 144°.
>
> The exterior angle is 180 – 144 = 36°.
>
> Exterior angles always sum to 360°, so there must be 10 of them and the shape must have 10 sides.

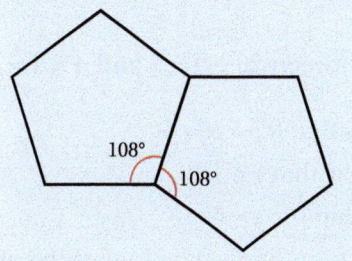

c A regular decagon can be surrounded by regular pentagons.

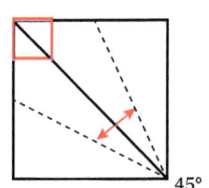

15

> What angles can be worked out?

360° ÷ 45° = 8, so 8 of the kites will fit together.

> Because of the way the paper has been folded you know the marked angle is 45°.

16 a 40 × 30 = 1200 unit squares

> You could start by working out the area of the rectangle.

$\frac{4}{5}$ of 1200 = 960

> Now you can work out the shaded area.

$\frac{5}{6}$ of 1200 = 1000 shaded, so need to shade an extra 40 unit squares.

b 960 is shaded from the first rectangle.
$\frac{2}{3}$ of 1200 = 800 is shaded from the second rectangle.

> One way to do this is to work out the total area and the total amount that is shaded.

The fraction of the whole thing that is shaded is:
$\frac{960 + 800}{1200 + 1200} = \frac{1760}{2400} = \frac{11}{15}$

c $\frac{3}{4}$ of 2400 = 1800, so an extra 40 unit squares need to be shaded.

> You already know that 1760 unit squares are shaded.

17 $6 \div 0.5 = 12$

$6 \div 0 =$ Error

There is a link between $20 \div 4 = 5$ and $4 \times 5 = 20$.

> There are lots of ways to explain why. Here is one.

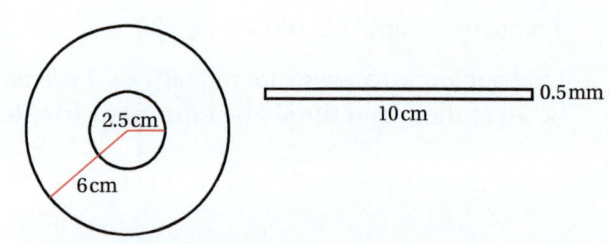

$6 \div 0.5 = x$ means that $0.5 \times x = 6$

This makes it clear that $x = 12$

$6 \div 0 = y$ means that $0 \times y = 6$

It is not possible to multiply 0 by something and to get the answer of 6, so $6 \div 0$ does not have an answer.

18

[Diagram: a ring with inner radius 2.5 cm and outer radius 6 cm; a rectangle 10 cm by 0.5 mm representing the side view of a piece of paper.]

> The width of the paper is irrelevant. You only need to worry about the area of the end of the roll.

The diagrams show the end of the roll of paper and the side view of a single piece of paper.

$\pi \times 6^2 - \pi \times 2.5^2 = 93.46238 \, \text{cm}^2$

> The area of the 'ring'.

$10 \times 0.05 = 0.5 \, \text{cm}^2$

> The area of the side of one piece of paper.
>
> Convert 0.5 mm into 0.05 cm.

$93.46238 \div 0.5 = 186.92476$

> Work out how many pieces of paper have the same area as the ring.

This means there are approximately 187 sheets on the roll. We cannot tell whether this is exact because the sheets might be compressed when they are rolled up.

If there are 200 sheets then they must be slightly thinner, so they aren't as high quality as was claimed.

19

θ	$\sin\theta$	$\cos\theta$	$\sin\theta \div \cos\theta$
0°	0	1	0
30°	$\frac{1}{2}$	$\frac{\sqrt{3}}{2}$	$\frac{1}{2} \div \frac{\sqrt{3}}{2} = \frac{1}{2} \times \frac{2}{\sqrt{3}} = \frac{1}{\sqrt{3}}$
45°	$\frac{\sqrt{2}}{2}$	$\frac{\sqrt{2}}{2}$	1
60°	$\frac{\sqrt{3}}{2}$	$\frac{1}{2}$	$\frac{\sqrt{3}}{2} \div \frac{1}{2} = \frac{\sqrt{3}}{2} \times \frac{2}{1} = \sqrt{3}$
90°	1	0	$1 \div 0$, which is undefined

It seems sensible to start by following the instructions and filling in the missing boxes in the table!

The values in the final column do look like $\tan\theta$.

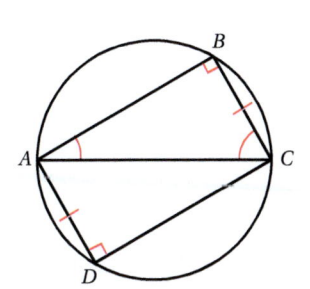

In a right-angled triangle: $\sin\theta = \frac{\text{opp}}{\text{hyp}}$ and $\cos\theta = \frac{\text{adj}}{\text{hyp}}$

This means that

$$\frac{\sin\theta}{\cos\theta} = \frac{\text{opp}}{\text{hyp}} \div \frac{\text{adj}}{\text{hyp}} = \frac{\text{opp}}{\text{hyp}} \times \frac{\text{hyp}}{\text{adj}} = \frac{\text{opp}}{\text{adj}}$$

$\frac{\text{opp}}{\text{adj}} = \tan\theta$,

so it is the case that $\sin\theta \div \cos\theta = \tan\theta$

20

$A\hat{B}C = 90°$ and $A\hat{D}C = 90°$

Because the angle in a semicircle is a right angle.

$AD = BC$

Compare triangles ABC and CDA.

AC is common to both triangles and is the hypotenuse.

So, by RHS, triangles ABC and CDA are congruent.

RHS refers to the RHS congruence theorem.

This means $B\hat{A}C = A\hat{C}D$. But $B\hat{A}C + A\hat{C}B = 90°$ (because angles in a triangle add up to 180°), so $D\hat{C}B = 90°$

For a similar reason, $D\hat{A}B = 90°$

All four angles in the quadrilateral ABCD are 90°, so it is a rectangle.

21 a

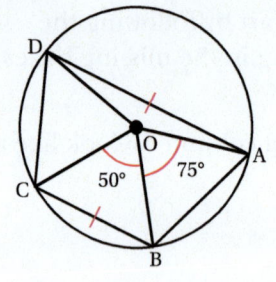

$O\hat{C}B = O\hat{B}C = (180° - 50°) \div 2 = 65°$

$O\hat{A}B = O\hat{B}A = (180° - 75°) \div 2 = 52.5°$

$C\hat{B}A = 65° + 52.5° = 117.5°$
$B\hat{A}D = 180° - 117.5° = 62.5°$

$O\hat{A}D = O\hat{D}A = 62.5° - 52.5° = 10°$

$A\hat{O}D = 180° - 20° = 160°$

$C\hat{O}D = 360° - 50° - 75° - 160° = 75°$

You need to show which angles you are looking at, so first draw in lines from each vertex of the trapezium to the centre of the circle and label the angles given in the question.

Each of the four triangles is isosceles (because the lines OA, OB, OC are radii).

Use this to calculate the other angles in triangles BOC and AOB.

Because AD is parallel to CB (trapezium), DAB + ABC = 180°.

Now calculate OÂD in the isosceles triangle OAD.

Now calculate AÔD, remembering to subtract both OÂD and OD̂A.

Angles around a point sum to 360°.

b OA = OB = OC = OD because they are all the radius of the circle, and so by SAS, triangle COD is congruent to triangle AOB. This means CD is equal to AB, so ABCD is an isosceles trapezium.

22 $\frac{2}{16}$ of the woodlice had a dot, which is $\frac{1}{8}$ of Nadine's sample.

That means the 16 she caught were about $\frac{1}{8}$ of the population, so there are $16 \times 8 = 128$ altogether, which is below the limit of 150.

As long as the woodlice she marked had mixed themselves up with the others, the fraction with dots the second time is the fraction she caught.

23 In the original pentagon all the angles were 108° (angles in a regular pentagon) and in the equilateral triangles the angles are all 60°.

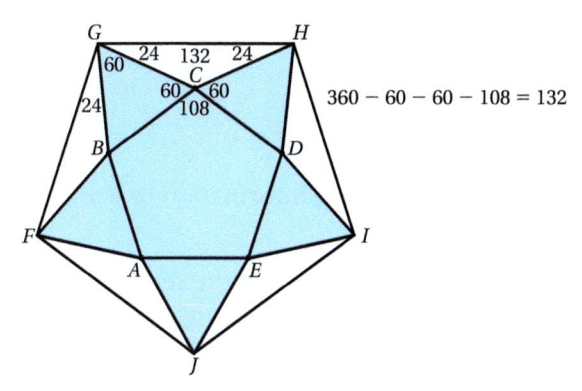

> There are lots of ways to explain this.
>
> Draw the pentagon in and then look at the diagram. To show that the outer pentagon is regular you need to show that the angles are all equal and that the sides are all the same length.

$360 - 60 - 60 - 108 = 132$

The angles in the isosceles triangles around the edge are therefore 132°, 24°, 24°.

The angles in the outer pentagon are therefore $24 + 60 + 24 = 108°$, which are the angles for a regular pentagon.

All the sides of the original pentagon are equal (because it is regular), so the equilateral triangles are all congruent. The isosceles triangles are all congruent (by SAS) so the sides of the outer pentagon are all the same.

Because the sides are all equal and the angles are equal the outer pentagon is regular.

24 a

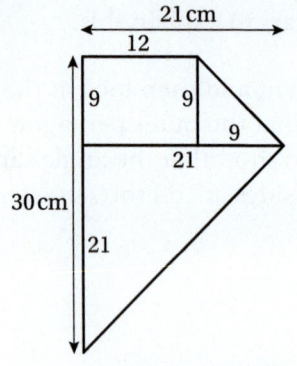

Rectangle: $12 \times 9 = 108$

Small triangle: $\frac{1}{2} \times 9 \times 9 = 40.5$

Large triangle: $\frac{1}{2} \times 21 \times 21 = 220.5$

Total area = 369 cm^2

b Area of the original sheet is $21 \times 30 = 630 \text{ cm}^2$

The fraction is $\dfrac{369}{630} = \dfrac{41}{70}$

> Draw a good diagram and then work out the lengths of the sides.
>
> The two right-angled triangles are each half a square and this helps you to work out the lengths.

> Now there is enough information to work out the areas.
>
> Either work out the area of the rectangle and the two triangles and add them, or work out the area of the original sheet of paper and subtract two triangles.

25

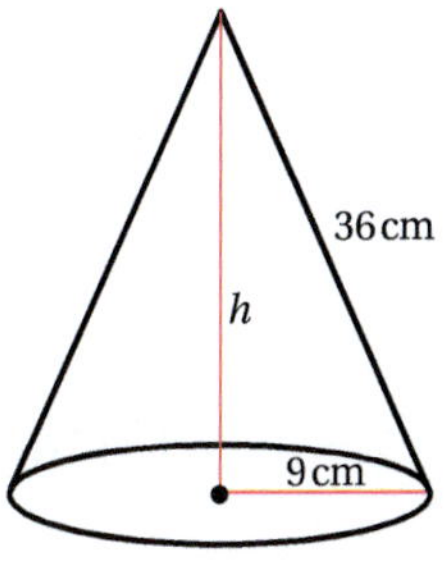

Circumference of the base is π × 2r = 18π, and when the hat is unrolled, this is the length of the arc.

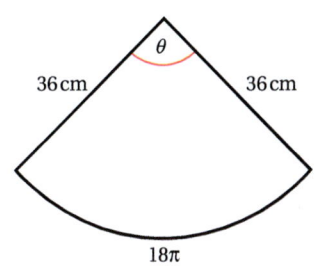

> Start with a labelled diagram of the hat.
> Circumference = π × 2r

> This is a sector of a circle.

The radius of the sector = 36 cm, so the circumference of a full circle would be 72 π.

The arc is 18 π, which is $\frac{1}{4}$ of the circumference, so the angle is $\frac{1}{4}$ of 360° = 90°.

Hence the sector required will be a quarter of a circle of radius 36 cm.

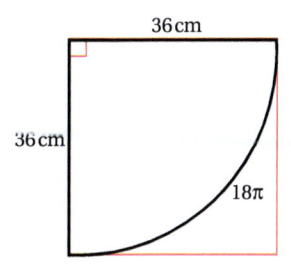

This will fit on a square of side 36 cm.

---

26 Radius = 16 cm ÷ 2 = 8 cm

Volume = $\frac{4}{3}$ × π × 8³ ÷ 2 = 1072.33 cm³ (2 d.p.)

Radius = 11 cm ÷ 2 = 5.5 cm

$\frac{4}{3}$ × π × 5.5 cm³ ÷ 2 = 348.45 cm³ (2 d.p.)

1072.33 cm³ − 348.45 cm³ = 723.88 cm³ (2 d.p.)

723.98 ml ÷ 100 = 7.2388

7.2388 × 59 = 427 kcal saved (to the nearest kcal).

> Volume of large bowl (hemisphere) = $\frac{4}{3}$ π r³ ÷ 2

> Volume of small bowl

> Difference between volumes of larger and smaller bowls

> Number of kcal in 723.88 of soup.

27 1 minute = 60 s
1 hour = 60 minutes = 60 × 60 s = 3600 s
1 day = 24 hours = 24 × 3600 s = 86 400 s
1 year = 365 days = 365 × 86 400 s = 31 536 000 s

2.99×10^5 km/s × 31 536 000 s = $9.429... \times 10^{12}$ km

$4.22 \times 9.429... \times 10^{12}$ km = $3.979... \times 10^{13}$ km

$3.979... \times 10^{13}$ km = $3.979... \times 10^{16}$ m

$3.979... \times 10^{16}$ m ÷ 400 m = $9.947... \times 10^{13}$

You would need to run approximately 10×10^{13} or 1×10^{14} or 100 000 000 000 000 laps of a standard 400 m running track to cover the distance from Earth to Proxima Centauri.

> First calculate the number of km in a light year.
> To do this, calculate the number of seconds in 1 year.

> Now calculate the number of km travelled by light in one year.

> Convert 4.22 light years into km.

> Convert this into metres.

> Calculate the number of laps of a 400 m track that are required to cover this distance.

28

> Draw an accurate version of the diagram on a grid.

> Then work out the length of each of the sides, using Pythagoras' theorem.

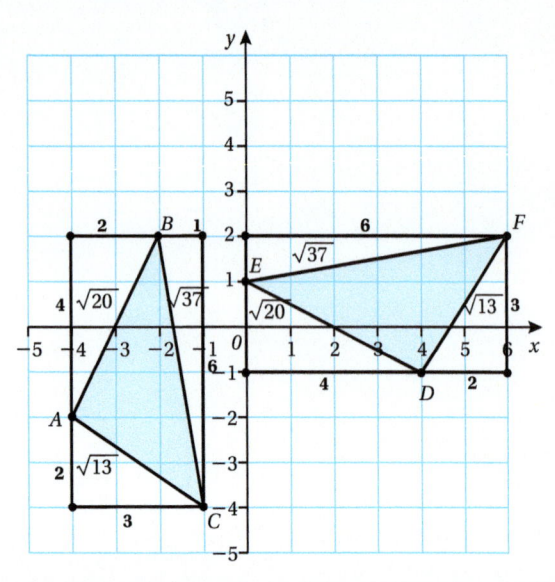

The two triangles have identical sides, so by SSS they are congruent.

29

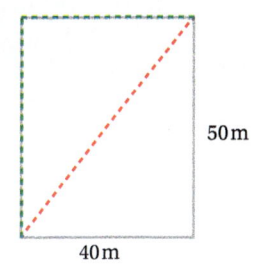

[Diagram: rectangle 40 m by 50 m with diagonal]

The tortoise travels $\sqrt{40^2 + 50^2} = \sqrt{4100}$

The hare travels $40 + 50 = 90$

Time $= \dfrac{\sqrt{41\,000}}{0.1} = 640.312\,\text{s}$

The hare only needs to travel 90 m in 640.312 seconds, so the lowest speed it can go at and still beat the tortoise is $\dfrac{90}{640.312} = 0.1405\,\text{m/s}$

> It seems sensible to work out the distances the two animals travel.

> You know how fast the tortoise moves, so you can work out how long it takes the tortoise to complete the race.
>
> Time = distance ÷ speed

3 Change your point of view

1

$2a + 1300 = 2280$

$a = 490$ m, so the value of a required is 0.49 km.

> Add some lines to make it into a rectangle.

> This makes it easy to see that the perimeter of the shape (which is the same as the perimeter of the rectangle) is $a + a + 650 + 650 = 2a + 1300$
>
> This is the same as 2.28 km, so (after converting that to 2280 m) you can make an equation.

2 Approach 1:

The interior angle of an octagon = 135°

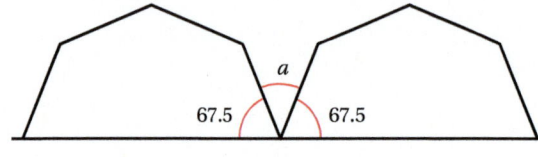

$135° \div 2 = 67.5°$

$67.5° + 67.5° + a = 180°$

$a = 180° - 135° = 45°$

Approach 2:

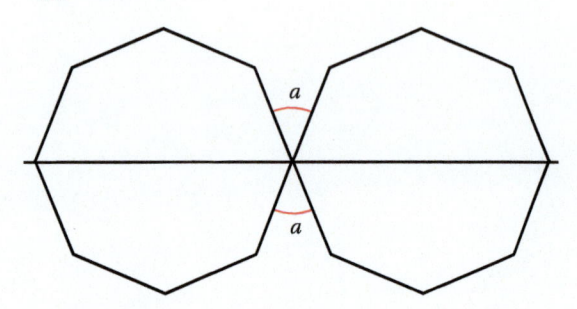

Exterior angle of an octagon = $360° \div 8 = 45°$

> There are several ways to approach this problem.

> The octagon has been cut in half so the angles adjacent to the one labelled a will each be half of the interior angle of the octagon.

> The sum of angles on a straight line is 180°.

> Making a copy of the half-octagons and rotating it creates two octagons. The angle a is the exterior angle.

3 a

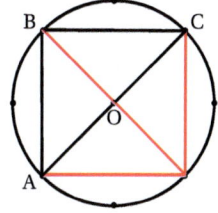

The inner shape is a square, so the angle ABC is 90°.

b

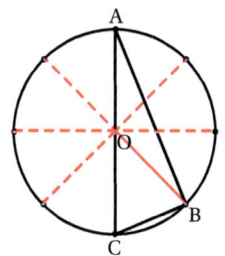

The extra lines show that there are 8 equal angles around the centre of the circle.

Each angle is therefore 360° ÷ 8 = 45°.

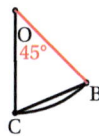

Triangle OBC is isosceles and the angle OBC = (180 − 45) ÷ 2 = 67.5°

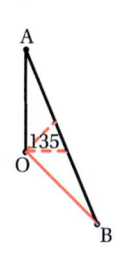

Triangle OAB is also isosceles and the angle AOB = 135° (three lots of 45°). Angles A and B are equal and add up to 45°, so each one is 22.5°.

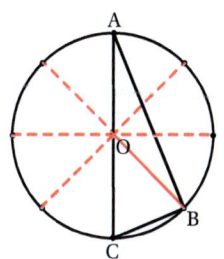

Angle ABC is 67.5° + 22.5° = 90°

c

When you choose a point for B you will make isosceles triangles and can work out the other angles as in part **b**. Angle ABC will again = 90°. Angles BAC and BCA form the other two angles of the triangle, so they will sum to 90°.

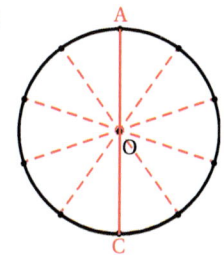

The angles around the centre are all 36° (360° ÷ 10).

Cambridge IGCSE Mathematics Extended Problem-solving Book

4

First, you could work out the actual answer. You could draw extra lines on the diagram.

It shows that $\frac{9}{16}$ of the diagram is coloured.

Team A have given an area rather than a proportion: 0 marks

Team B have got the wrong fraction. Maybe they saw that $\frac{3}{4}$ of this part was shaded:

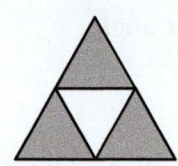

But that is not the whole thing: 0 or 1 mark

Team C are correct. Maybe they used the idea that the inner big white triangle is not included (leaving $\frac{3}{4}$ of the whole diagram) and then $\frac{3}{4}$ of that is shaded, which is $\frac{3}{4} \times \frac{3}{4}$. This equals $\frac{9}{16}$. But Team C have not completed their calculation: 3 marks

Team D are correct. $\frac{9}{16} = 0.5625$: 4 marks

5 a

[Diagram: circle with inner diameter 15 m and outer diameter 17 m]

The length of the fence is:

π × 17 = 53.407075 … m

= 53.4 m

> A copy of the diagram with the extra line added will help.

> Circumference of circle = π × diameter

> Round the answer to 3 s.f.

b semicircle with diameter of 23 m

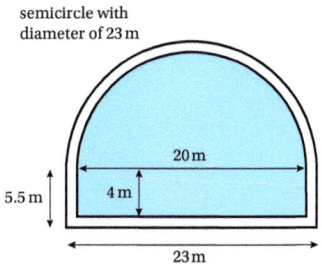

[Diagram: semicircle with inner width 20 m, outer width 23 m, inner height 4 m, outer height 5.5 m]

Length of fence:

5.5 + 23 + 5.5 + semicircle with diameter of 23 m

Semicircle:

π × 23 ÷ 2

Total length is 70.1 m

70.1 m − 53.4 m = 16.7 m

Arjun will need to buy 16.7 m more fencing than Gerry.

> Calculate the difference in lengths of fencing.

> Conclusion.

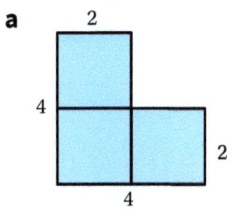

6

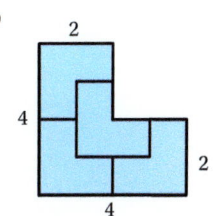

> You need to divide the area into congruent shapes. Congruent shapes have the same area, so you could start by working out the area of the original diagram, which is 12 square units.

a

[Diagram: L-shape made of two squares, each 2×2 above and 4×4 on side, dimensions 2, 4, 2, 4]

> To have three congruent shapes the area of each one must be 4 square units. An easy way to make an area of 4 is to have a square.

b

[Diagram: L-shape with dimensions 2, 4, 2, 4]

> To make four congruent shapes the area of each one must be 3 square units. If you try to use three straight lines it doesn't work, either with rectangles or with triangles. There are other shapes that have an area of 3 square units, and these will work here.

7 **a** 3.6 m = 360 cm

360 cm ÷ 18 cm = 20 stairs in the staircase.

> The stairs must cover a vertical distance of 3.6 m. Each step is 18 cm high.

b Base length of staircase = 20 × 28 cm = 560 cm

$a^2 + b^2 = c^2$

$560^2 + 360^2 = c^2$

$443\,200 = c^2$

$c = 665.73\ldots$ cm

> The banister rail will go diagonally up the stairs. It will need to be the same length as the diagonal length of the staircase. Use Pythagoras' theorem to calculate this.

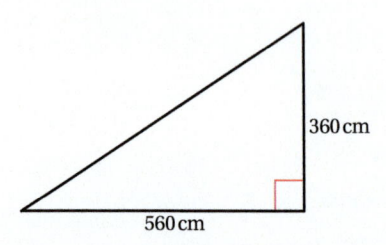

[Right-angled triangle with vertical side 360 cm and horizontal side 560 cm]

The hand rail will need to be 6.66 m in length (to the nearest cm).

---

8 The sides of the triangle are all tangents to the circle.

> A good extra line to try is one from the centre of the circle to the tangent point (because this does some special things, like forming right angles).

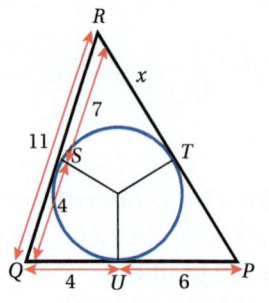

[Triangle PQR with inscribed circle; tangent points S (on QR), T (on PR), U (on QP). Lengths marked: RS = 7, ST (along RQ above S) labelled 11, SQ = 4, QU = 4, UP = 6, and RT = x]

SQ = UQ, so SQ = 4.

RS is equal to RT, so $x = 7$.

> You know this because two tangents from the same point are the same length.

9 **a** The horizontal line is 6 – x

> The perimeter is 12, so the horizontal line and the side together add up to 6.

The area is therefore $(6 - x)x$, which can also be written as $6x - x^2$.

b The area is equal to $6.3\,\text{m}^2$, so you get the equation (using the area from part **a**):

$6x - x^2 = 6.3$

> The area of the tablecloth is big enough, but it might not be the right dimensions to fit neatly on the table, so you need to work out the dimensions of the table.

$10x^2 - 60x + 63 = 0$

> Rearrange and multiply through by 10.

$x = 4.64$ or $x = 1.36$

> Use the quadratic formula.

These are the dimensions of the table (because $6 - 4.64 = 1.36$).

The tablecloth won't fit.

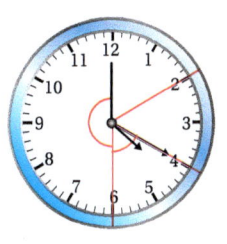

10 **a**

240°

> It seems to be a good plan to draw the angle you need to work out.
>
> Then a couple of extra lines will make the calculations easier.

> The extra lines on the diagram show that you need 180° plus a third of 180° (60°), which is 240° in total.

b $\frac{1}{12}$ of 240° = 20°

> When the minute hand makes a full turn the hour hand moves one hour, which means the hour hand moves at $\frac{1}{12}$ of the speed.

11

The coordinates of point B are (0.5, 0).

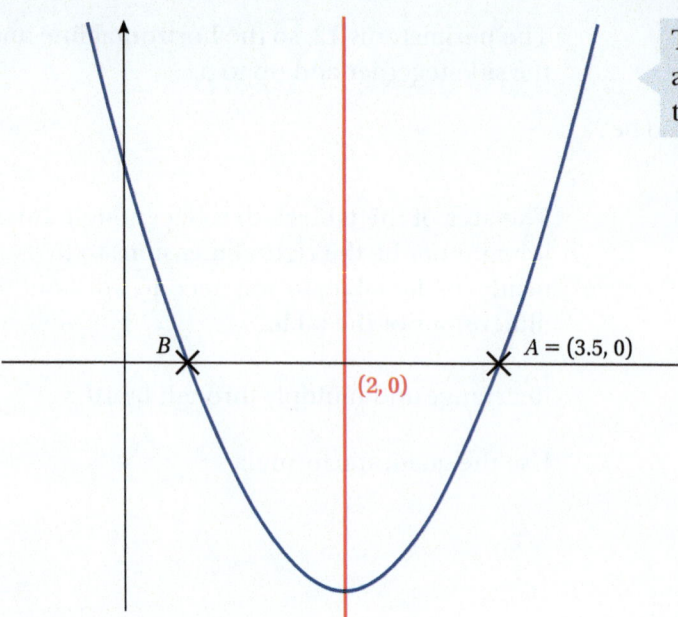

The question says that the graph is symmetrical about the line $x = 2$, so it makes sense to draw that line on a copy of the graph.

Now you can see that the crossing value for point A is 1.5 to the right of the line of reflection, so point B must cross at 1.5 to the left of the line.

C is (3.5, 0) and D is (0.5, 0).

In the second diagram the quadratic has been reflected in the x-axis so the crossing points are the same.

---

12 If Z, S and P are collinear then $\overrightarrow{SP}$ is parallel to $\overrightarrow{ZS}$ and they are multiples of each other.

$\overrightarrow{SP} = 2u + 3v$

$\overrightarrow{ZS} = \tfrac{1}{2}u + 2v$

$4\overrightarrow{ZS} = 2u + 8v$

There is no way to express $\overrightarrow{SZ}$ as a multiple of $\overrightarrow{SP}$.

Hence Z, S and P are not collinear.

It is worth adding these extra lines to the diagram.

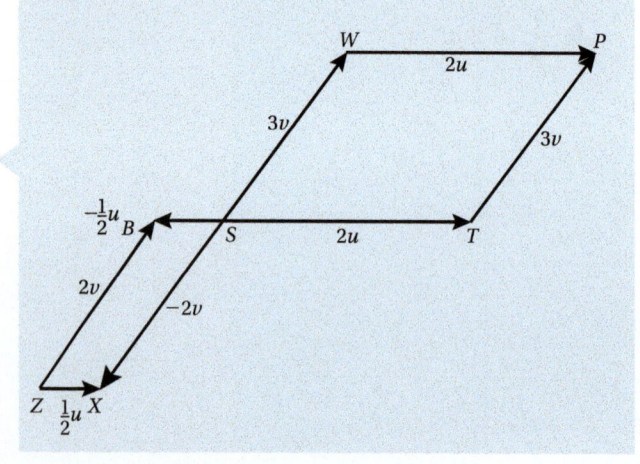

13 a

[Diagram: paperclip on ruler with labels: radius = 0.9, 2 × 1.2, 4 × 2.9, radius = 0.6, 2 × 1.8, radius = 0.7]

The straight parts add up to 17.6

$0.9\pi + 0.6\pi + 0.7\pi = 2.2\pi$

The total length is 24.5 cm (1 d.p.).

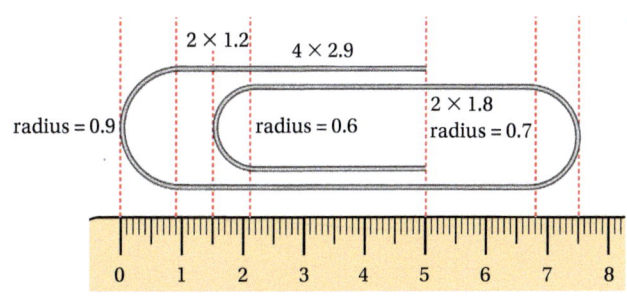

> Chop the diagram up into sections and label them.

> Work out the perimeter of a semicircle.

b

[Diagram: pointed paperclip on ruler with labels: 2 × 1.4, 4 × 2.6, 2 × 1, radius = 0.4, 1]

The diagonal parts are the hypotenuse because of a right-angled triangle.

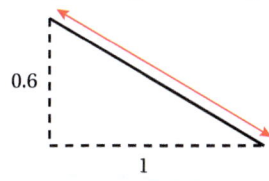

[Right triangle with legs 0.6 and 1]

$h = \sqrt{1^2 + 0.6^2} = 1.166\ldots$

The total length of wire is 19.8 cm (1 d.p.), which means the first paperclip contains more wire.

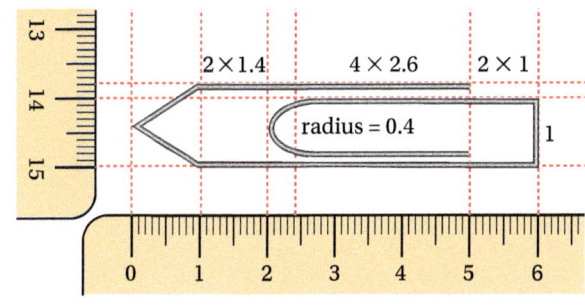

> Use the same process as in part **a** to work out the length of the straight parts and the semicircle.

> The total length will be:
> straight parts + diagonal parts + semicircle

14 a

[Two triangles: isosceles with sides $2x-1$, $2x-1$ and base $2x-4$; right triangle with hypotenuse $2x-1$ and base $x-2$]

$h = \sqrt{(2x-1)^2 - (x-2)^2}$

$h = \sqrt{(4x^2 - 4x + 1) - (x^2 - 4x + 4)}$

This simplifies to $h = \sqrt{3x^2 - 3}$

The perpendicular height of the triangle is $= \sqrt{3x^2 - 3}$.

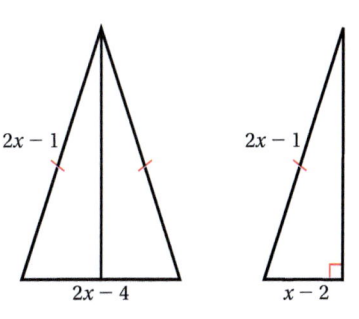

> Put in the extra line – this makes two right-angled triangles.

> Work out the height of the triangle, using Pythagoras' theorem.

b $h = 12$

$\sqrt{3x^2 - 3} = 12$

$3x^2 - 3 = 12^2$

$3x^2 = 144 + 3$

$x^2 = 49$

$x = 7$

Area of triangle $= \frac{1}{2}(2 \times 7 - 4) \times 12$
$= 60 \text{ cm}^2$

> You are told the height is 12.

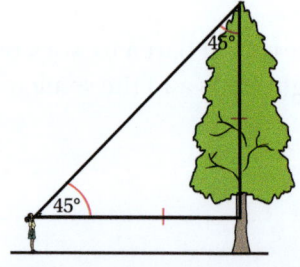

15 a

> Draw the extra lines on the diagram so you can see what is going on.

If they are looking up at an angle of 45°, then they create a right-angled, isosceles triangle. (Isosceles because if one angle is 90° and another is 45° then the remaining angle will also be 45°.)

Assuming that the child's height is small compared to the height of the tree, then the horizontal distance along the ground is approximately the same as the height of the tree (two equal sides in an isosceles triangle).

b

> A good diagram will help.

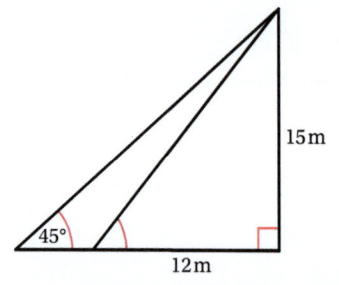

Opposite side = height of tree = 15 m

Adjacent side = 12 m

Guy's angle $= \tan^{-1} \frac{15}{12} = 51.34\ldots°$

Guy's angle is approximately 51°.

16

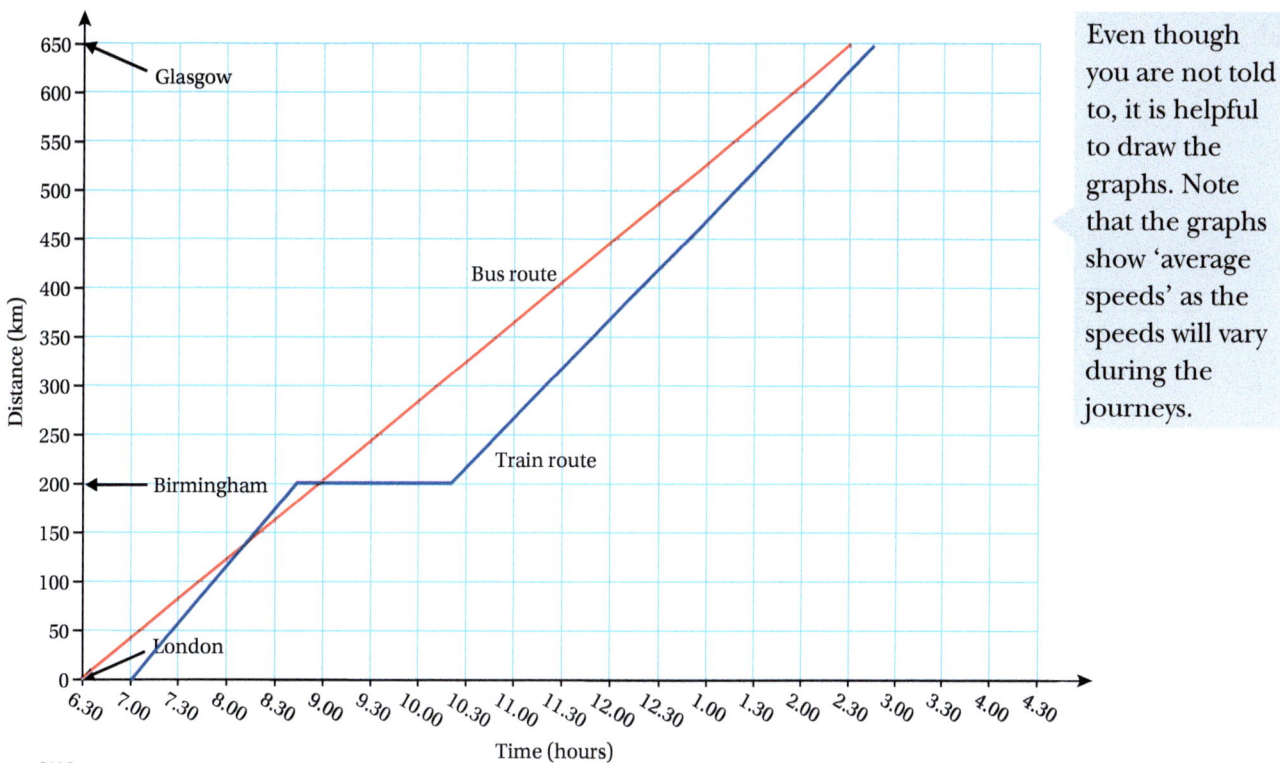

[Graph showing Distance (km) vs Time (hours) with Bus route and Train route from London to Glasgow via Birmingham]

Even though you are not told to, it is helpful to draw the graphs. Note that the graphs show 'average speeds' as the speeds will vary during the journeys.

a $\dfrac{650}{8} = 81.25$ km/h

b 7 h 40 min is $7\frac{2}{3}$ h

Work out the total time for the train journey in hours.

$650 \div 7\frac{2}{3} = 84.8$ km/h

17

The diagram, with its extra lines, shows that 3 straight lines (each $4r$ in length) and 3 arcs, are needed.

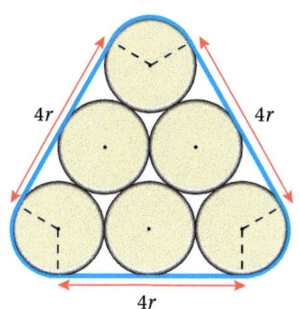

The 3 arcs together make a circle, so the total length is $12 \times r + 2\pi r$.

The radius is 2.7 cm, so the length is 49.36 cm.

18 a

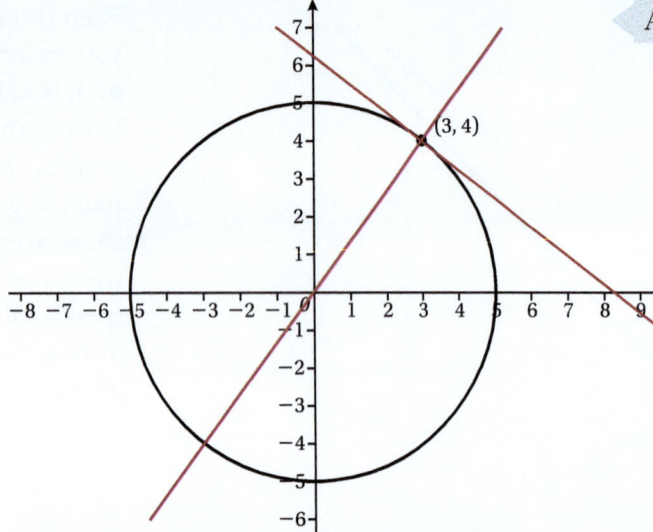

> Add some extra lines to help.

The equation of the line passing through $(0, 0)$ is $y = \frac{4}{3}x$

This means the equation of the tangent has a gradient of $-\frac{3}{4}$

$y = -\frac{3}{4}x + c$ passes through the point $(3, 4)$.
Substituting in those values

gives: $4 = -\frac{3}{4} \times 3 + c$, which rearranges to give $c = \frac{25}{4}$, which is $6\frac{1}{4}$

This means the equation of the tangent is $y = -\frac{3}{4}x + 6\frac{1}{4}$

> The extra lines show that you have the radius and the tangent, so the gradients of the two lines multiply together to give -1.

b

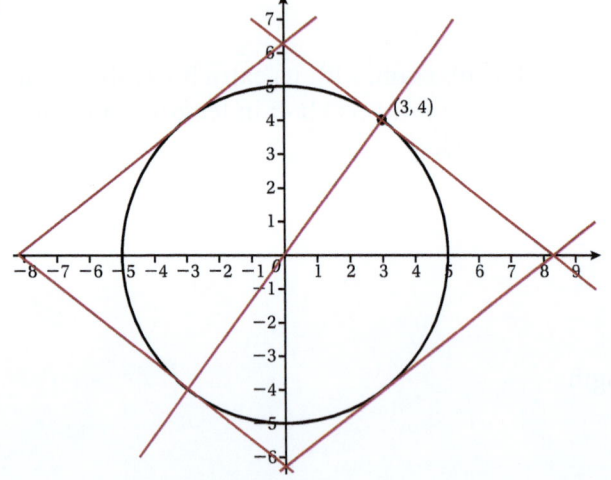

> There are lots of other tangent lines that you could write down equations for, but the three shown here seem to be the easiest.

The original tangent was $y = \frac{-3}{4}x + 6\frac{1}{4}$

The tangent parallel to it is $y = \frac{-3}{4}x - 6\frac{1}{4}$

The reflection of the original tangent in the y-axis gives $y = \frac{3}{4}x + 6\frac{1}{4}$

The reflection of the original tangent in the x-axis gives $y = \frac{3}{4}x - 6\frac{1}{4}$

19

A well-labelled diagram might help.

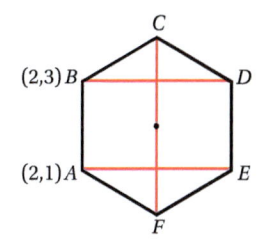

a $\overrightarrow{DE}$ is the same vector as $\overrightarrow{BA}$. This is $\begin{pmatrix} 0 \\ -2 \end{pmatrix}$ (the same numbers as $\overrightarrow{AB}$ but with the opposite sign).

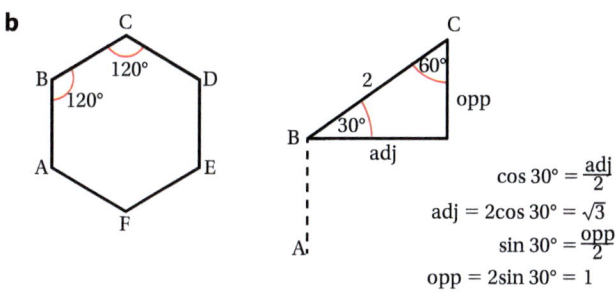

b

In a regular hexagon the interior angles are each $120°$.

By drawing a right-angled triangle where the hypotenuse side is of length 2 units, you can use the edge of the hexagon and trigonometry to calculate the other lengths.

$\cos 30° = \dfrac{\text{adj}}{2}$

adj $= 2\cos 30° = \sqrt{3}$

$\sin 30° = \dfrac{\text{opp}}{2}$

opp $= 2\sin 30° = 1$

Coordinates:
- $A(2, 1)$
- $B(2, 3)$
- $C(2 + \sqrt{3}, 4)$
- $D(2 + 2\sqrt{3}, 3)$
- $E(2 + 2\sqrt{3}, 1)$
- $F(2 + \sqrt{3}, 0)$

$(2 + \sqrt{3}, 4)$

c The vector $\overrightarrow{BC} = \begin{pmatrix} \sqrt{3} \\ 1 \end{pmatrix}$

To get from B to C you need to go right by $\sqrt{3}$ and up by 1.

d The vector $\overrightarrow{FC} = \begin{pmatrix} 0 \\ 4 \end{pmatrix}$.

F is immediately below C. C is 1 above B, so F must be 1 below A, which means the distance from F to C is 4.

e The vector $\overrightarrow{AE} = \begin{pmatrix} 2\sqrt{3} \\ 0 \end{pmatrix}$

The vector $\overrightarrow{AE}$ is the same as the vector $\overrightarrow{BD}$. D is level with B, so you just need to look at how far D is to the right of B. To get from B to C you go right by $\sqrt{3}$, so you need to double this.

f The vector $\overrightarrow{AC}$ is the same as $\overrightarrow{AB} + \overrightarrow{BC}$. This is $\begin{pmatrix} 0 \\ 2 \end{pmatrix} + \begin{pmatrix} \sqrt{3} \\ 1 \end{pmatrix} = \begin{pmatrix} \sqrt{3} \\ 3 \end{pmatrix}$

g $\overrightarrow{EF}$ is the same vector as $\overrightarrow{CB}$. This is $\overrightarrow{EF} = \begin{pmatrix} -\sqrt{3} \\ -1 \end{pmatrix}$

20

Triangle A (right triangle with legs $\sqrt{6}$ and $\sqrt{2}$, hypotenuse $\sqrt{8}$)

Triangle B (isosceles triangle with equal sides $\sqrt{6}$, base $\sqrt{8}$, height 2)

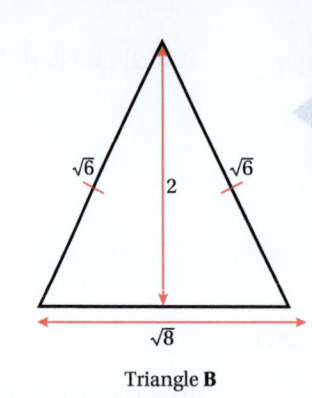

> The base of the first triangle is $4^{\frac{1}{4}}$ (4 to the power of $\frac{1}{4}$), which is the same as $(4^{\frac{1}{2}})^{\frac{1}{2}}$
>
> This is equal to $\sqrt{2}$.

> In Triangle **A** the hypotenuse is $\sqrt{(6)^2 + (2)^2} = \sqrt{8}$
>
> In Triangle **B** the two equal sides are $\sqrt{\left(\frac{\sqrt{8}}{2}\right)^2 + (2)^2} = \sqrt{6}$

a The perimeter of Triangle A is $\sqrt{8} + \sqrt{6} + \sqrt{2}$

The perimeter of Triangle B is $\sqrt{8} + \sqrt{6} + \sqrt{6}$

Because $\sqrt{6} > \sqrt{2}$ Triangle B has the bigger perimeter.

b The area of Triangle A is $\frac{1}{2}\sqrt{2}\sqrt{6}$

$= \frac{1}{2}\sqrt{12} = \frac{1}{2}\sqrt{4}\sqrt{3} = \sqrt{3}$

The area of Triangle B is $\frac{1}{2}\sqrt{8} \times 2 = \sqrt{8}$

Because $\sqrt{8} > \sqrt{3}$ Triangle B has the bigger area.

21 a

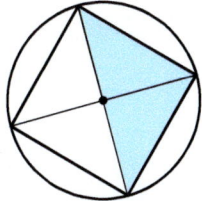

The radius is 1cm so the area of the shaded triangle is $\frac{1}{2}$ and the area of the whole square is 2 cm².

You are told the radius of the circle is 1cm, so it makes sense to draw in the radius.

b

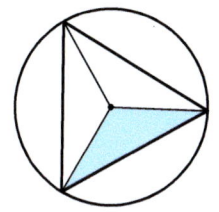

The shaded triangle has two sides of 1cm and the angle between them is 120°.

The area, using $\frac{1}{2}ab\sin C$ is $\frac{1}{2}\sin 120$.

The total area of the equilateral triangle is therefore 1.299.

The ratio of the area of the triangle to the area of the square is 1.299 : 2.

This is 1.299 ÷ 2 : 1 – then multiply by 3 to get 1.9485 : 3, which is approximately 2 : 3.

c

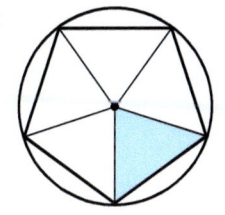

The shaded triangle has two sides of 1cm with an angle between them of 72°.

The area, using $\frac{1}{2}ab\sin C$ is $\frac{1}{2}\sin 72$.

The total area of the regular pentagon is therefore 2.3776…

Divide this area by the area of the square to get 1.18882… This is approximately 1.2, which is the $\frac{6}{5}$ referred to in the question.

22

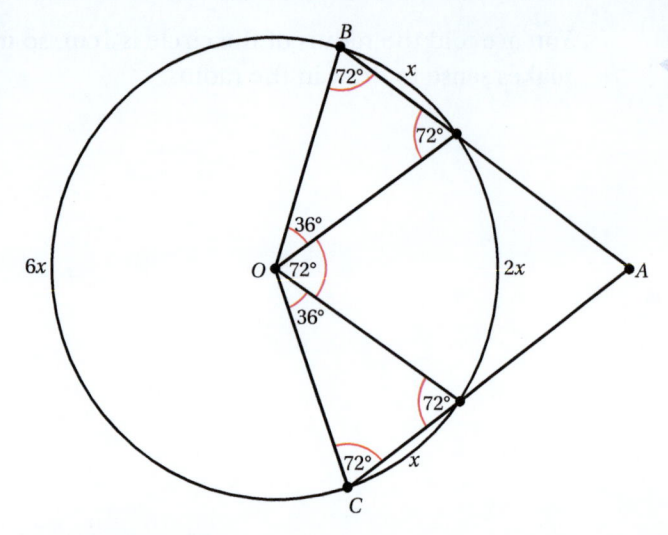

Angle BAC = 72°

Draw in the radius of the circle. This gives two isosceles triangles.

The total circumference of the circle is $10x$, which means that x is $\frac{1}{10}$ of the circumference and the angle at the centre of the circle formed by each of the arcs of x is $360 \div 10 = 36°$.

The angle at the centre of the arc of $2x$ is therefore 72°.

Use the fact that there are isosceles triangles to work out the other angles in those triangles.

Now focus on the biggest quadrilateral in the picture. The angles must add up to 360° so angle BAC must be 72°.

23

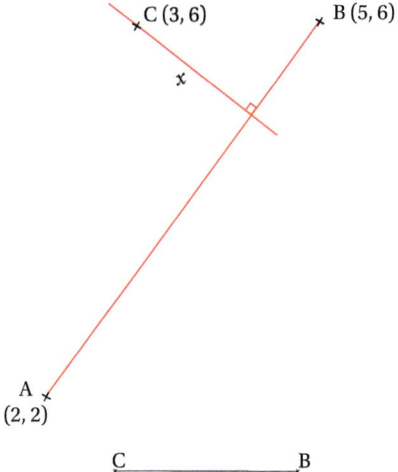

Draw a simple version of the diagram first. Add the distance that you are trying to calculate and call this x. This can be shown by drawing a line through C that is perpendicular to AB.

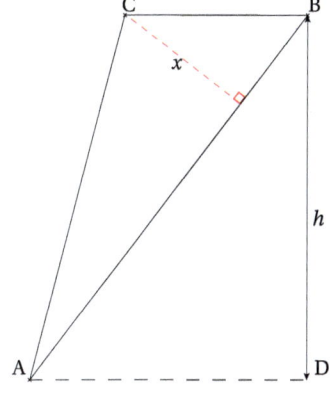

Adding extra lines gives you more ways in which you can proceed. Notice that B and C have the same y-coordinate giving a natural base, BC, for triangle ABC. If BC is the base (which has length 2) then the height will be h as shown here. Height h can now be seen to be 4 and we can calculate the area of the triangle ABC.

$$\text{Area of ABC} = \frac{1}{2} \times 2 \times 4 = 4$$

$$AB = \sqrt{3^2 + 4^2}$$
$$= 5$$

By using the right-angled triangle, ADB, we can use Pythagoras' theorem to find the length AB.

$$\frac{1}{2} \times 5 \times x = 4$$

But we know the area of the triangle and can now calculate that using the distance x that we are trying to find.

So
$$x = \frac{8}{5}$$

24

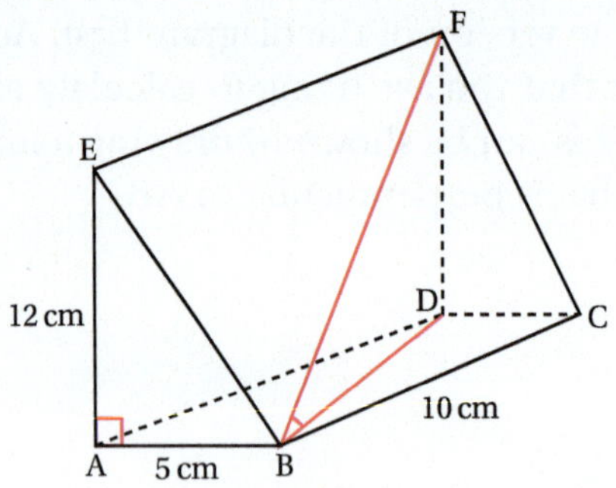

Draw a right-angled triangle that includes DF and a line in the base, specifically the line BD. The angle between the lines BD and BF is the angle that you need.

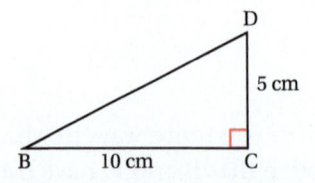

We already know that DF is 12 cm, so we now need to find the length BD. Draw the right-angled triangle BCD to help you. Now use Pythagoras' theorem to calculate the length BD.

$$BD = \sqrt{5^2 + 10^2} = \sqrt{125}$$

$\sqrt{125}$ does not give an exact decimal answer. If you evaluate it, you must remember to use all the digits on your calculator in the next stage of the working. It is better to leave this as a root.

Now we will draw the triangle BDF and include the lengths that we have calculated.

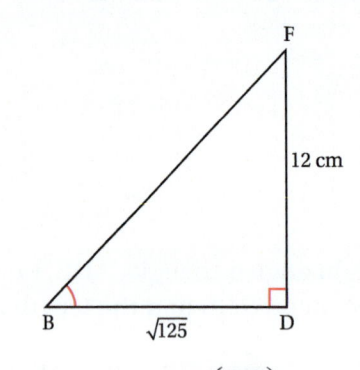

Angle DBF = $\tan^{-1}\left(\dfrac{DF}{BD}\right)$

$= \tan^{-1}\left(\dfrac{12}{\sqrt{125}}\right)$

$= 47.0°$

Use the tangent ratio to calculate the angle DBF.

25

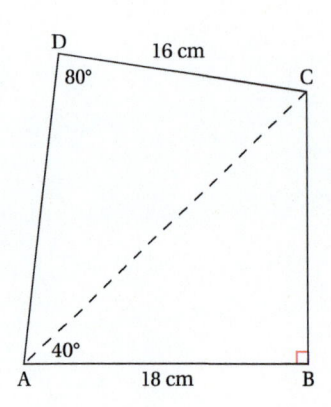

It is clear that you need to draw the quadrilateral ABCD. The question asks for angle ACD, which is a clue. Add the line AC so that you can see this angle.

Angle ACB = 180 − 40 − 90 = 50°

Now calculate angles and lengths as far as you can.

Length AC = $\dfrac{18}{\cos 40}$

Using straightforward trigonometry.

Notice that length AC lies opposite the 80° angle, and CD = 16 cm lies opposite the angle CAD.

$$\dfrac{\sin(CAD)}{16} = \dfrac{\sin 80}{\left(\dfrac{18}{\cos 40}\right)}$$

Use the sine rule to calculate CAD.

So

Angle CAD = $\sin^{-1}\left(\dfrac{16 \sin 80}{\left(\dfrac{18}{\cos 40}\right)}\right)$

$= 42.11212\ldots°$

Then angle ACD = 180 − 80 − 42.11212... = 57.9°

4 Simplify the problem

1

The two semicircles make a circle, radius 2.25 cm.

Area of circle = π × 2.25² = 15.9043 … cm²

Height of triangle = 13 − 2.25 = 10.75 cm

Area of triangle = $\frac{1}{2}$ × 9 × 10.75 = 48.375 cm²

9 × 13 − 15.9043 − 48.375 = 52.7 cm² (3 s.f.)

> Start by working out the areas of the different parts of the heart.

> Subtract the areas of the circle and triangle from the area of the rectangle to find the total area of card removed.

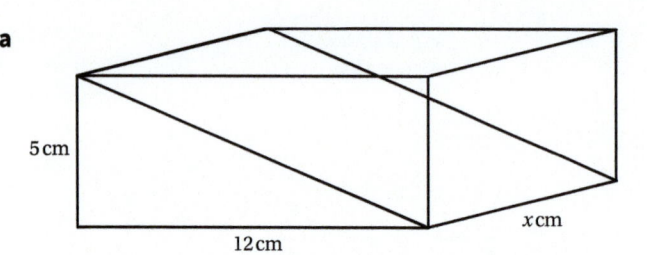

2 a

The diagram shows two wedges. That means 20 of these pairs total a metre long, so *x* must be 5.

b To make $30 profit and cover the cost of the wood ($5), Ahmed has to take at least $35.

As he has 40 wedges to sell, the minimum cost to achieve this is $35 ÷ 40 = 87.5¢.

This rounds to 88¢.

3 a Principal × 1.08^{10}

= Principal × 2.16

Yes, he would more than double his money.

b $40 000 × 1.08^{10}

$86 357 to the nearest pound.

c $30 000 × 1.08^{10} = $64 767.75

$31 000 × 1.08^{10} = $66 926.67

$32 000 × 1.08^{10} = $69 085.60

$33 000 × 1.08^{10} = $71 244.52

$34 000 × 1.08^{10} = $73 403.45

$35 000 × 1.08^{10} = $75 562.37

She must invest at least $35 000.

> 8% interest is an increase with a multiplier of 1.08

> The bank only gives this deal for $30 000 or more so start checking from this amount.
> Another way to work it out is to divide $75 000 by 1.08^{10}.

4 1 000 000 ÷ 60 = 16 666.666… minutes

16 666.666… ÷ 60 = 277.777… hours

277.777… ÷ 24 = 11.574 days

Some numbers will be much quicker to say than others. It is quick to say 'three' or 'five hundred thousand,' but it takes much longer to say 'two hundred and twenty-two thousand, two hundred and twenty-two.' If each number takes about 2 seconds to say (on average), then it will take about 23 days to say them all.

Even allowing for breaks for sleeping and eating, you could easily do this in your lifetime.

> This method starts by working out how many days is the same as 1 million seconds.

5 $\frac{9}{10} \times \frac{3}{4} \times \frac{1}{3} = \frac{27}{120}$

$1 - \frac{27}{120} = \frac{93}{120}$

This simplifies to give $\frac{31}{40}$.

> A simpler problem would be to work out the probability she doesn't have to stop.
> You can then work out the probability she does have to stop at least once.

6 a

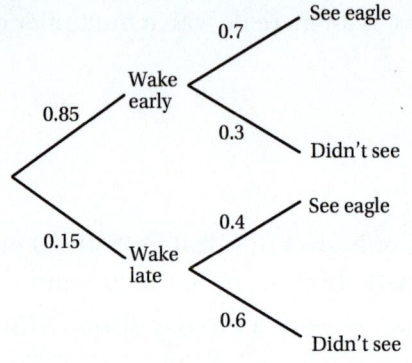

```
        0.7  See eagle
   Wake
   early
0.85     0.3  Didn't see
         
         0.4  See eagle
0.15 Wake
     late
         0.6  Didn't see
```

$(0.85 \times 0.7) + (0.15 \times 0.4)$

$= 0.655$

Nilesh could see an eagle if he wakes up early, but he could also see one if he wakes up later.

b

```
              Sister      0.7  See
              wakes
         0.75 early       0.3  Didn't see
   Nilesh
   wakes
   early 0.25 Sister      0.4  See
              wakes
0.85          late        0.6  Didn't see

              Sister      0.4  See
              wakes
0.15     0.75 early       0.6  Didn't see
   Nilesh
   doesn't
   wake
   early 0.25 Sister      0.4  See
              wakes
              late        0.6  Didn't see
```

If Nilesh wakes up late then it doesn't matter whether his sister wakes up early or late.

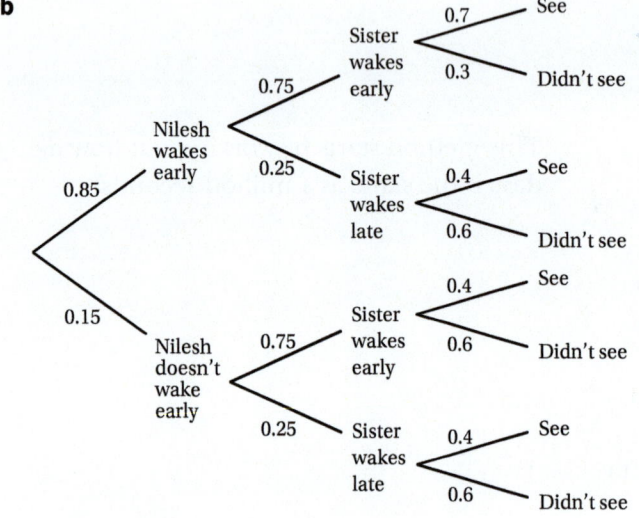

$(0.85 \times 0.75 \times 0.7) + (0.85 \times 0.25 \times 0.4)$
$+ (0.15 \times 0.4)$

$= 0.59125$

This is the probability that they will see an eagle.

$1 - 0.59125 = 0.40875$

This is the probability that they won't see an eagle.

c $0.655 - 0.591 = 0.064$

The probability goes down from about 0.7 to about 0.6.

Without his sister, Nilesh's chance of seeing an eagle is 0.655.

With her, his chance of seeing an eagle is 0.591.

7

a $4^3 = 4 \times 4 \times 4$ which is even

$3^4 = 3 \times 3 \times 3 \times 3$ which is odd

Even + odd = odd

So $4^3 + 3^4$ is odd

b 6^7 is even

3^7 is odd

So $6^7 + 3^7$ is odd

> Think about what happens when you add odd and even numbers.
>
> Show that:
>
> Even + even = even
>
> Odd + odd = even
>
> Even + odd = odd
>
> Then do the same for multiplication:
>
> Even × even = even
>
> Odd × odd = odd
>
> Even × even × even… = even
>
> Odd × odd × odd… = odd
>
> An even number raised to any integer power is even.
>
> $(\text{even})^x$ = even
>
> An odd number raised to any integer power is odd.
>
> $(\text{odd})^x$ = odd

8 a

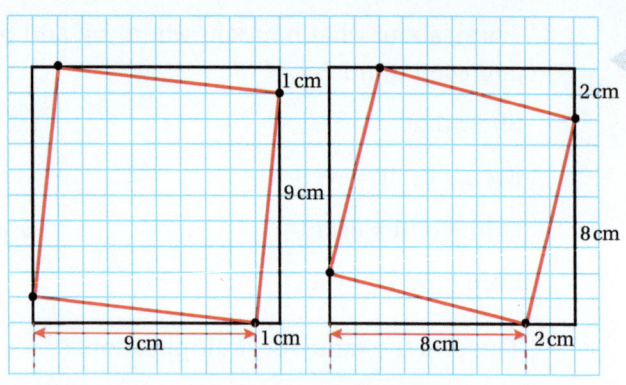

> Label what you know. Use the squares on the paper to find the lengths.

> Now focus on a triangle. Use Pythagoras' theorem to calculate the side length of the titled square.

$a^2 + b^2 = c^2$

$9^2 + 1^2 = c^2$

$82 = c^2$

$c = \sqrt{82} = 9.055\ldots$ cm

$a^2 + b^2 = c^2$

$8^2 + 2^2 = c^2$

$68 = c^2$

$c = \sqrt{68} = 8.246\ldots$ cm

A line in the first logo is longer than a line in the second logo, so the total line length of the first logo is greater.

b

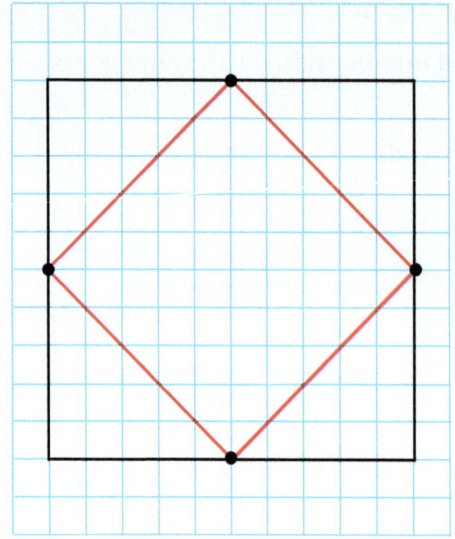

> To make a square of half the area you can rotate it.

> How can you be sure this has half the area?

Worked solutions: 4 Simplify the problem

9
a $140 \div 1\frac{1}{2} = 93.3$ km/h

b $140 \div 1\frac{1}{3} = 105$ km/h

c 10 minutes

d 12 noon

e 4.5 hours, 62.2 km/h

f 3 hours 40 minutes, 76.36 km/h

g 105 km/h is only 65.6 miles per hour, so no one was speeding at any point as long as the speed limit was 70 mph.

10

It is sensible to multiply the number of years by 365 to work out the approximate number of days and to round off the final answer for the following reasons:

- You don't know what time of day they were born, so you don't know whether it is an exact number of days.
- You don't know which month to start with for Ross (some are longer than others).
- You also don't know how many leap years have been involved.

	Pia	Ross	Jemima
Number of months		169 months	
Number of months / 12 = number of years	14.2 years	14.0833333 years	
Number of years × 365 = number of days	5183 days	5140.41667 days	5293 days
Number of days × 24 = number of hours	124 392 hours	123 370 hours	127 032 hours
Number of hours × 60 = number of minutes	7 463 520 minutes	7 402 200 minutes	7 621 920 minutes
Number of minutes × 60 = number of seconds	447 811 200 seconds	444 132 000 seconds	457 315 200 seconds
Rounded to 3 s.f.	448 000 000 seconds	444 000 000 seconds	457 000 000 seconds

Jemima is the eldest (and is older than Arindam by 7 million seconds).

11 a

	12 muffins	30 muffins	fat	sugar
eggs	2	5	4.6 × 5 = 23	trace
caster sugar	200 g	500 g		500
milk	250 ml	625 ml	0.02 × 625 = 12.5	0.05 × 625 = 31.25
vegetable oil	125 ml	312.5 ml	312.5	0
flour	400 g	1000 ml	7/500 × 1000 = 14	1/1000 × 1000 = 1
salt	1 tsp	2.5 tsp		
			total fat for 30 muffins: 362 g	total sugar for 30 muffins: 532.25 g
			fat for 1 muffin: 12.1 g	sugar for 1 muffin: 17.7 g

b Fat: 12.1 ÷ 70 × 100 = 17% of GDA.

Sugar: 17.7 ÷ 30 × 100 = 59% of GDA.

12 $V_{hemisphere}$ is $\frac{4}{3}\pi r^3 \div 2 = \frac{2}{3}\pi r^3$ — Work out the volume of a hemisphere.

V_{cone} is $\frac{1}{3}\pi r^2 h$ — Work out the volume of a cone.

$V_{cone} = \frac{1}{3}\pi r^2 \times 2r = \frac{2}{3}\pi r^3$ — The conical hanging basket has a height equal to its diameter. Therefore $h = 2r$.

That is the same as for the hemisphere, so the volumes are identical.

13 Area of A is $\sqrt{2}a$ — Start by working out what you know.

Area of B is
$2\sqrt{5} \times \sqrt{10} = 2\sqrt{5} \times \sqrt{5} \times \sqrt{2} = 2 \times 5 \times \sqrt{2} = 10\sqrt{2}$

The areas of the two rectangles are the same, so $\sqrt{2}a = 10\sqrt{2}$ and it is clear that $a = 10$.

14 $\sqrt{28} \times \sqrt{12}$

$\sqrt{28} \times \sqrt{12} = \sqrt{4} \times \sqrt{7} \times \sqrt{4} \times \sqrt{3} = 4\sqrt{21}$

$\sqrt{7} \times \sqrt{3} = \sqrt{21}$

The fraction that is left is $= \dfrac{3\sqrt{21}}{4\sqrt{21}} = \dfrac{3}{4}$

> Start by working out the area of the bigger rectangle.
>
> It's easier to simplify this now.
>
> Now work out the area of the smaller rectangle.

15

> Start by considering the fact there are five squares. 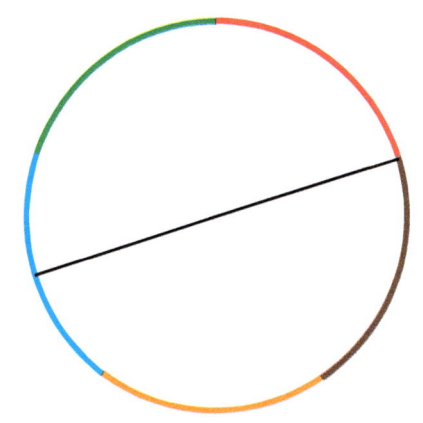
>
> Five of the squares fit around the mug, so start with five lines that are the same length around the mug.
>
> The black line is the diameter (9 cm).

The circumference of the circle is 9π, so each coloured line is = 5.654867…

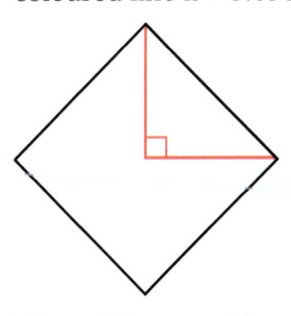

The red lines on this square are half of 5.654867….

$\sqrt{2.827^2 + 2.827^2} = 3.9985946…$

The perimeter is four times this:
15.99436 = 16.0 cm (3 s.f.).

> You can use Pythagoras' theorem to work out the hypotenuse of the right-angled triangle.

16 a Let $a = x + y$ and $b = p - q$ — Make things simpler by writing terms as single letters.

So

$(x+y)^2(p-q)^3 + (x+y)^3(p-q)^2$

$= a^2 b^3 + a^3 b^2$ — Now factorise.

$= a^2 b^2 (b + a)$

$= (x+y)^2 (p-q)^2 (x+y+p-q)$ — Return to original form.

b Let $a = x^2 + 3x - 10$ and $b = x^2 - 3x - 10$ — Use a single letter to help you see the problem more clearly, then factorise.

So $(x^2 + 3x - 10)^2 - (x^2 - 3x - 10)^2$

$= a^2 - b^2$

$= (a - b)(a + b)$

$= \{x^2 + 3x - 10 - (x^2 - 3x - 10)\}\{x^2 + 3x - 10 + (x^2 - 3x - 10)\}$

$= \{x^2 + 3x - 10 - x^2 + 3x + 10\}\{x^2 + 3x - 10 + x^2 - 3x - 10\}$

$= (6x)(2x^2 - 20)$

So now $(6x)(2x^2 - 20) = 0$ — This is now a straightforward factorisation problem.

$\Rightarrow 6x = 0$ or $2x^2 - 20 = 0$

$\Rightarrow x = 0$ or $x^2 = 10$ — Remember ±

$\Rightarrow x = 0$ or $x = \pm \sqrt{10}$

17 $f(x) = x^2 - 7x + 12$

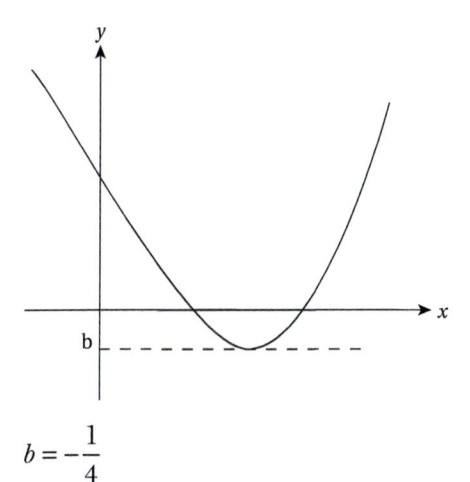

> Think about drawing the graph of $y = f(x)$. What points do you need to plot?

$x^2 - 7x + 12 = 0$
$\Rightarrow (x-3)(x-4) = 0$
$\Rightarrow x = 3$ or $x = 4$
$x = 0 \Rightarrow y = 12$
So

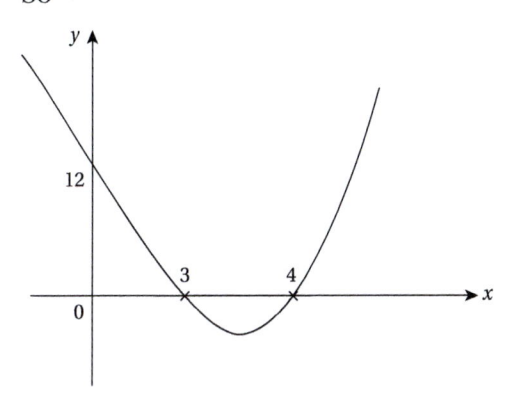

> Solve $f(x) = 0$ to find out where the graph crosses the x-axis.

$f(3.5) = f\left(\dfrac{7}{2}\right)$

> Use symmetry to find out the y-coordinate of the lowest point of the graph. (3.5 is exactly half way between 3 and 4.)

$= \left(\dfrac{7}{2}\right)^2 - 7 \times \dfrac{7}{2} + 12$

$= \dfrac{49}{4} - \dfrac{49}{2} + 12$

$= \dfrac{49}{4} - \dfrac{98}{4} + \dfrac{48}{4}$

$= -\dfrac{1}{4}$

> This is the smallest value of y.

> When you solve the equation $f(x) = b$, you look for all the points on the curve where $y = b$.
>
> Draw the line $y = b$ so that there is only one solution.

$b = -\dfrac{1}{4}$

5 Consider different cases

1 a A diagram shows that 12 chairs are required.

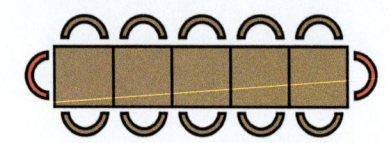

b Every table has 2 chairs, and there are 2 extra on the ends (shown in red).

A diagram like this shows the structure of the algebra.

This means there are $2n + 2$ chairs, where n is the number of tables.

c If it is possible to use 55 chairs then $2n + 2 = 55$, so $n = 26.5$.

Presumably you can't have half a table, so this is not possible.

d Each big group will contain 16 people. $2n + 2$ means that $n = 7$, so each group will require 7 tables and 14 tables will be needed in total.

This just involves a tweak to the rule from part b.

2 a e.g. $\frac{1}{50}, \frac{1}{49}, \frac{1}{48}, \frac{1}{47}, \frac{1}{46}$

This question can be answered in many ways, but making changes to the original set of fractions works well.

b e.g. $\frac{2}{6}, \frac{2}{5}, \frac{2}{4}, \frac{2}{3}, \frac{2}{2}$

c e.g. $\frac{6}{2}, \frac{7}{2}, \frac{8}{2}, \frac{9}{2}, \frac{10}{2}$

or

$\frac{5}{3}, \frac{7}{4}, \frac{9}{5}, \frac{8}{3}, \frac{9}{2}$

You could sprinkle some unrelated fractions around (such as in this final example), but it is easier to work in a systematic way and to make use of some patterns.

3 a 400 mg = 0.4 g
    400 g + 400 mg = 400.4 g

    0.5 kg = 500 g
    0.5 kg + 90 g = 590 g

    400 g + 400 mg < 0.5 kg + 90 g

> Change the quantities so they use the same units. It makes sense to work in grams.
> 1 kg = 1000 g and 1 g = 1000 mg.

b 0.1 km = 100 m
    150 cm = 1.5 m
    0.1 km + 150 cm = 101.5 m

> Convert everything to metres. 1 km = 1000 m and 1 m = 100 cm.

    900 cm = 9 m
    110 m + 900 cm = 119 m

    0.1 km + 150 cm < 110 m + 900 cm

c 0.75 hours = 45 minutes
    600 seconds = 10 minutes
    0.75 hours + 600 seconds = 55 minutes

> Convert everything to minutes.

    0.1 hours = 6 minutes
    50 minutes + 0.1 hours = 56 minutes

    0.75 hours + 600 seconds < 50 minutes + 0.1 hours

4 a $\frac{3}{7}$ of the balls in the bag = 9 balls
    $\frac{1}{7}$ of the balls in the bag = 3 balls

> Consider what you know.

   The number of balls in the bag = 3 × 7 = 21 balls.

   $\frac{3}{7}$ of the balls are red and half of the rest are green, which means there are 6 green ones.

b $\frac{3}{25}$ of the balls in the bag = 6 green balls
    $\frac{1}{25}$ of the balls in the bag = 2 balls

   The number of balls in the bag = 2 × 25 = 50 balls.

5 a Raise 0.9975 to the power of 82 to find out the proportion that will be left after 82 years.

$0.9975^{82} = 0.814438$ so about 81% remains, which means about 19% has been lost.

> Consider the numbers in the question. What happens if you change any of them? The rate of growth of the hair doesn't make a difference to the number of actual hairs that are lost.
>
> The number of strands of hair that people start with doesn't affect the proportion that they lose.
>
> So you just need to look at the proportion that is lost each year.
>
> If you wanted to reduce something by 10% every year then you would instead decide to keep 90% and would multiply by 0.9 for each year.
>
> In this case the average person loses 0.25% per year so they keep 99.75% per year.

b $0.9975^{50} = 0.882359$

$0.9975^{40} = 0.904724$

$0.9975^{42} = 0.900206$

$0.9975^{43} = 0.8979556$

It would take 43 years for at least 10% of the hair to be lost.

> If you lose 10% then you have 90% left, which is 0.9. You need to know what n is when $0.9975^n \leq 0.9$.
>
> You can use trial and improvement.

6 Method 1

Rounding the numbers to 1 significant figure in this calculation gives:

$20 \times 800 = 16\,000$, which is about 10 times the size of 1903.02. The answer is likely to be incorrect.

> Here is one convincing method that involves making changes to the problem.

Method 2

Start with $23.64 \times 805 = 1903.02$.

If $23.64 \times 805 = 1903.02$ is true, then:

$2.364 \times 805 = 190.302$

and $2.364 \times 8.05 = 1.90302$

The left-hand side must be bigger than 16, so the calculation can't be correct.

> Here is a second convincing method that involves making different changes.

7 **a** $1 + 2 + 3 = 6$, which is 2×3

$2 + 3 + 4 = 9$, which is 3×3

$3 + 4 + 5 = 12$, which is 4×3

$(n-1) + (n) + (n+1)$

$n - 1 + n + n + 1 = 3n$

Yes, this is true for all integers.

b $n + (n+1) + (n+2) + (n+3) = 4n + 6$

c

Number of numbers	Rule based on the first number being n
2	$2n + 1$
3	$3n + 3$
4	$4n + 6$
5	$5n + 10$
6	$6n + 15$
7	$7n + 21$
8	$8n + 28$

First, try it out with some more sets of three consecutive integers. You could work systematically.

Once you are convinced that it works, try to think about why.

There are several different ways of explaining this. To start with, think about a general set of three consecutive numbers.

Using algebra you can simplify this expression.

The expression simplifies to $3n$ ($3 \times$ the middle number). So it must be true for all integers.

You could do this algebraically, where n is the first number.

The method for part **b** can be extended for any number of numbers.

8 **Snail 1** 36 000 mm/h (÷ 10)

3600 cm/h (÷ 60)

60 cm/min (÷ 60)

1 cm/s

Snail 2 0.01 m/s (× 100)

1 cm/s

Snail 3 5 km/day (× 1000)

5000 m/day (× 100)

500 000 cm/day (÷ 24)

20 833.333… cm/h (÷ 60)

347.222… cm/min (÷ 60)

5.787… cm/s (= 5.8 cm/s to 1 d.p.)

Snail 4 700 cm/h (÷ 60)

11.666… cm/min (÷ 60)

0.19444… cm/s (= 0.2 cm/s to 1 d.p.)

Snail 3 finishes first (and is a fast snail!).

> To compare the snails' speeds they must be measured in the same units.
>
> In this question it might be sensible to convert all the speeds into cm per second (cm/s).

9 a Circular pens: C = πd

Fences with 2 m gap between:

Inner fence, diameter = 20 m, C = 20π

Outer fence, diameter = 24 m, C = 24π

Difference = 4π

> The formula for the circumference C of a circle with diameter d is C = πd.

b Fences with 3 m gap between:

Outer fence, diameter = 26 m, C = 26π

Difference = 6π

> Now work out the difference for a 3 m gap between the fences.

c Fences with 4 m gap between:

Outer fence, diameter = 28 m, C = 28π

Difference = 8π

> … and a 4 m gap.

The outer fence, diameter = 20 + 2x,
C = (20 + 2x)π = 20π + 2πx

The difference between this and the inner fence involves subtracting 20π, which leaves 2πx where x is the width of the gap. In general, the outer fence will be 2πx m longer than the inner fence.

d This diagram shows what happens for any rectangles, where the inner one is a by b and there is a gap of x all the way around.

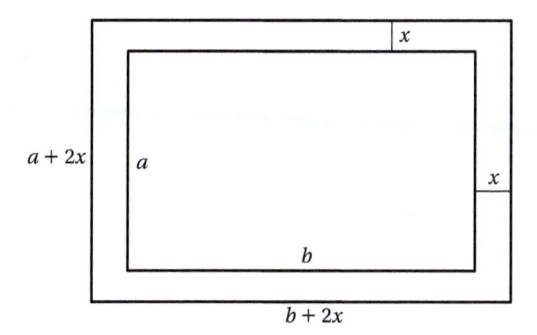

The perimeter of the inner rectangle is
$a + b + a + b = 2a + 2b$

The perimeter of the outer rectangle is
$(a + 2x) + (b + 2x) + (a + 2x) + (b + 2x)$
$= 2a + 2b + 8x$

The difference between these is 8x.

10 a Delia can move her shape up and down.
A translation using any vector $\begin{pmatrix} 0 \\ a \end{pmatrix}$ will do this.

This is a translation where the x-coordinate doesn't change but the y-coordinate can change to be anything.

b A translation using any vector $\begin{pmatrix} b \\ b \end{pmatrix}$ will do this. This can also be written as $b\begin{pmatrix} 1 \\ 1 \end{pmatrix}$.

This time Delia moves her shape diagonally. If she moves it right then she also has to move it up by the same amount.

c

A good diagram will help here.

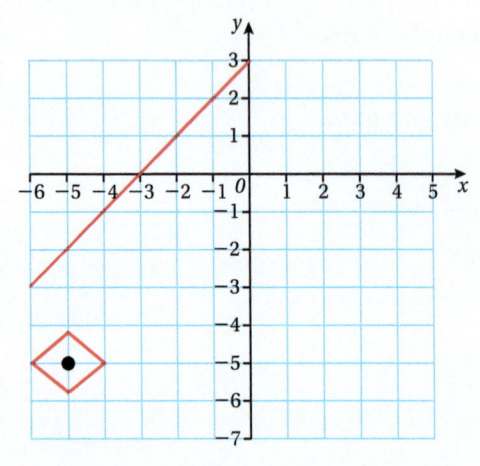

To get the black dot onto this line we could use the vector $\begin{pmatrix} 0 \\ 3 \end{pmatrix}$ or $\begin{pmatrix} 1 \\ 4 \end{pmatrix}$ or $\begin{pmatrix} 2 \\ 5 \end{pmatrix}$.

We always need to go up three more than we go right, so the vector $\begin{pmatrix} c \\ c+3 \end{pmatrix}$ will cover all the possibilities (including those with decimals).

11

$28\,\text{cm} \times 17\,\text{cm} \times 5\,\text{cm} = 2380\,\text{cm}^3$ — Volume of Choc Flakes packet.

$21\,\text{cm} \times 15\,\text{cm} \times 9\,\text{cm} = 2835\,\text{cm}^3$ — Volume of BioWheat packet.

The volume of the BioWheat packet is greater than the volume of the Choc Flakes packet; therefore, Kiefer is wrong. — Conclusion part 1.

$2 \times (28 \times 17) + 2 \times (28 \times 5) + 2 \times (17 \times 5) = 1402\,\text{cm}^2$ — Surface area of Choc Flakes packet.

$2 \times (21 \times 15) + 2 \times (21 \times 9) + 2 \times (15 \times 9) = 1278\,\text{cm}^2$ — Surface area of BioWheat packet.

The surface area of the Choc Flakes packet is greater than the surface area of the BioWheat packet; therefore, Arpad is correct. — Conclusion part 2.

Raymon is wrong as the packet with the greater volume does not have the greater surface area. — Conclusion part 3.

Work out the volume and surface area of each packet.

12 a 1 Try a different starting shape.

2 Try a different pair of perpendicular mirror lines.

3 Try a different starting position for the shape.

Micah has looked at one example and drawn his conclusion based on this.

b

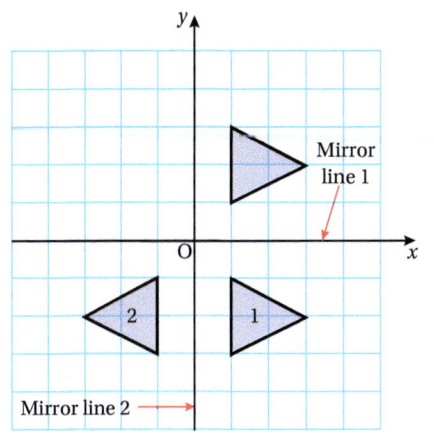

If we carry out the reflection in Micah's chosen mirror lines ($y = 0$ and $x = 0$) with this new shape it becomes clear that something else is happening – the shape has been rotated 180° about the origin.

Because Micah's original shape was a rectangle, it has rotational symmetry and he therefore did not notice that the rotation had happened.

His conclusion was not incorrect, but it was not the full answer. That depends on the nature of the starting shape.

Cambridge IGCSE Mathematics Extended Problem-solving Book

13 The perimeter of the big semicircle is
$\pi \times \frac{6}{2} = 9.42\ldots$ cm.

> Treat this as a large semicircle and a smaller circle.

(Right-angled triangle with legs 2 and 3, hypotenuse d)

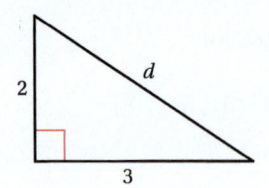

$d^2 = 2^2 + 3^2$

$d = \sqrt{13} = 3.60555\ldots$ cm

> Now find the diameter of the smaller circle.
>
> This is the hypotenuse of a right-angled triangle.

Circumference = $\pi \times 3.60655\ldots$ cm = $11.327\ldots$ cm
Total perimeter = $9.42478\ldots + 11.327\ldots$
= 20.75 cm (2 d.p.)

14

> To work out the mean of three numbers, add them together and divide by three. As this is a non-calculator question you will need to combine the surds by hand.

$24 = 4 \times 6$, so $\sqrt{24} = \sqrt{4} \times \sqrt{6} = 2\sqrt{6}$

$54 = 9 \times 6$, so $\sqrt{54} = \sqrt{9} \times \sqrt{6} = 3\sqrt{6}$

> To simplify surds, look for square numbers.

Both of these involve 6, so check whether 96 is divisible by 6.

$96 \div 6 = 16$

$96 = 16 \times 6$, so $\sqrt{96} = \sqrt{16} \times \sqrt{6} = 4\sqrt{6}$

This means $\dfrac{\sqrt{24} + \sqrt{54} + \sqrt{96}}{3} = \dfrac{2\sqrt{6} + 3\sqrt{6} + 4\sqrt{6}}{3}$

$= \dfrac{9\sqrt{6}}{3} = 3\sqrt{6}$

15 a

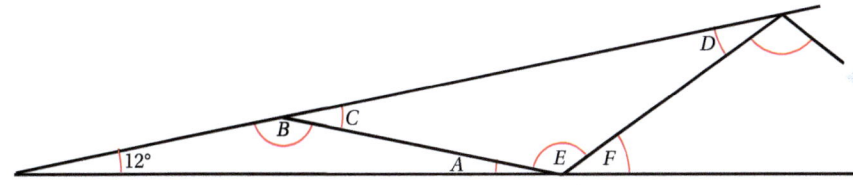

> It is possible to work out every angle in the diagram. Start on the left hand side of the diagram.

Angle A is 12°.

> Base angles in an isosceles triangle are equal.

Angle B is 156°.

> Angles in a triangle add up to 180°.

Angle C is 24°.

> Angles on a straight line add up to 180°.

Angle D is 24°.

> Base angles in an isosceles triangle are equal, and so on.

> Check whether the angles at ABC and ACB are equal, and so on.

> This will mean the outer triangle is isosceles.

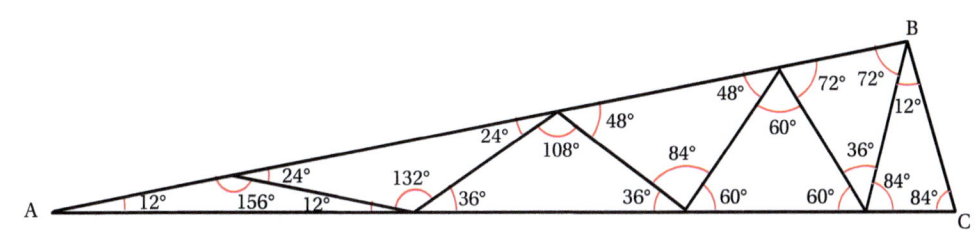

So: Helen is correct.

b Repeating with a starting angle of 10° gives the following triangle since angle ABC ≠ angle ACB.

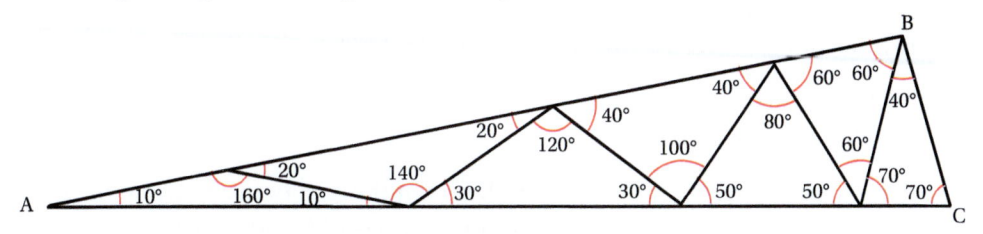

Pete's suggestion of starting with an angle of 10° does not work since angle ABC ≠ angle ACB.

c

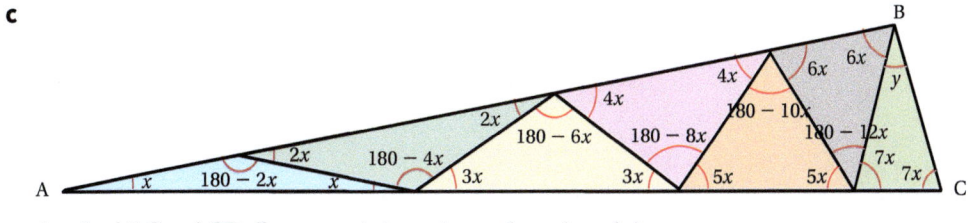

> This is an algebraic solution, starting with angle x.

Angle ABC = ACB (because it is an isosceles triangle)

This means that $6x + y = 7x$, so $x = y$.

The three angles in triangle ABC add up to $15x$, so $15x = 180°$

This means that the only starting value that works is 12°.

16 a

Fraction	Decimal
$\frac{1}{9}$	0.1111…
$\frac{1}{99}$	0.01010…
$\frac{1}{999}$	0.001001001…
$\frac{1}{9999}$	0.000100010001…
$\frac{1}{99999}$	0.0000100001000010000100001…
$\frac{1}{999999}$	0.000001000001…

> It seems sensible to use a calculator and to work out the decimal equivalents.

All of the fractions have a denominator that is a multiple of 9.

All of the fractions have equivalent decimals that are eventually recurring.

The recurring part of each decimal includes only 1s and 0s.

The number of recurring digits (the period) is the same as the number of digits in the denominator.

> Similarities.

The denominator of each fraction is different. In fact the denominator is getting larger with each fraction.

The equivalent decimal of each fraction is smaller than the previous one.

The number of zeros in the recurring part of the fraction increases with the denominator.

> Differences.

b i $\frac{1}{9} = 0.1111…$

Therefore $0.7777… = \frac{7}{9}$

> Look for similarities between the number and the fractions considered above.
>
> This is similar to the recurring decimal for. In fact it is seven times bigger.

ii $\frac{1}{9} = 0.1111…$

$0.333… = \frac{3}{9} = \frac{1}{3}$

Therefore $5.3333… = 5\frac{1}{3}$

This is also equal to $\frac{16}{3}$

iii 0.14444… is the same as 0.44444… − 0.3

$0.44444… = \frac{4}{9}$ so you need to do $\frac{4}{9} - \frac{3}{10}$

This is $\frac{40}{90} - \frac{27}{90} = \frac{13}{90}$

iv 2.5000900090009... is

2.5 + (0.000100010001...) × 9 ÷ 10

$2 + \frac{5}{10} + \left(\frac{1}{9999} \times \frac{9}{10}\right)$

$= 2 + \frac{5}{10} + \frac{1}{11110}$

$= 2 + \frac{5555}{11110} + \frac{1}{11110}$

$= 2 + \frac{5556}{11110} = 2\frac{2778}{5555}$

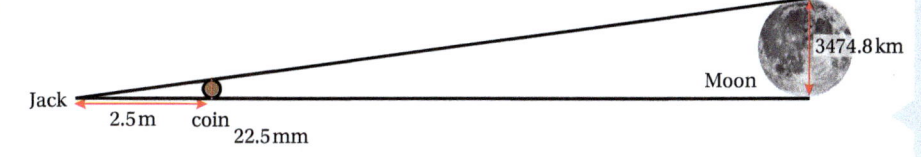

17

Jack — 2.5 m — coin 22.5 mm — Moon 3474.8 km

Draw a diagram to illustrate the situation. This is a problem about similar triangles (the triangle from Jack to the coin and the triangle from Jack to the Moon).

The question says Jack is about 2.5 m away from the coin, so it seems sensible to round off the value for the diameter of the Moon to 3500 km.

3500 km = 3 500 000 m = 350 000 000 cm

22.5 mm = 2.25 cm

Calculate the scale factor of enlargement from the coin to the Moon.

Scale factor = 350 000 000 cm ÷ 2.25 = 155 555 555

2.5 m × 155 555 555 = 388 888 889 m

Use the scale factor to enlarge the distance.

Distance to the Moon = 390 000 km (rounded off to 2 s.f.)

---

18 $(2^x)^2 - 20(2^x) + 64 = 0$

Substitute $y = 2^x$ to make the equation look more familiar. This doesn't change the equation; it just gives you an easier way to work with it.

put $y = 2^x$

$\Rightarrow y^2 - 20y + 64 = 0$

$\Rightarrow (y-16)(y-4) = 0$

Solve for y by factorising.

$\Rightarrow y = 16$ or $y = 4$

But $y = 2^x$

So $2^x = 16 \Rightarrow x = 4$

Or $2^x = 4 \Rightarrow x = 2$

Return to the definition of y and then solve for x.

19 The sequence 1, 4, 9, 16, 25, ... has nth term n^2.

> You should recognise this as the sequence of square numbers from previous work.

Differences term by term:

Table of sequence values with arrows connecting consecutive terms of differences on last row.

Term number (n)	1	2	3	4	5
Sequence	9	17	27	39	53 ...
n^2	1	4	9	16	25 ...
Difference	8	13	18	23	28
		+5	+5	+5	+5

> Look at how these terms differ from your new sequence. Organise your answers carefully.

> Notice that the differences increase by five each time.

Sequences of differences:

nth term = $5n + k$

$n = 1 \Rightarrow 5 \times 1 + k = 8$

So $k = 3$

> Use standard methods to find the nth term in the sequence of differences.

nth term of sequence = n^2 + difference

$= n^2 + 5n + 3$

> Add the nth terms of the two sequences.

6 Make connections

1 It might be sensible to assume a working day of 8 hours (9 am – 5 pm).

> Clearly this is a joke, but assume it is accurate. You need to make some assumptions about Nick's 'normal' working hours.

a 5% of 8 hours is 0.4 of an hour.
Nick works 8 × 60 minutes = 480 minutes.
5% of this is 24 minutes.

> Calculate the amount of time spent working on Friday. 0.4 of an hour doesn't mean very much, so change 8 hours into minutes.

b 2 hours, 14 minutes and 24 seconds.

> One way to do this is to work out that on Wednesday it would be 40% of 480 mins (192 mins) and then to subtract 12% of 480 mins (57 mins and 36 seconds). Then subtract to get 134 mins and 24 seconds (2 hours 14 mins 24 seconds).

c It might look as if it must be Nick because he works for 23% compared to Bernard's 18%, but if Bernard's working hours are longer then 18% of a larger amount could be bigger than 23% of something smaller.

2 a 225 minutes = 3 hours 45 minutes

> A lot of information in the question is irrelevant. The carving time is the same for both birds. The turkey weighs 4.5 kg more, so it needs to be in the oven for 50 minutes × 4.5 longer.

b $t = 50m + 30$

c 5 × 60 + 5 = 305 minutes

(305 − 30) ÷ 50

5.5 kg

d 9.25 am if no carving time is required.

9.05 am if 20 minutes of preparation time is needed.

3 a 12 m × 8 m = 96 m², so the cost is $4 × 96 = $384.

> The first lawn has an area of 80 m² and this costs $320, so each square metre costs $4.
>
> The second lawn has an area of 144 m² and, as expected, the cost is $4 × 144.

b 560 ÷ 4 = 140, so the area is 140 m².

Any pair of integers that multiply to give 140 will work:
1 × 140, 2 × 70, 4 × 35, 5 × 28, 7 × 20, 10 × 14.

4

> Do you recognise the equations of perpendicular graphs?

a +1, −1

$y = -\frac{1}{2}x - 3$

c The product of the gradients of two perpendicular lines is −1.

5

```
         0.48 ── Number 1 (0.62 × 0.48)
    0.62 Thurs
   ╱         ╲── Not
  ╱              Number 1
 ╲        0.18 ── Number 1 (0.38 × 0.18)
  0.38 Not
       Thurs ╲── Not
              Number 1
```

> This type of question can be solved using a tree diagram.

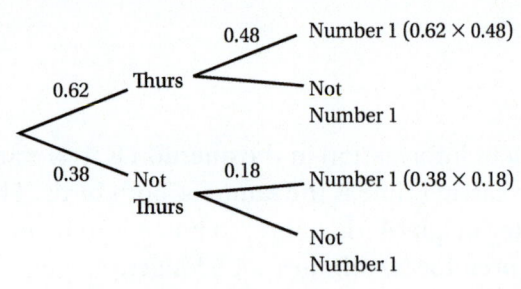

The probability of a number one hit is 0.366.

6

Sample 1		Sample 2
8	57	
9 8 5	58	1 7 8 9 9
5 5	59	1 3 3 4
6 1	60	2 4
3 1	61	
3	62	

Key: 57 | 4 = 57.4 g

> A stem and leaf diagram would be a good way to display the data.

This shows that there are more packets that are less than 60 g than are 60 or more.

The median is 59.5 g for Sample 1 and 59.1 g for Sample 2.

It might be better to label the packets as being 59 g instead.

Worked solutions: 6 Make connections

7

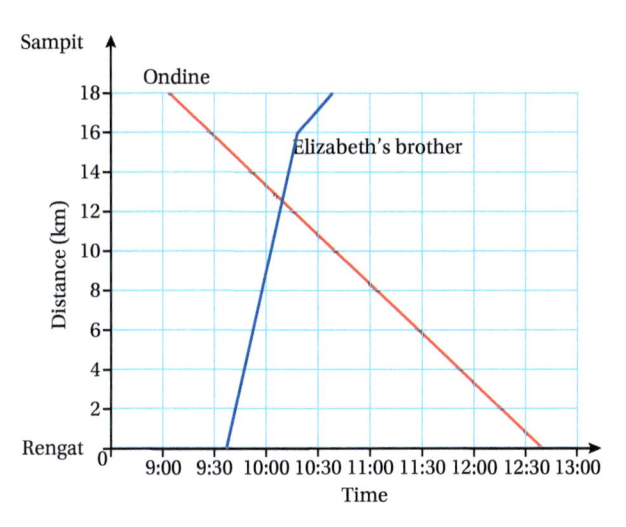

[Travel graph showing Distance (km) from Rengat (0) to Sampit (18) vs Time from 9:00 to 13:00. Ondine's line goes from (9:00, 18) down to (13:00, 0). Elizabeth's brother's line goes from (9:30, 0) up to (10:30, 18).]

> It is useful to recognise that a travel graph is likely to help here.

a 10:12
b 5.2 km
c 12.6 km
d 12:46
e 6 km/h
f 4 km

---

8 a 10 km

> Use the travel graph to help you answer the questions.

b 20 minutes
c 2 stops, 20 minutes
d First stage of the return journey.

> The graph is steepest at this point.

e 30 km in 10 minutes, means 180 km/h
f 20:55
g about 37 km
h 90 km ÷ 3 h = 30 km/h
i 90 km/h

9 $y + 7 = 2x + 4 + 7 = 2x + 11$,
which has y-intercept of 11.

> This could be explained using algebra.

> Alternatively, you could draw a graph.

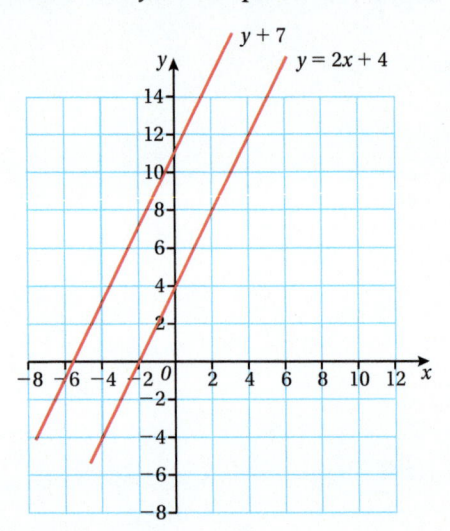

---

10 **a** 42, 56, 72

b $(n - 1) \times n$

This can be written as $n(n - 1)$, or as $n^2 - n$.

> These numbers have lots of factors. For example:
>
> | 0 | 2 | 6 | 12 | 20 | 30 |
> |---|---|---|----|----|----|
> | 0×1 | 1×2 | 2×3 | 3×4 | 4×5 | 5×6 |
>
> It is always two adjacent numbers.

c $n(n - 1)$ is always a number multiplied by the previous number. One of those two numbers must be even, so the answer must be even too.

---

11 **a** All the quickest journeys involve one of the edges of each length: $4.5\,\text{m} + 3\,\text{m} + 2\,\text{m} = 9.5\,\text{m}$.

b $GD = \sqrt{4.5^2 + 2^2} = 4.92\,\text{m}$

> Find GD using Pythagoras' theorem. 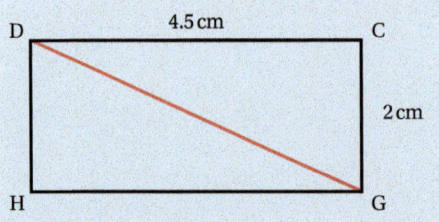
>
> (Rectangle DCGH with D top-left, C top-right (4.5 cm), G bottom-right, H bottom-left; CG = 2 cm; diagonal DG drawn.)
>
> From D to A = 3 m
>
> Total distance walked = $4.92\,\text{m} + 3\,\text{m} = 7.92\,\text{m}$

This is $9.5 - 7.92 = 1.58\,\text{m}$ shorter.

> Don't forget to work out the difference between the two path lengths as this is what was asked for in the question.

Worked solutions: 6 Make connections

12

You might think that the maximum difference in the two areas will happen when the area of the circle is smallest and the area of the square is biggest.

However, the circle is drawn to fit exactly inside the square so it will always have a diameter equal to the side length of the square, whatever that is.

Think about the area between the square and the circle. As the square and circle both get bigger, the area will get bigger (if this is not clear you could imagine a very big square/circle and a very small square/circle.

The upper bound of 7.0 is 7.05 cm.

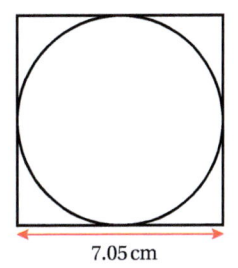

7.05 cm

The biggest difference between the areas must happen when you use the upper bound.

$7.05 \times 7.05 = 49.7025 \text{ cm}^2$

Calculate the upper bound for the area of the square.

$\pi \times r^2 = \pi \times (7.05 / 2)^2 = 39.036... \text{ cm}^2$

Calculate the area of the circle for the upper bound of the square side length.

Area of square − area of circle

Calculate the difference between the two areas.

$49.7025 \text{ cm}^2 - 39.036... \text{ cm}^2 = 10.666... \text{ cm}^2$

The maximum difference between the area of the square and the area of the circle is 10.7 cm² (to 3 s.f.).

13

Work out the volumes of the cylinders.

$8.5 \div 2 = 4.25 \text{ cm}$

Radius of small bottle.

$\pi \times 4.25^2 \times 23 = 1305.14 \text{ cm}^3$ (2 d.p.)

Volume of small bottle (cylinder) = area of circular base × height.

$\pi \times 5.5^2 \times 25 = 2375.83 \text{ cm}^3$ (2 d.p.)

$2375.83 - 1305.14 = 1070.69 \text{ cm}^3$ (2 d.p.)

Difference between the volumes of the large and small bottles.

To the nearest ml, the large bottle holds 1071 cm³ or 1071 ml or 1.071 litres more than the smaller bottle.

Conclusion.

14 $\sqrt{15}$ is a surd that cannot be simplified, so cannot possibly be an integer. This means C and D must be wrong.

B is correct.

What do you know about surds?

---

15 a $\vec{AB} + \vec{BC} = \vec{AC}$

$\vec{AC} = 2\mathbf{a} - \mathbf{b} - (\mathbf{a} + 2\mathbf{b})$

$= \mathbf{a} - 3\mathbf{b}$

b $3(2\mathbf{a} - \mathbf{b}) = 6\mathbf{a} - 3\mathbf{b}$

$\vec{CB} = \mathbf{a} + 2\mathbf{b}$ and $\vec{C_1B_1} = 3\mathbf{a} + 6\mathbf{b}$, so the lengths in triangle $A_1B_1C_1$ are 3 times bigger than the lengths in triangle ABC.

Hence $\vec{A_1B_1}$ must be 3 times bigger than $\vec{AB}$.

---

16 a

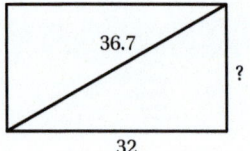

Height = 18 inches (to nearest inch)

32 : 18

This simplifies to 16 : 9

To calculate the aspect ratio you need to know the height of Carlos's TV.

You know the diagonal length and the width so you need to apply Pythagoras' theorem.

b

$(9x)^2 + (16x)^2 = 1764$

$337x^2 = 1764$

$x^2 = 1764 \div 337$

$x = \sqrt{1764 \div 337} = 2.287...$ inches

Width = $16x = 16 \times 2.287... = 36.6$ inches (to 1 d.p.)

Height = $9x = 9 \times 2.287... = 20.6$ inches (to 1 d.p.)

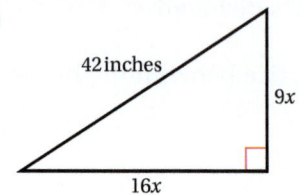

The aspect ratio of the TV is 16 : 9 (width : height).

We know the diagonal length so will have to apply Pythagoras' theorem.

17 a

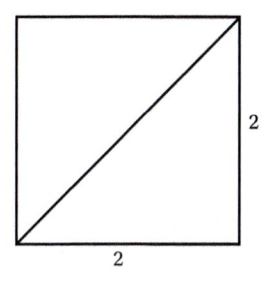

Diagonal = $\sqrt{2^2 + 2^2} = \sqrt{8}$

$\sqrt{8} = 2\sqrt{2}$

Use Pythagoras' theorem.

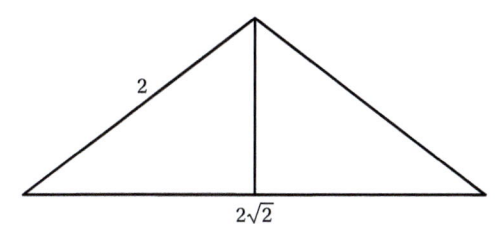

Now use that as the base of an isosceles triangle.

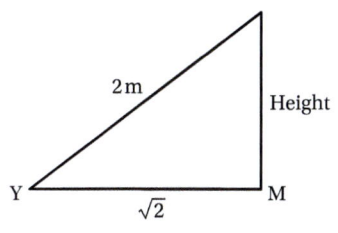

There are lots of ways to do this. One is to work out the length of the diagonal of the square base and then to use this with the slanted height.

Height = $\sqrt{2^2 - (\sqrt{2})^2} = \sqrt{4-2} = \sqrt{2}$

The height of this triangle is the height of the pyramid. You need to halve the diagonal to get the base of the triangle.

b Height = $\frac{3}{2}\sqrt{2}$

You could repeat all the calculations from part **a**, but an alternative is to note that all of the lengths will change in the same way. To turn the 2-pyramid into a 3-pyramid you need to multiply by $\frac{3}{2}$.

c Height = $\frac{a}{2}\sqrt{2}$

To turn the 2-pyramid into an a-pyramid you need to multiply by $\frac{a}{2}$.

18

> Angle ACB is a right angle (because the tongs form a tangent to the circle).
>
> Draw in some lines and see whether that helps.
>
> Now it is clear there is a right-angled triangle and you can work out some angles.

$\tan BAC = \frac{2.5}{25}$

Angle BAC = 5.710593

The angle made by the tongs is double that: 11.421186

The angle has been reduced by 60 − 11.421186 = 49° (to the nearest integer).

---

19 a You would expect a weak negative correlation.

> It is likely that Year 7 students go to bed earlier and therefore have more sleep than Year 11 students.

b Here is an example:

"Year 11 students have less sleep than Year 7 students."

c An example:

Question 1: "What year group are you in?"

Tick one box:

Yr 7 ☐ Yr 8 ☐ Yr 9 ☐ Yr 10 ☐ Yr 11 ☐

Question 2: "On average, how many hours of sleep do you have per night?"

Tick one box:

4hrs $< s \leqslant$ 5hrs ☐

5hrs $< s \leqslant$ 6hrs ☐

6hrs $< s \leqslant$ 7hrs ☐

7hrs $< s \leqslant$ 8hrs ☐

8+ hrs ☐

d A scatter diagram will show immediately if there is any correlation and possible outliers.

Worked solutions: 6 Make connections

20 a For the red bricks: $2t + 2c \leqslant 8$

Let t be the number of tables and c be the number of chairs.

b For the yellow bricks: $2t + c \leqslant 6$

c

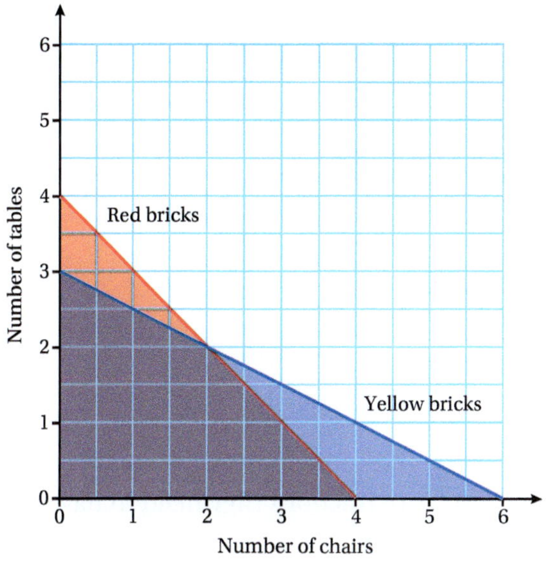

[Graph showing Number of tables (y-axis, 0-6) vs Number of chairs (x-axis, 0-6), with Red bricks line and Yellow bricks line, shaded feasible region]

The graphs cross at (2, 2).

21 a Shop A: Final percentage price = $\frac{209}{310} \times 100$
= 67.4% of original price

Shop A offers a 32.6% discount (3 s.f.)

Shop B: Final percentage price = $\frac{259}{310} \times 100$
= 83.5% of original price

Shop B offers a 16.5% discount (3 s.f.)

b Shop A: Original price of trainers = $\frac{62}{67.4} \times 100$
= $91.99

There are lots of ways to work this out, including by calculating the original price.

Shop B: Final price = 91.99 × 0.835 = $76.81

The trainers will cost $76.81 in Shop B.

22 $C = \pi \times$ diameter

Circumference (C) of dial is πd.

radius = 3.2 cm = 32 mm
$C = \pi \times (32 \times 2) = 64\pi$ mm
$121 \div 64\pi = 0.60$ to (2 d.p.)

Write the arc length as a fraction of the circumference.

The dial has been turned through 0.6 of a turn, which is equivalent to $\frac{3}{5}$ of a turn.

This means it ends up pointing at the Wool setting.

23 a Upper bound = 1.5 × 2.5 × 3.5 = 13.125 m²

Lower bound = 0.5 × 1.5 × 2.5 = 1.875 m²

Difference is 11.25 m²

> The biggest volume is calculated using the three upper bounds and the smallest is calculated using the lower bounds.

b Upper bound = 1.005 × 2.005 × 3.005 = 6.05515 m²

Lower bound = 0.9995 × 1.995 × 2.995
= 5.97204 m²

Difference is 0.083 m²

c Upper bound = 1.0005 × 2.0005 × 3.0005
= 6.0055015 m²

Lower bound = 0.9995 × 1.9995 × 2.9995
= 5.9945015 m²

Difference is 0.011 m²

---

24 a $\frac{3}{\sqrt{5}} \times \frac{2}{2} = \frac{6}{2\sqrt{5}}$

so $\frac{3}{\sqrt{5}} \left(= \frac{3}{\sqrt{5}}\right) > \frac{5}{2\sqrt{5}}$

so $\frac{3}{\sqrt{5}}$ is larger.

> To compare fractions they need to have the same denominator.

b $\sqrt{8} = \sqrt{(4 \times 2)} = \sqrt{4} \times \sqrt{2} = 2\sqrt{2}$

$\sqrt{50} = \sqrt{(25 \times 2)} = \sqrt{25} \times \sqrt{2} = 5\sqrt{2}$

> Again you need to have the same denominator.
>
> It isn't easy to see how to do this for this question. First you could see whether you can simplify the surds.

$\frac{4}{\sqrt{8}} = \frac{4}{2\sqrt{2}} = \frac{2}{\sqrt{2}}$

$\frac{25}{\sqrt{50}} = \frac{25}{5\sqrt{2}} = \frac{5}{\sqrt{2}}$

$\frac{2}{\sqrt{2}} < \frac{5}{\sqrt{2}}$

so $\frac{25}{\sqrt{50}}$ is larger.

> Now you can see that to find a common denominator you can multiply the top and bottom of the first fraction by 5 and the top and bottom of the second fraction by 2.

c This could be worked out by finding a common denominator for the two fractions in the same way as in parts **a** and **b**. An alternative way would be to note that $\frac{10}{\sqrt{7}+3}$ is a positive number (because the numerator and the denominator are both positive), but that $\frac{6}{\sqrt{7}-3}$ is a negative number (because the numerator is positive but the denominator is negative), so $\frac{10}{\sqrt{7}+3}$ is larger.

25   Let n = number of red counters

So 120 − n = number of blue counters

P(choosing a red counter on any turn) = $\frac{n}{210}$

P(choosing a blue counter on any turn) = $\frac{120-n}{210}$

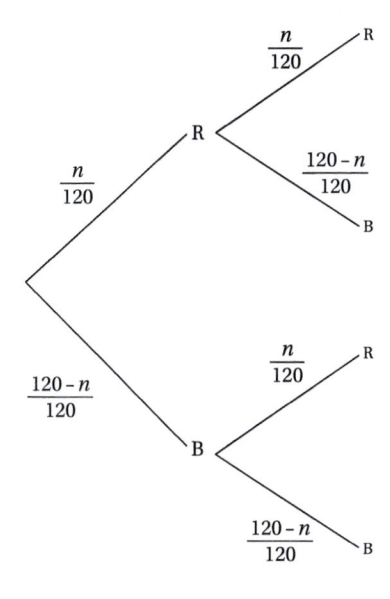

> This is simply a question of taking items and replacing them.
>
> You have solved many similar problems in the past. Don't let the algebra put you off.

> This is a standard tree diagram.

P(exactly one red) = P(red, blue) + P(blue, red)

$= \frac{n}{120} \times \frac{120-n}{120} + \frac{120-n}{120} \times \frac{n}{120}$

$= 2 \times \frac{n(120-n)}{120^2} = 0.42$

So $n(120-n) = \frac{0.42 \times 120^2}{2}$

$\Rightarrow 120n - n^2 = 3024$

So

$n^2 - 120n + 3024 = 0$

$(n-36)(n-84) = 0$

$\Rightarrow n = 36$ or $n = 84$

But more red than blue $\Rightarrow n = 84$

> Now, think of this as a question about algebraic fractions. What method can you use to solve it?

26 a i 5   8   11   14   17…
         +3 +3 +3 +3

nth term = $3n + k$

But $n = 1$: $3 + k = 5$
              $k = 2$

So nth term = $3n + 2$

ii 3   5   7   9   11…
       +2 +2 +2 +2

Similarly nth term = $2n + 1$

b   15   40   77   126   …
       (5 × 3)   (8 × 5)   (11 × 7) (14 × 9)

nth term = nth term of 1st sequence × nth term of 2nd sequence
           = $(3n+2)(2n+1)$

Check: $n = 3$ gives

$(9 + 2)(6 + 1)$
$= 11 × 7$
$= 77$ ✓

So, for 10th term, put $n = 10$

$(3 × 10 + 2)(2 × 10 + 1)$
$= 32 × 21$
$= 672$

c $(3n + 2)(2n + 1) = 15960$

$6n^2 + 3n + 4n + 2 = 15960$

$6n^2 + 7n - 15958 = 0$

$n = \dfrac{-7 \pm \sqrt{49 - 4 × 6 × (-15958)}}{2 × 6}$

$n = -52.2$ or $n = 51.0$

n is not a whole number, so 15 960 is not in the sequence.

You should recognise the type of sequence you see in both part **a** and part **b**. The terms increase by a fixed number each time.

This is the standard method for finding the nth term.

How does this sequence relate to the previous two?

You can see that each term is the product of corresponding terms from the sequences in **a i and ii**.

If the number is in the sequence, the nth term will equal 15 960 for an integer value of n.

It is not enough for n to be *nearly* a whole number: for the number to be in the sequence, n must be an exact integer.

Worked solutions: 6 Make connections

27 $x + y = a \times 10^n + b \times 10^n$

$ = (a + b) \times 10^n$

But $\left.\begin{array}{l} 5 < a < 10 \\ 5 < b < 10 \end{array}\right\} \Rightarrow 10 < a + b < 20$

> First, write down what $x + y$ actually is!

> For standard form, the number before the power of 10 must be greater than or equal to 1 but less than 10. $a + b$ is between 10 and 20, so we can divide by 10. Remember to increase the power of 10 by one to balance the change.

So $1 < \dfrac{a + b}{10} < 2$

So $x + y = (a + b) \times 10^n$

$ = \dfrac{a + b}{10} \times 10^{n+1}$

This is now in standard form since

$\left(1 < \dfrac{a + b}{10} < 2\right) < 10$

7 Use logical reasoning

1 a 1500 m ÷ 200 m = 7.5

Mikhail will need to run 7.5 laps of the indoor running track and 3.75 laps of the outdoor running track to cover 1500 m.

> Given that the other track is twice as long, he will need half as many laps.

b 5 km = 5000 m

5000 m ÷ 200 m = 25

Kenji will have to run 25 laps of the indoor track and 12.5 laps of the outdoor track to cover 5 km.

The 10 km is double the 5 km race, so Kenji will have to run 50 laps of the indoor track and 25 laps of the outdoor track to cover 10 km.

2 a $t = 40k + 25$, where t is the number of minutes and k is the number of kilograms.

b No – he needs to put it in the oven at 9.25 am

> $40 \times 3.75 + 25$ plus an extra 10 minutes of time is 185 minutes. This is the same as 3 hours and 5 minutes.

3 a In the original recipe there is 150 g + 120 g = 270 g dark chocolate.

270 g × 2.5 = 675 g

> You need to convert a recipe for 8 people to a recipe that serves 20 people.
>
> You could divide by 8 to find the ingredients for one serving and then multiply by 20.
>
> Alternatively, you could multiply by $\frac{20}{8}$, which is the same as multiplying by $2\frac{1}{2}$.

b 4 bars of 200 g each (because 3 bars is only 600 g)

c 800 g – 675 g = 125 g

675 : 125

27 : 5

d $\frac{3}{4}$ of 400 g is 300 g.

Nadira needs 300 g of chocolate spread

> To serve 6 people you can divide by 8 and multiply by 6, or you can multiply by $\frac{6}{8}$.
>
> $\frac{6}{8}$ is the same as $\frac{3}{4}$.

4 a

		Day 1		
		Swim	Jog	Cycle
Day 2	Swim	SS	JS	CS
	Jog	SJ	JJ	CJ
	Cycle	SC	JC	CC

This is one way to list all the possibilities in a systematic way.

b $\frac{1}{9}$

c $\frac{6}{9}$ = all of the combinations except SS, JJ and CC. This is the same as $\frac{2}{3}$. This is sensible because whichever one is chosen for Day 1, there are 2 out of the 3 that can be chosen on Day 2.

5 a Each cleaner works for 2 hours 45 mins, which is 165 minutes. 5 cleaners work a total of $5 \times 165 = 825$ minutes.

If there are 3 workers then it will take $825 \div 3 = 275$ minutes, which is 4 hours and 35 minutes each.

The same amount of work needs to be done regardless of how many people are doing it. If payment is made by the hour then the total cost should be the same. While that is not the same scenario that applies here, it is a useful starting point.

b 5 cleaners are paid for 3 hours.

3 cleaners are paid for 5 hours.

The total is the same.

6 a 183 cm

b Coach Cooksey will have the more accurate mean height as he is using the actual height of each of his players. Coach McKay is finding the estimated mean using the midpoints of each class. By using the midpoints he is giving each player in each class interval the same height.

Height (cm)	Midpoint	Frequency	Midpoint × frequency
$145 \leqslant h < 155$	150	1	150
$155 \leqslant h < 165$	160	2	320
$165 \leqslant h < 175$	170	2	340
$175 \leqslant h < 185$	180	8	1440
$185 \leqslant h < 195$	190	3	570
$195 \leqslant h < 225$	210	4	840
	Totals:	20	3660

$3660 \div 20 = 183$

7 a $(x-6) \times (x-1)$
$= x^2 - 7x + 6$

So Valerie is correct.

> Area involves multiplying, so it is likely that x^2 will be involved, so Valerie's expression looks more plausible. To work out the area of a rectangle we do length × width.

b and c $x^2 - 7x + 6 - 2 = 2(2x - 7)$

$x^2 - 7x + 4 = 4x - 14$

$x^2 - 11x + 18 = 0$

$(x - 9)(x - 2) = 0$

so $x = 9$ or $x = 2$

If $x = 2$ then one of the sides has negative length (which Fritz found funny).

Using $x = 9$ the rectangle measures $3\,\text{cm} \times 8\,\text{cm}$.

---

8 a Glass 1 contains $\frac{1}{4}$ units of squash.

Glass 2 contains $\frac{1}{6}$ units of squash.

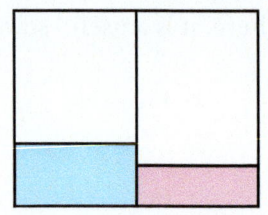

> With questions like this it can help to assign a volume to the glass, be it a numerical value or an algebraic one.
>
> Assume the volume of each glass is 1 unit so that you can just work with the fraction in the question.

Pouring the two glasses together results in a total volume of 2 units.

The squash from glass 1 now represents $\frac{1}{8}$ of the combined drink.

The squash from glass 2 now represents $\frac{1}{12}$ of the combined drink.

$\frac{1}{8} + \frac{1}{12} = \frac{3}{24} + \frac{2}{24} = \frac{5}{24}$

So the resulting drink is $\frac{5}{24}$ squash.

> Notice that this will produce a drink that is weaker than glass 1 and stronger than glass 2.

b The strength of the final drink will be between the two strengths of the original drinks. $\frac{2}{5}$ and $\frac{3}{10}$ are both less than $\frac{1}{2}$ so it is not possible to make a drink that is exactly $\frac{1}{2}$ apple juice.

9 a

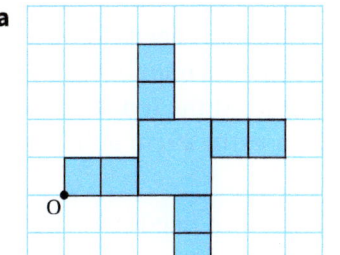

b 0 lines of symmetry

c rotational symmetry order 4

d 1 Draw a circle of radius 1 cm.
2 Enlarge this circle by a scale factor of 2 about the centre of the circle.
3 Translate the small circle 2 cm to the left.
4 Translate the small central circle 2 cm to the right.

> There are several ways this image could be created. Here is one possible set of instructions.

10 Grace needs to gain $\frac{5}{95}$ whereas Meg needs to lose $\frac{5}{105}$

> The percentages are not the same even though the amounts of chocolate buttons involved are equal.

$\frac{5}{95} = 5.263\%$

$\frac{5}{105} = 4.762\%$

11 a $\left(\frac{6}{20}\right)^2 + \left(\frac{5}{20}\right)^2 + \left(\frac{7}{20}\right)^2 + \left(\frac{2}{20}\right)^2 = \frac{114}{400} = \frac{57}{200}$

b $1 - \frac{57}{200} = \frac{143}{200}$

> The easiest way to do this is to realise that picking a different colour the second time is like not picking the same colour.

c $\left(\frac{6}{20} \times \frac{5}{19}\right) + \left(\frac{5}{20} \times \frac{4}{19}\right) + \left(\frac{7}{20} \times \frac{6}{19}\right) + \left(\frac{2}{20} \times \frac{1}{19}\right) = \frac{94}{380} = \frac{47}{190}$

d $\frac{57}{200} = 0.285$ and $\frac{47}{190} = 0.2473...$

When he forgets to put the first pen back in, the probability that he gets two the same colour goes down.

This makes sense because if green was chosen first and then put back in, there is a higher chance green will be picked again than if there were fewer green pens available.

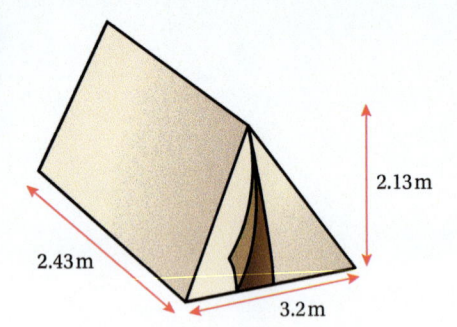

Cambridge IGCSE Mathematics Extended Problem-solving Book

12

2.13 m
2.43 m
3.2 m

Peter is 2.03 m tall so the tent needs to be at least this long. You might assume that to be comfortable Peter will need the tent to be a little longer, for example an extra 20 cm at his head and at his feet.

To decide how wide the tent needs to be you have to make an assumption about the 'width' of Peter and his three friends. You want it to be comfortable so you should be generous with your estimate. Perhaps allowing 80 cm per person is reasonable.

Peter also needs to be able to stand up in the tent. If the tent is 2.03 m tall then Peter would just about be able to stand up in the middle (but his head would touch the top). So again, make it more comfortable and given him a little extra room, say 10 cm.

---

13 a $\$15\,000 = 20\,m^2 \times k$

$k = \dfrac{15\,000}{20}$

$k = \$750$ per square metre

Cost = area × constant of proportionality

Rearrange the equation to calculate the value of k.

$a = \dfrac{23\,000}{750} = 30.666666\,m^2$

But as the area must be an integer value,
$a = 30\,m^2$.

b 4 men would take 4 weeks, meaning there are 16 man-weeks of work.

To get the job done in 3 weeks there would need to be $16 \div 3 = 5.33333$ men. So the builder could employ 5 labourers (making 6 men in total) to finish the job in less than 3 weeks.

c The total number of hours is 4 men × 4 weeks × 5 days per week × 9 hours per day = 720 man-hours of work.

With 6 workers that means each worker needs to do $720 \div 6 = 120$ hours of work.

They work 9 hours per day, which means they need $120 \div 9 = 13\frac{1}{3}$ days.

This is two 5-day weeks, 3 days and 3 hours. If they start on a Monday they will do two full weeks and will finish on the following Thursday at 11 o'clock.

d The 3 hours that the 6 people would need to work on that final day is a total of 18 hours. The builder can do that by himself over two 9-hour days and still finish by the end of the three weeks (assuming there are no jobs that require two people to do them together, such as lifting heavy objects).

e 26 + 39 + 25 = 90 parts altogether, of which 25 parts are profit.

This means the profit is $\frac{25}{90}$ = 27.7777%

Job price includes nearly 28% profit.

> You could work out how much the work costs, or you could just use the ratio that is given.

14 a Total number of students = 720

$\frac{20}{720}$ = 0.0278

Year 7 = 243 × 0.0278 = 6.76, which rounds off to 7 students.

Year 8 = 176 × 0.0278 = 4.89, which rounds off to 5 students.

Year 9 = 162 × 0.0278 = 4.5, which rounds off to 5 students.

Year 10 = 88 × 0.0278 = 2.45, which rounds off to 2 students.

Year 11 = 51 × 0.0278 = 1.42, which rounds off to 1 student.

> Take a stratified sample.

b The stratified sampling method ensures that bigger year groups have more representatives.

Year 11 students are quite important in any school. Only having one Year 11 student on the council might not be a good idea, as that one might not share the same opinions as the majority. Year 7 students are new and might not have mature ideas about particular ideas/needs of older students. Hence for such a council it might be considered best to have 4 students from each year group.

> There are lots of things you might write here. Think about the scenario and decide what would be sensible.

15 a Carpet Lay = $85, Underfoot = $105
  b Underfoot
  c 6 m²
  d Underfoot
  e $125

> The answers to parts **d** and **e** assume that the lines on the graph continue as straight lines.

16 a

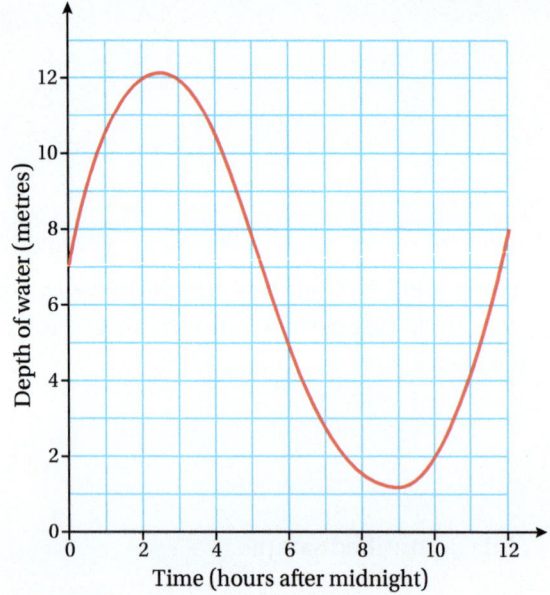

(Graph: Depth of water (metres) vs Time (hours after midnight), showing a sinusoidal curve starting at ~7m at 0h, peaking around 12m near 2h, reaching a low of ~1m near 9h, and rising to ~8m at 12h.)

b Just after 6 am and just before 11 am (need to read off the graph as accurately as possible).

c Yes, in the second low tide period.

> You know that the tide goes in and out roughly twice a day. Use this fact to help you answer the question.

17

(Graph: Number of microbes vs Time (minutes), showing data points rising from near 0 at 2 minutes up to about 1200 at 20 minutes, joined by a smooth curve.)

> It is sensible to draw a graph.
>
> This graph has a smooth slope, so it can be joined with a curve.

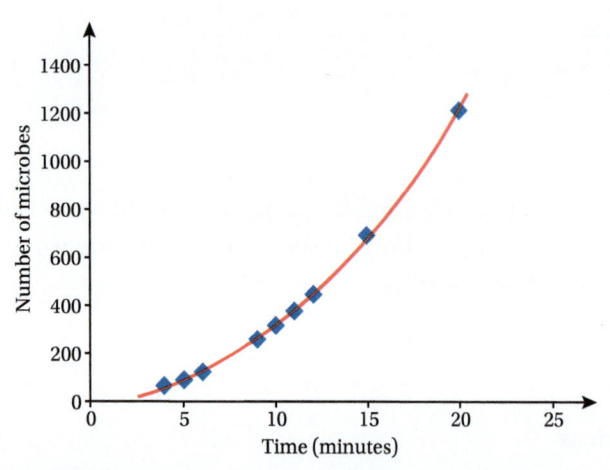

a Reading off the graph at 8 minutes there are about 200 microbes.

b 50 minutes is a long way away from the data, so the pattern might not continue (for example the microbes might get too hot and begin to die off).

18 a There are two possibilities:

Rotate A 180° about (0, 3).

Enlarge A by a scale factor of ⁻1 about point (0, 3).

b There are a lot of possibilities:

Do two reflections (e.g. in the line $x = 0$ and then in the line $y = 3$).

Do a rotation and a translation (e.g. rotate A 180° about (-2, 3) and then translate it 4 units to the right.

Do a translation and then a rotation, or two enlargements, or an enlargement and a translation.

> There are lots of ways to answer part **b**.

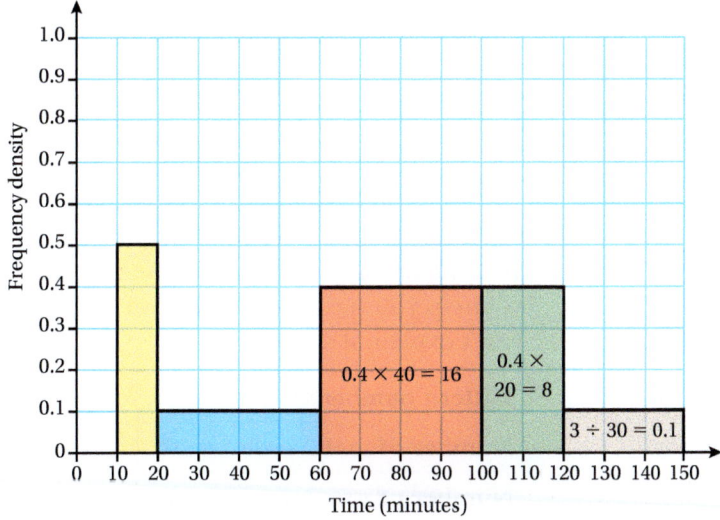

19 a

[Histogram with Frequency density on y-axis (0 to 1.0) and Time (minutes) on x-axis (0 to 150). Annotations show: 0.4 × 40 = 16, 0.4 × 20 = 8, 3 ÷ 30 = 0.1]

b The missing number in the table is 24.

c On the histogram, to the right of 100 mins there are 8 + 3 = 11 people. Because the data has been grouped we don't know for certain about the 8, but there are at least 3 students who play games for longer than 100 minutes (they are the ones in the 120-150 minute group).

> Use the graph and some common sense to help you with this part of the question.

8 Use equations, formulae or ratios

1 a $x = 4 + \dfrac{5}{x}$ — You could start with some algebra.

$x^2 = 4x + 5$ — Multiply by x.

$x^2 - 4x - 5 = 0$

$(x+1)(x-5) = 0$ — Factorise.

so $x = -1$ or $x = 5$

We are told that a positive number is required, so $x = 5$.

b $5 = 4 + \dfrac{5}{5}$ — Look back at part **a**.

Now $y = 5 + \dfrac{6}{y}$, and it is clear that $y = 6$ will work.

c This means that if $z = (n-1) + \dfrac{n}{z}$ then $z = n$.

2

You could draw a few more diagrams and could then make a table of results to see whether that will help you see what is going on (although it won't explain it).

Pattern number	1	2	3	4
Number of metal rods	6	12	18	24
Number of wooden rods	7	12	17	22

a 18

The number of metal rods goes up by 6 each time because each new panel has 6 metal rods in it.

b 22

The number of wooden rods goes up by 5 each time because when a new panel is added, the left-hand side is joined to the previous panel.

c $6n$

d The $6 \times 12 = 72$ metal rods will cost \$144, and the $5 \times 12 + 2 = 62$ wooden rods will cost \$155.

The total cost is \$299.

3 a 80% of $10 is $1 × 8 = $8. 75% of $12 is $\frac{3}{4}$ of $12 = $9. 75% of $12 is greater.

> There are lots of ways of carrying out these comparisons. Some of them are shown here.

b 50% of 1 is a half. 25% of 2 is also a half. They are the same.

c A 10% discount would be $1.299, which is less than the $1.99 delivery charge, so a 5% discount is not enough to cancel out the delivery charge. The online cost is greater.

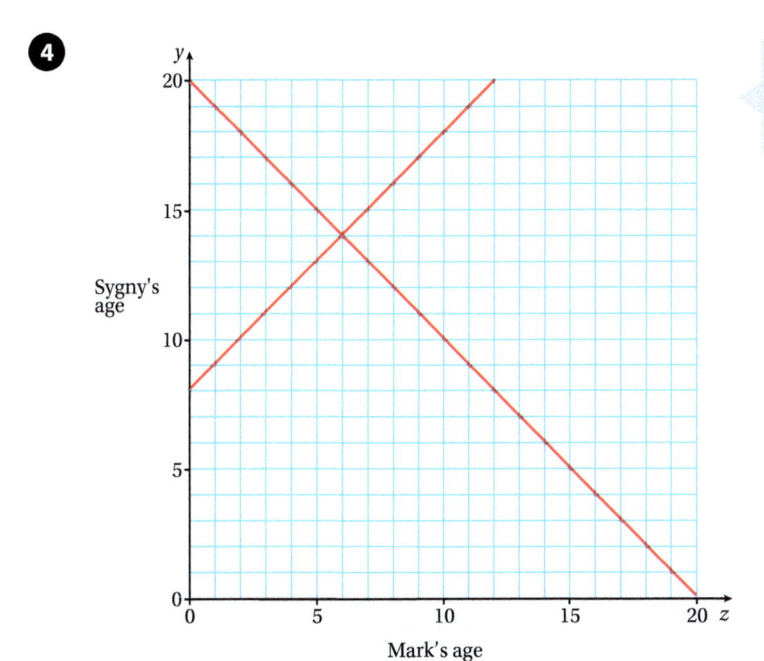

> We don't need to do any difficult calculations.

4

> You could draw a graph as in this example solution. An alternative would be to solve the equations.

Their ages total 20, so $z + y = 20$.

Sygny is 8 years older than Mark so $y = z + 8$.

The lines cross at $z = 6$ (Mark's age) and $y = 14$ (Susan's age).

5 $a^2 + b^2 = c^2$

$2.1^2 + 1.05^2 = c^2$

$5.5125 = c^2$

$c = \sqrt{5.5125} = 2.347\ldots$ m

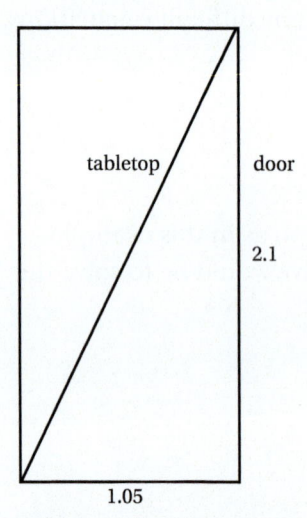

> 2.4 metres is more than the height of the door. Even when it is tilted it will be a close-run thing as to whether it will fit.

Abdul's new table has a diameter of 240 cm. Even if Abdul turns the table to try to go through the door diagonally, it will not fit – it is more than 5 cm too big.

---

6 a We know it is inversely proportional, so it must look like this:

$y = \dfrac{k}{x}$

$20\,000 = \dfrac{k}{4}$

$k = 80\,000$

> If it is inversely proportional then one quantity goes up while the other goes down.

A possible formula is: number of bacteria = $\dfrac{80\,000}{\text{number of hours}}$

b $\dfrac{80\,000}{8} = 10\,000$

c There will be problems when the time is very small. At zero hours it doesn't work at all.

7 a The blue graph is Move It Builders, the red graph is JCE

b Move It Builders = $15

c $14 $70 for 5 days, daily rate = $70 ÷ 5

d Less, by $2 per day   Move It Builders $75 for 5 days (75 − 15 = 60, 60 ÷ 5)

e $75

f $183   15 + (12 × 14)

g Move It Builders   14 × 14 = 196, so the cost from JCE is $196, which is more than $183.

h $13 cheaper

---

8 $y = (x-2)(x+2) = x^2 - 4$

You could answer this question algebraically.

$y + 4 = (x-2)(x+2) + 4$

$y + 4 = x^2 + 2x - 2x - 4 + 4$

$y + 4 = x^2$

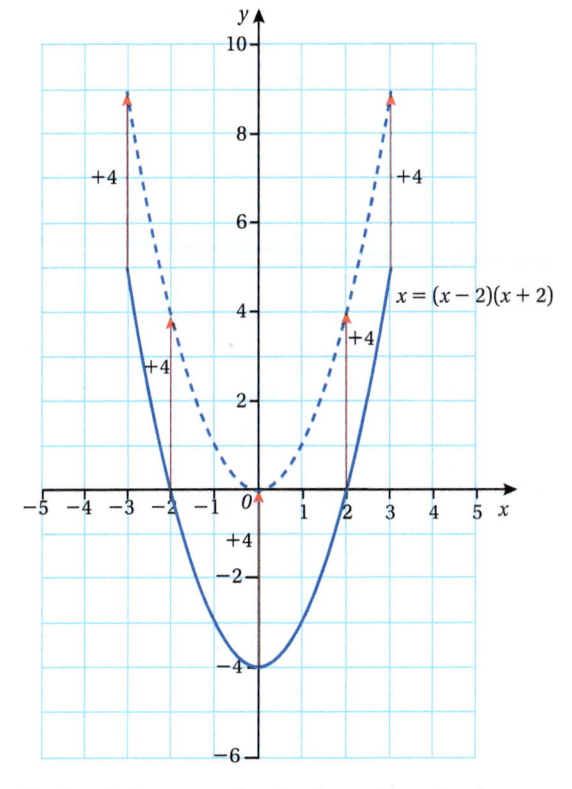

You could answer it graphically.

Both of these methods show that she is correct.

Cambridge IGCSE Mathematics Extended Problem-solving Book

9

a and b $h = 3c + 1$ and $h = 4(c - 1)$

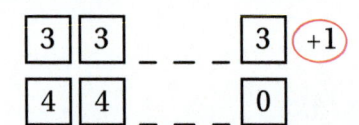

| 3 | 3 | _ | _ | _ | 3 | +1 |
| 4 | 4 | _ | _ | _ | 0 | |

The three chickens from the final cage, and the extra one, have been shared out and put into the other cages. That means there are now 4 cages with 4 chickens each and one empty cage.

There are 5 cages and 16 chickens.

> You don't know how many chickens there are, or how many cages, which makes this difficult.
>
> You could write two equations and then solve them (using h for the number of chickens and c for the number of cages).
>
> An alternative would be to use some diagrams.

10

a If three consecutive even numbers add up to 228 then the middle one is $\frac{1}{3}$ of 228, the smallest one is 2 less than that and the biggest one is 2 more.

This gives 76 as the middle number so the answers are:

74, 76, 78

b Similar reasoning gives the middle number as $291 \div 3 = 97$.

The three numbers are 95, 97, 99.

c Half of 1301 is 650.5, so the two numbers must be either side of $\sqrt{605.5}$. This is 25.504... so the two numbers are 25 and 26.

> You could make a quadratic using $x^2 + (x+1)^2 = 1301$ and solve it. An alternative would be to look for a rough average, as in this example.

d Alternatively, if the two numbers were equal then they would each be 40 (because their sum is 80). To get a difference of 6 we need to subtract 3 from one and add 3 to the other, giving 37 and 43.

> You could make two equations and solve them (e.g. $x - y = 6$ and $x + y = 80$).

11 a The first number in each product is n and the second one is $3n - 1$.

The nth term is therefore $n(3n - 1)$ or $3n^2 - n$.

b 234 is divisible by 9, so work out $234 \div 9 = 26$.

Those two numbers work: $9 \times 26 = 234$

> Knowing the factors of 234 is helpful here.

12

> This involves several steps. Start with what you know: the square has area $4x^2 - 12x + 9$.

$4x^2 - 12x + 9 = (2x - 3)(2x - 3)$

> Usually you would square root the area to work out the length of a side. If you don't know how to square root the algebra you could factorise it.

[square with sides labelled $2x - 3$]

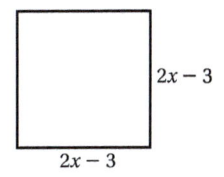

This is helpful because it means the sides of the square are all $2x - 3$. The perimeter is therefore $4(2x - 3)$ or $8x - 12$.

13 a

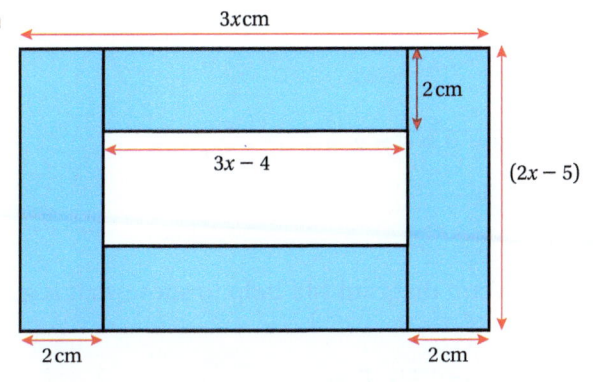

[diagram of rectangle with outer dimensions $3x$ cm by $(2x - 5)$, inner cut-out $3x - 4$ by 2 cm, borders 2 cm on left, right, and top]

> This is one way to split up the shape.
> The top rectangle has area: $2(3x - 4) = 6x - 8$
> The left rectangle has area: $2(2x - 5) = 4x - 10$

Altogether all four rectangles add up to $20x - 36$.

b $20x - 36 = 204$

$20x = 240$

$x = 12$

This means $3x$ is 36 and $(2x - 5)$ is 19.

The dimensions are 36 cm by 19 cm.

14 a $4x + 5y = 205$ (equation 1)

$3x + 7y = 235$ (equation 2)

> Let x be the price of each apple in cents, and y be the price of each banana in cents.

b and c

> One way to solve this is to get the same number of xs in each equation.

$12x + 28y = 940$

> Multiply equation 2 through by 4.

$12x + 15y = 615$

> Multiply equation 1 through by 3.

$13y = 325$

> Subtract.

$y = 25$

> Divide by 13.

This means a banana costs 25 cents.

$4x + 5 \times 25 = 205$

> Substitute $y = 35$ into equation 1.

$4x = 80$

$x = 20$ so an apple costs 20 cents.

d

> You can draw graphs of each of the lines and find the coordinates of the point where they cross.

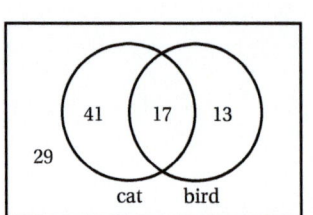

15

> A Venn diagram will help to show what is going on.
>
> Fill the 17 in first.
>
> Then use the information about how many people own a bird.
>
> Then use the information about how many people own either a bird or a cat but not both.
>
> Finally, fill in the ones who own neither a bird nor a cat.

Venn diagram: cat and bird circles. cat only: 41, intersection: 17, bird only: 13, outside: 29.

a $\dfrac{29}{100}$

b $\dfrac{41}{100}$

16 a If a to the power of something $= 1$ then the power equals zero.

$(a^x)^y = a^{xy}$, so either $x = 0$ or $y = 0$, the other one can be anything.

The only exception is if $a = 1$, then x and y can be anything.

b $(a^x)^y = a^1$ means that $x \times y = 1$.

> You might find that there are some other restrictions. For example, if a is zero or negative.

c $(a^x)^y = \sqrt{a}$ means that $x \times y = \frac{1}{2}$.

---

17 a $24.6 : 24$

$246 : 240$

$123 : 120$

b The ratios of times is $123 : 120$ whatever units are used.

> You could start again, having converted the times to minutes, but these ratios don't have units.

c $6.4 \times 10^{23} : 6.0 \times 10^{24}$

$64 : 600$

$8 : 75$

d $27 : 9$

$3 : 1$

> The two mountains are approximately $27\,\text{km}$ and $9\,\text{km}$ tall.

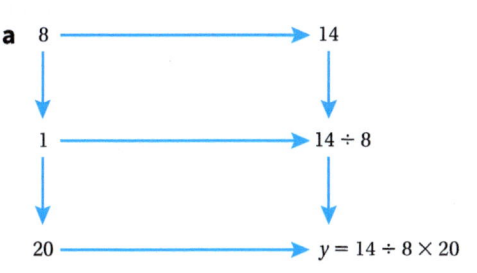

---

18 a

8 ⟶ 14

↓   ↓

1 ⟶ 14 ÷ 8

↓   ↓

20 ⟶ $y = 14 \div 8 \times 20$

Triangle ABC has area $80\,\text{cm}^2$.

Triangle XYZ has area $245\,\text{cm}^2$.

b The ratio is $80 : 245$, which simplifies to $16 : 49$.

c 16 and 49 are both square numbers.

The ratio of the sides is $4 : 7$.

The ratio of the areas is $4^2 : 7^2$.

19 a

x	-2	-1	0	1	2	3	4	5	6
y	11	2	-5	-10	-13	-14	-13	-10	-5

b The turning point is at (3, −14).

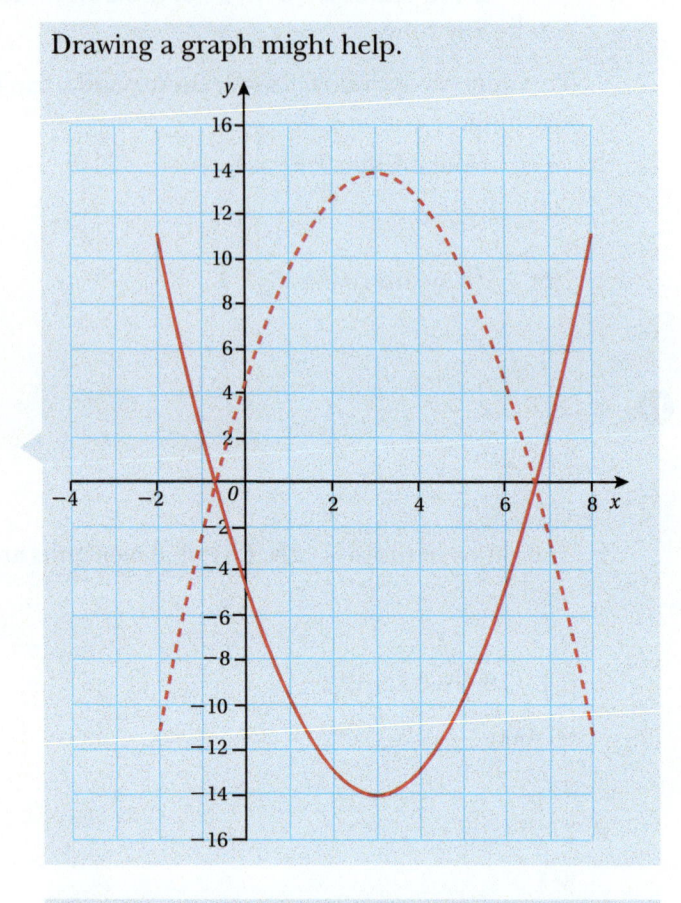

> Drawing a graph might help.

c $x^2 - 6x - 5 = 0$

$(x-3)^2 - 9 - 5 = 0$

$(x-3)^2 - 14 = 0$

$(x-3)^2 = 14$

$x - 3 = \pm\sqrt{14}$

$x = 3 \pm \sqrt{14}$

> The graph only gives approximate versions of where it crosses the x-axis. You could complete the square or use the formula to get these answers.

d The graph of $-y = x^2 - 6x - 5$ shows that the turning point is at (3, 14).

e This is the same as part **c**.

---

20 a The vector moves the original graph down by 8, whereas a transition of 8 units to the right transforms $y = x^3$ to the graph of $y = (x-8)^3$.

b Now he needs to move it back up by 8 and then to the right by 8, so the vector is $\binom{8}{8}$

> If this is not clear then you could draw the two graphs.

21 a

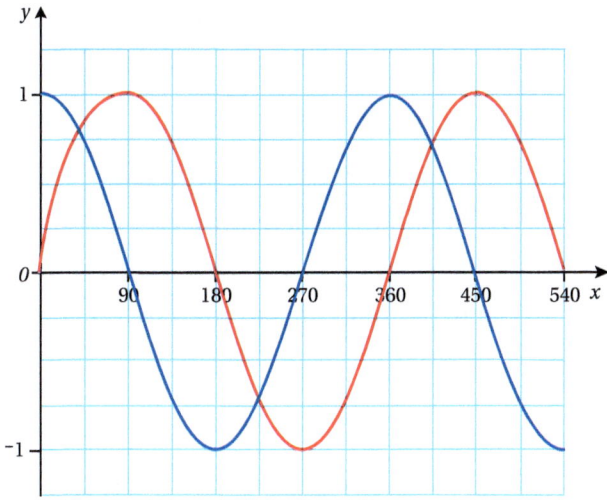

y = sin(x) is shown in red.

y = cos(x) is shown in blue.

b $y = \cos(x - 90°)$

c $y = \sin(x + 90°)$

> Here is one way to do it. There are alternatives that will also work.

d Translations.

---

22 a Each tile looks like this:

$3x - 2$ by $x - 1$

The area is $(3x - 2)(x - 1) = 3x^2 - 5x + 2$

Four of them have area $= 12x^2 - 20x + 8$

b The big square has sides of $4x - 3$, so the area is $(4x - 3)^2 = 16x^2 - 24x + 9$

c $4x^2 - 4x + 1$

$(2x - 1)^2 = 4x^2 - 4x + 1$

> To work out the area of the inner square you can subtract part **a** from part **b**.
>
> Or you could see on the diagram that the side of the inner square is $2x - 1$.

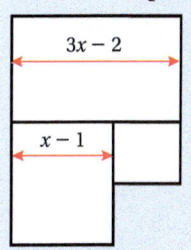

Cambridge IGCSE Mathematics Extended Problem-solving Book

23 **a** The area of the semicircle is
$\pi \times 25 \div 2 = 39.269... \text{cm}^2$ – this is not the same as the student's answer of $39.3\,\text{cm}^2$.

$\sqrt{75} = 8.660...\,\text{cm}$ – this is not the same as the student's answer of $8.7\,\text{cm}$.

the student has rounded too early in each calculation.

> There are lots of things that might have gone wrong. You could work through the student's calculations and check the following:
>
> Did he use the radius and not the diameter?
>
> Did he halve the area of the circle?
>
> Did he subtract when using Pythagoras' theorem?
>
> Did he work out the area of the triangle incorrectly?

b $12.5\pi + 5\sqrt{75} = 82.571...\,\text{cm}^2$, which is $82.6\,\text{cm}^2$ to 1 d.p.

---

24 **a** For the triangles to be similar they must have the same angles.

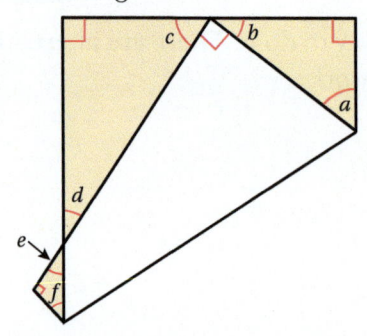

> This is likely to have something to do with angles. Mark on the angles you know and then see which angles are equal to each other.
>
> Start with the top right-hand triangle. Label the non-right angles a and b, as shown.

$a + b + 90° = 180°$, so $b = 90° - a$

$c + 90° + 90° - a = 180°$

$c = a$

> Now look at the middle of the top of the diagram. It is a straight line.

$a + d + 90° = 180°$, so $d = 90° - a$

> Next focus on the top left-hand triangle.

$d = e$, so $e = 90° - a$

> d and e are vertically opposite angles.

$f + 90° + 90° - a = 180°$

> Finally, look at the smallest triangle.

$f = a$

In all three triangles the angles are a, $90°$ and $90° - a$.
This means the triangles are all similar.

b

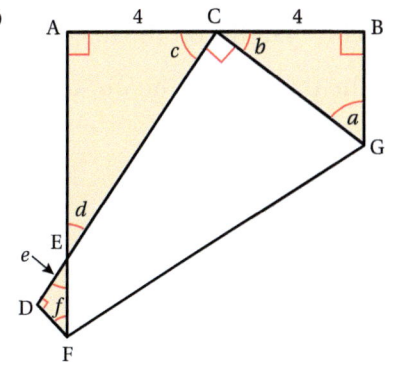

> Move between thinking about each right-angled triangle to thinking about the square.

The square has sides of 8 cm so we know that:

CG + BG = 8

CE + ED = 8

AC and CB are both 4

$CG^2 = BG^2 + 4^2$ (by Pythagoras' Theorem).

> Focus on the top-right triangle.

But CG = 8 − BG (because BG and CG were originally one side of the square).

This gives $(8 - BG)^2 = BG^2 + 4^2$

This simplifies to $64 - 16BG + BG^2 = BG^2 + 16$

48 = 16BG

BG = 3

Pythagoras' theorem tells us that CG = 5.

The top-right triangle has sides of 3, 4 and 5.

We know from part **a** that all the triangles are similar, so triangle ACE is similar to triangle BGC and the 4 in triangle ACE corresponds to the 3 in triangle BGC.

> Now focus on the top-left triangle.

The scale factor of the enlargement is $\times \frac{4}{3}$.

CE is therefore $5 \times \frac{4}{3} = 6\frac{2}{3}$

$AE = 4 \times \frac{4}{3} = \frac{16}{3}$.

This means $DE = 1\frac{1}{3}$ (because CD was a side of the original square so CE + DE = 8).

Compare DE and AE.

$\frac{1}{4}$ of $\frac{16}{3} = \frac{4}{3}$, which is $1\frac{1}{3}$.

This means the sides of the smallest triangle are indeed a quarter of the size of the sides of the largest triangle.

25 a

> Work out the other lengths on the diagram.
>
> The height of the triangle can be worked out using Pythagoras' theorem.

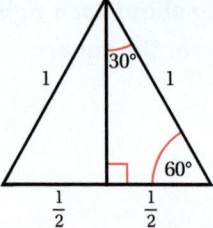

Perpendicular height is: $\sqrt{1^2 - \left(\frac{1}{2}\right)^2}$

$= \sqrt{\left(\frac{3}{4}\right)} = \frac{\sqrt{3}}{2}$

i $\tan 60° = \frac{opp}{adj} = \frac{\sqrt{3}}{2} \div \frac{1}{2} = \sqrt{3}$

ii $\sin 60° = \frac{opp}{hyp} = \frac{\sqrt{3}}{2} \div 1 = \frac{\sqrt{3}}{2}$

iii $\cos 60° = \frac{adj}{hyp} = \frac{1}{2} \div 1 = \frac{1}{2}$

b To work out $\sin 60°$ you need $\frac{\sqrt{3}}{2} \div 1$

To work out $\cos 30°$ you need $\frac{\sqrt{3}}{2} \div 1$

The opposite side needed to work out $\sin 60°$ is the adjacent side needed to work out $\cos 30°$.

The same argument holds true for $\sin 30°$ and $\cos 60°$.

26

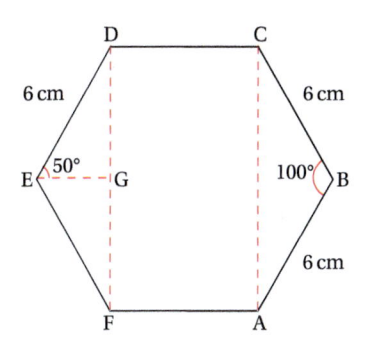

Area of triangle ABC = Area of triangle DEF

$= \dfrac{1}{2} \times 6 \times 6 \times \sin 100°$

$= 18 \sin 100°$

> Simplify the problem by considering the shape as two triangles and a rectangle.

> These are two of the possible triangles: they are congruent.

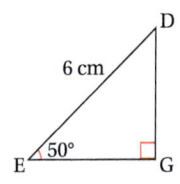

$\dfrac{DG}{6} = \sin 50°$

$\Rightarrow DG = 6 \sin 50°$

> Now find the height of the rectangle.
> You can find half the height using trigonometry.

Area of ACDF $= 6 \times 2 \times 6\sin 50°$

$= 72 \sin 50°$

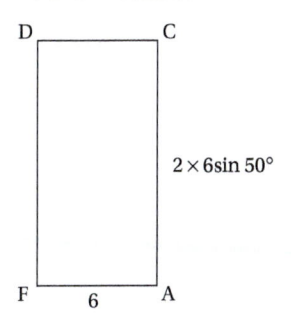

> Now find the area of the rectangle using length × width.

Total area $=$ Area ABC + Area DEF + Area ACDF

$= 18\sin 100° + 18\sin 100° + 72\sin 50°$

$= 90.6 \text{ cm}^2$ (3 s.f.)

> Now find the total area.

27 Volume of hemisphere $= \dfrac{1}{2} \times \dfrac{4}{3} \times \pi \times 5^3$

$\qquad\qquad\qquad\qquad = \dfrac{250}{3}\pi$

Volume of cone $= \dfrac{1}{3} \times \pi \times 5^2 \times h$

$\qquad\qquad\quad = \dfrac{25}{3}\pi h$

So $\dfrac{25}{3}\pi h = \dfrac{250}{3}\pi$

$\Rightarrow h = 10$ cm

Curved surface area of hemisphere
$= \dfrac{1}{2} \times 4 \times \pi \times 5^2$
$= 50\pi$

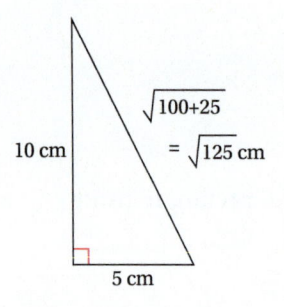

Triangle: 10 cm (vertical), 5 cm (base), hypotenuse $\sqrt{100+25} = \sqrt{125}$ cm

Curved surface of cone $= \pi \times$ radius $\times$ slant height

$\qquad\qquad\qquad\qquad = \pi \times 5 \times \sqrt{125}$
$\qquad\qquad\qquad\qquad = \pi \times 5 \times 5\sqrt{5}$
$\qquad\qquad\qquad\qquad = 25\sqrt{5}\pi$

Total surface area $= \left(50 + 25\sqrt{5}\right)\pi$ cm^2

Work out the other lengths on the diagram.

The height of the triangle can be worked out using Pythagoras' theorem.

Let h be the height of the cone.

Make the volume of the cone equal to the volume of the hemisphere.

Find the height of the cone.

Always look for triangles in cones: the radius of the base, the slant height and the vertical height form a right-angled triangle. The slant height can be found using Pythagoras' theorem.

28

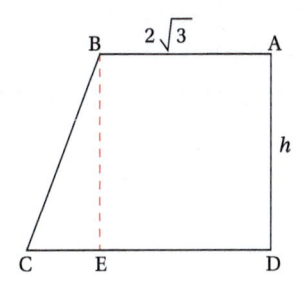

$\sqrt{27} = \sqrt{9} \times \sqrt{3} = 3\sqrt{3}$

Let AD = h

So $\left(\dfrac{2\sqrt{3} + 3\sqrt{3}}{2}\right) \times h = \sqrt{75}$

$\therefore \dfrac{5\sqrt{3}h}{2} = \sqrt{25} \times \sqrt{3}$

$\therefore \dfrac{5\sqrt{3}h}{2} = 5\sqrt{3}$

$\Rightarrow h = 2$ cm

$= BE$

CE $= 3\sqrt{3} - 2\sqrt{3}$

$= \sqrt{3}$

$\therefore BC^2 = \left(\sqrt{3}\right)^2 + 2^2$

$= 3 + 4$

$= 7$

$\Rightarrow BC = \sqrt{7}$

So, perimeter = AB + BC + CD + AD

$= 2\sqrt{3} + \sqrt{7} + 3\sqrt{3} + 2$

$= \left(5\sqrt{3} + \sqrt{7} + 2\right)$ cm

> First, use the formula for the area of a trapezium. This will help you to find the distance between the parallel sides, labelled h in this diagram.

> Always look for triangles in cones: the radius of the base, the slant height and the vertical height form a right-angled triangle. The slant height can be found using Pythagoras' theorem.

> Now, consider the trapezium as a rectangle joined to a right-angled triangle.

> Use Pythagoras' theorem to find length BC.

1 a

+	1	2	3	4	5	6	7	8	9
1									
2									
3									
4									
5									
6									
7									
8									
9									

Systematically pair up every integer with every other integer.

The table illustrates all the possible calculations that can be made.

Notice that these are different calculations. They do not necessarily represent different answers.

The answer is 43.

There are 45 different calculations, but as two were already given then the answer is 43.

b

	–9	–8	–7	–6	–5	–4	–3	–2	–1
–9	–18	–17	–16	–15	–14	–13	–12	–11	–10
–8	–17	–6	–15	–14	–13	–12	–11	–10	–9
–7	–16	–15	–14	–13	–12	–11	–10	–9	–8
–6	–15	–14	–13	–12	–11	–10	–9	–8	–7
–5	–14	–13	–12	–11	–10	–9	–8	–7	–6
–4	–13	–12	–11	–10	–9	–8	–7	–6	–5
–3	–12	–11	–10	–9	–8	–7	–6	–5	–4
–2	–11	–10	–9	–8	–7	–6	–5	–4	–3
–1	–10	–9	–8	–7	–6	–5	–4	–3	–2

The shaded cells show the 17 further possible answers you can get.

The sum of positive and negative numbers must also be considered, yielding 0 and –1 as solutions in addition to this. In total there are 64 possible answers to addition calculations.

2 $+ - \times$: $5 + 2 - 10 \times -3 = 5 + 2 - -30 = 5 + 2 + 30 = 37$

$+ \times -$: $5 + 2 \times 10 - -3 = 5 + 20 + 3 = 28$

$- + \times$: $5 - 2 + 10 \times -3 = 5 - 2 - 30 = -27$

$- \times +$: $5 - 2 \times 10 + -3 = 5 - 20 - 3 = -18$

$\times + -$: $5 \times 2 + 10 - -3 = 10 + 10 + 3 = 23$

$\times - +$: $5 \times 2 - 10 + -3 = 10 - 10 - 3 = -3$

You can achieve a negative result in three different ways.

Make a systematic list of the arrangements of the three operations and then calculate the answers.

3 **a** If a and b are not negative and have to be whole numbers then either $a = 1$ and $b = 0$ or $a = 0$ and $b = 1$.

b This time they are positive, so 0 cannot be used.

> Make a systematic list.

1: $0.1 + 0.9 = 1$

2: $0.2 + 0.8 = 1$

3: $0.3 + 0.7 = 1$

…

9: $0.9 + 0.1 = 1$

There are 9 of them.

c 1: $0.01 + 0.99 = 1$

2: $0.02 + 0.98 = 1$

3: $0.03 + 0.97 = 1$

…

99: $0.99 + 0.01 = 1$

There are 99 of them.

d If a and b are allowed to be negative then $a + b = 1$ with the only restriction being that they are both integers. Whatever you choose as the value for a you can choose a value for b that works, because b is $1 - a$.

4 a i

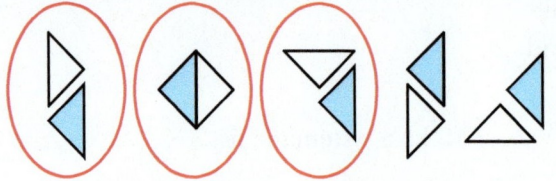

With two sandwiches it is possible to create three polygons: a right-angled isosceles triangle, a parallelogram and a square.

> If you have two sandwiches (two triangles) then it might make sense to keep one of them fixed and move the other around it. Here the blue one is fixed and the white one moves.
>
> There are three different positions in which the second sandwich could be placed.

ii

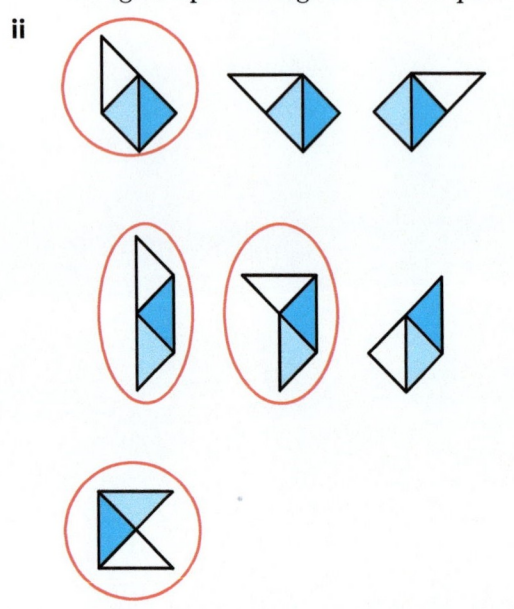

> If you have three sandwiches (three triangles) then it makes sense to start with the three arrangements for two sandwiches and move the third sandwich around these.
>
> The second and third ones are congruent to the first one – and the others that start with a square will also all be congruent.
>
> The third one is congruent to the ones above. All the others that start with the parallelogram will be congruent to others that we have already got.
>
> This is the only new one.

With three sandwiches it is possible to create four polygons: two different trapezia and two different irregular pentagons.

> Conclusion.

iii

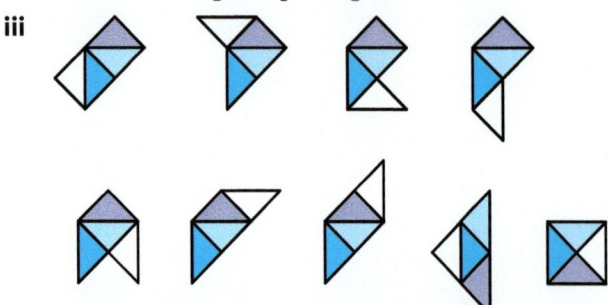

> If you have four sandwiches (four triangles) then it makes sense to start with the four arrangements for three sandwiches and move the fourth sandwich around these.
>
> Again, some of these are identical or are reflections of each other.
>
> These are the ones that are distinct.

With four sandwiches it is possible to create nine polygons: a rectangle, an irregular pentagon, three different irregular hexagons, an isosceles trapezium, a parallelogram, an isosceles triangle and a square.

b Yes.

> This is almost a trick question. A square is an example of all the special quadrilaterals (it is also a rectangle, a parallelogram, a rhombus, a kite and a trapezium), so the original sandwich works for all of them.

5

$$\frac{2}{3} + \frac{1}{5} = \frac{10}{15} + \frac{3}{15} = \frac{13}{15}$$

$$\frac{2}{3} - \frac{1}{5} = \frac{7}{15}$$

$$\frac{1}{5} - \frac{2}{3} = -\frac{7}{15}$$

$$\frac{2}{3} \times \frac{1}{5} = \frac{2}{15}$$

$$\frac{2}{3} \div \frac{1}{5} = \frac{2}{3} \times \frac{5}{1} = \frac{10}{3}$$

$$\frac{1}{5} \div \frac{2}{3} = \frac{1}{5} \times \frac{3}{2} = \frac{3}{10}$$

a The biggest answer is $\frac{10}{3}$ (which comes from $\frac{2}{3} \div \frac{1}{5}$)

b The smallest positive answer is $-\frac{7}{15}$ (which comes from subtracting the largest fraction from the smallest)

---

6 a Box 1: four cylinders of radius 10 cm and height 15 cm

Box 2: one cylinder of radius 20 cm and height 15 cm

Box 3: sixteen cylinders of radius 5 cm and height 15 cm

b Students' guesses.

c Box 1: vol. of cylinders = $\pi \times 10^2 \times 15 \times 4 = 6000\pi$

Box 2: vol. of cylinders = $\pi \times 20^2 \times 15 = 6000\pi$

Box 3: vol. of cylinders = $\pi \times 5^2 \times 15 \times 16 = 6000\pi$

Because the total volume of the cylinders is the same each time, the unused space is the same in each box.

> Did this answer surprise you? Or did you guess that all three boxes had the same amount of unused space?
>
> If you look at each calculation for the volume of the cylinders, you will notice that each has $\pi \times 15$. The rest of the calculation for each volume multiplies to give the same answer, 400.
>
> $4 \times 10^2 = 20^2 = 16 \times 5^2 = 400$

Cambridge IGCSE Mathematics Extended Problem-solving Book

7 a

	Second card				
First card		J_1	J_2	Q	K	A
J_1			J_1J_2	J_1Q	J_1K	J_1A
J_2				J_2Q	J_2K	J_2A
Q					QK	QA
K						KA
A						

> There are two jacks and because they are different suits it is useful to call them J_1 and J_2.

b Of these 10 possibilities 1 involves the two jacks: $\frac{1}{10}$

c From the table it is $\frac{3}{10}$

8 a _ _ _ _ 3 3 _ _ _ _

> Start by working through the information you are given in order.

The median is 3, and because the mode of 10 numbers is 3 and there are only three different numbers, there must be at least four 3s. The mean is 6, so the total is 60.

3 3 3 3 3 3 _ _ _ 13 and the other numbers must be 8, 8, 13.

> The range is 10, so if the lowest number is 3 you get this.

> If the lowest is 2 then the highest is 12 and there are no combinations of 2, 3 and 12 that fit the rules.

1 3 3 3 3 3 11 11 11 11 works.

> If the lowest is 1 then the highest is 11.

b 3 3 3 71 and

1 3 3 73 will work.

> The mode and the median are both 3 so the middle two numbers are both 3. The mean is 20 so they all add up to 80.

c 3, 3, 7, 67

> The mode is 3 so there must be at least two 3s. The median is 5, so you get this.

d 3, 3, 17, 57

e 3, 3, 27, 47

f As long as two of the numbers are 3 and the other two are both odd and add up to 74 then this will work.

Worked solutions: 9 Organise data and work systematically

9 a This table shows there are 78 pairs of numbers.

	1	2	3	4	5	6	7	8	9	10	11	12
1	1	1	1	1	1	1	1	1	1	1	1	1
2		2	1	2	1	2	1	2	1	2	1	2
3			3	1	1	3	1	1	3	1	1	3
4				4	1	2	1	4	1	2	1	4
5					5	1	1	1	1	5	1	1
6						6	1	2	3	2	1	6
7							7	1	1	1	1	1
8								8	1	2	1	4
9									9	1	1	3
10										10	1	2
11											11	1
12												12

This table, and the way it is shaded, is a good way of showing what is going on here.

b The number in each cell is the HCF of the pair of numbers. The co-prime numbers are shown with a 1. There are 46 pink cells, so $\frac{46}{78}$ of the pairs are co-prime. This simplifies to give $\frac{23}{39}$.

10 a The number 1 is used in four lines. So is the number 2.

All the numbers from 1 to 7 are used four times so the total is $(1 + 2 + 3... + 7) \times 4 = 28 \times 4 = 112$.

As an alternative method, you could add up the totals for each line.

b In a hexagon each number joins to three others, so the total is $(1 + 2 + 3... + 6) \times 3 = 21 \times 3 = 63$.

In a pentagon each number joins to two others, so the total is $(1 + 2 + 3 + 4 + 5) \times 2 = 15 \times 2 = 30$.

The total of $63 + 30 = 93$ is less than 112.

11 We know the triangles are equilateral because the sides are all radii of the circles. This helps to work out the angle of 240°.

> There are many ways to work this out. This method uses two sectors of circles (shown unshaded) and two equilateral triangles.

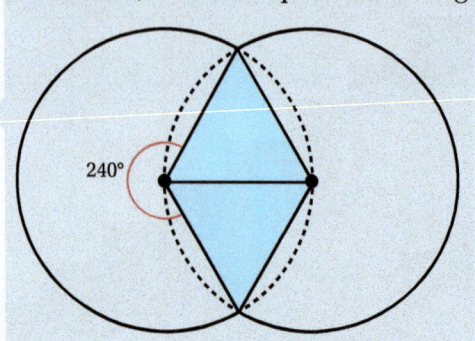

The perimeter is therefore: $\frac{240}{360} \times \pi \times d \times 2 = \frac{16}{3}\pi$.

The area of each sector is $\frac{2}{3} \times \pi r^2 = \frac{8}{3}\pi$.

The area of one triangle is
$\frac{1}{2}ab \sin C = \frac{1}{2} \times 2 \times 2 \times \sin 60°$.

This is $\frac{1}{2} \times 2 \times 2 \times \frac{\sqrt{3}}{2} = \sqrt{3}$

The total area is therefore $\frac{16}{3}\pi + 2\sqrt{3}$

The cost of the pool is
$\frac{16\pi}{3} \times \$225 + (\frac{16}{3}\pi + 2\sqrt{3}) \times \$800$
= \$19 945 to the nearest dollar.

---

12 We know that all powers of 1 are 1, so this means that $2^b + 3^c = 244$.

> This question can be worked out in several different systematic ways. Here is one.

We don't need to worry about negative powers of 2 and 3 because they will give fractions.

3^0	1
3^1	3
3^2	9
3^3	27
3^4	81
3^5	243

> You could make a list of powers of 2 and powers of 3, but consider for a moment that 3^c is always odd. The only way to get an even result (such as 244) is for 2^b to be odd.
> So this must be $2^0 = 1$ and $3^c = 243$.

This means that:

a can be anything

$b = 0$

$c = 5$

13

Use Pythagoras' theorem in the smallest triangle, but leave your answer as a surd because you will need to square it again to work out the hypotenuse of the second triangle, and so on.

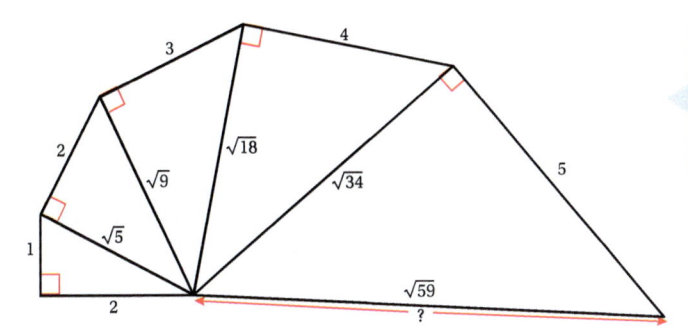

The final hypotenuse is the square root of
$2^2 + 1^2 + 2^2 + 3^2 + 4^2 + 5^2$

This is $\sqrt{59}$.

14

End of week number	1	2	3	4	5	6
Number of people	4	16	64	256	1024	4096

Mai gives the mixture away at the end of each week, so this table shows the number of people who have the mixture at the end of the week. Because each person shares theirs with 3 others it is multiplied by 4 each week.

a 256 people will have it after 4 weeks.

b 4096 people after 6 weeks.

c $4^{13} = 67\,108\,864$

So 13 weeks are required.

d Not everyone will pass it on or keep their own one going. Babies and children would find it difficult. After a while everyone you know will have it and you won't be able to find anyone new to pass it on to.

15

N	Fraction	Decimal	Recurring or terminating?
1	$\frac{1}{1}$	1	Terminating
2	$\frac{1}{2}$	0.5	Terminating
3	$\frac{1}{3}$	0.3333…	Recurring
4	$\frac{1}{4}$	0.25	Terminating
5	$\frac{1}{5}$	0.2	Terminating
6	$\frac{1}{6}$	0.1666…	Recurring
7	$\frac{1}{7}$	0.142857142857…	Recurring
8	$\frac{1}{8}$	0.125	Terminating
9	$\frac{1}{9}$	0.1111…	Recurring
10	$\frac{1}{10}$	0.1	Terminating

Four of the fractions, where N is any positive integer from 1 to 10, are recurring.

If the numerator is 1 then the terminating ones must have denominators whose only prime factors are 2 or 5.

16

Work on each triangle separately.

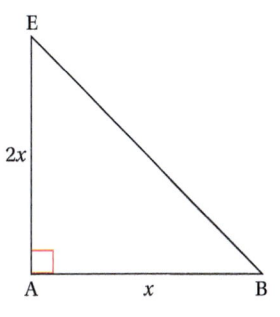

$x^2 + (2x)^2 = BE^2$

$\therefore BE^2 = x^2 + 4x^2$

$\qquad = 5x^2$

$\therefore BE = \sqrt{5x^2}$

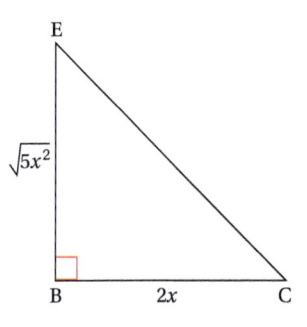

Use Pythagoras' theorem.

$(2x)^2 + \left(\sqrt{5x^2}\right)^2 = CE^2$

$\therefore CE^2 = 4x^2 + 5x^2$

$\qquad = 9x^2$

$\therefore CE = \sqrt{9x^2}$

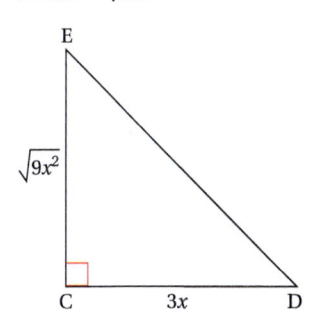

Remind yourself how to square a square root.

Repeat the process.

$(3x)^2 + \left(\sqrt{9x^2}\right)^2 = DE^2$

$\therefore DE^2 = 9x^2 + 9x^2$

$\qquad = 18x^2$

$\therefore DE = \sqrt{18x^2}$

$\qquad = \sqrt{2}\sqrt{9}\sqrt{x^2}$

$\qquad = \left(3\sqrt{2}\right)x$

17 **a** $y = x^2 - 4x + 3$

$y = 2x + 3$

$x^2 - 4x + 3 = 2x + 3$

$\Rightarrow x^2 - 6x = 0$

$\Rightarrow x(x - 6) = 0$

$\Rightarrow x = 0$ or $x = 6$

$x = 0 \Rightarrow y = 3$, so $(0, 3)$

$x = 6 \Rightarrow y = 15$, so $(6, 15)$

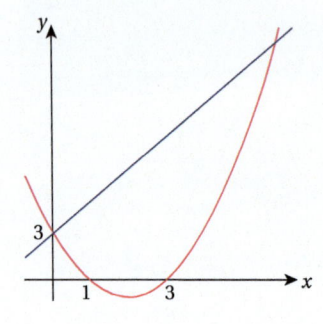

> Find where the curve meets the line.

> Factorise and solve for x.

b Solve $x^2 - 4x + 3 = 0$

$\Rightarrow (x - 3)(x - 1) = 0$

$\Rightarrow x = 1$ or 3

> Find where the curve crosses the x-axis: substitute $y = 0$ into the equation of the curve.

> Notice that both the line and the curve cross the y-axis at 3.

18

$ff(x) = \dfrac{1 - \left(\dfrac{1-x}{1+x}\right)}{1 + \left(\dfrac{1-x}{1+x}\right)}$

$= \dfrac{\left(\dfrac{1+x-(1-x)}{1+x}\right)}{\left(\dfrac{1+x+1-x}{1+x}\right)}$

$= \dfrac{\left(\dfrac{1+x-1+x}{1+x}\right)}{\left(\dfrac{2}{1+x}\right)}$

$= \dfrac{2x}{2}$

$= x$

> For this question, follow your method carefully. Don't let the fractions put you off.

> Clear, systematic working is very important.

10 Guess, test and improve

1   **a**   Jyoti's tower = 1 + 2 + 3 + 4 + 5 + 6 = 21 cm

Indira's tower = 7 + 8 + 9 + 10 + 11 + 12 = 57 cm

Indira's tower is 36 cm taller.

> One way to do this is to write out the heights of the two towers.

b   57 + 21 = 78 cm

One possible answer is 1 + 2 + 3 + 10 + 11 + 12 = 39
and 4 + 5 + 6 + 7 + 8 + 9 = 39

> The total height of all the cubes is 78 cm.
>
> 78 ÷ 2 = 39 cm gives the height when they are the same.
>
> Each girl must now have a combination that is 39 cm high.

2   **i**   False

ii   True

> If you add the digits of the number together you get 48, which is divisible by 3, so the number is also divisible by 3.

iii   False

> The number is a multiple of 3, so it cannot be prime. It is also even.

iv   True

> The number 12 345 678 910 is in the 5 times table, so if you divide 12 345 678 912 by 5 then the remainder is 2.

v   True

> The divisibility rule for 4 states that a number is divisible by 4 if the last two digits are divisible by 4. The last two digits are 12, which is divisible by 4. If a number is divisible by 4, it follows that it must be a multiple of 4.

3   Grandfather's age is $2x$, Dimitri's age is x and Paolo's age is $x - 29$.

> One way to do this is to call Dimitri's age x and to work out the other ages in terms of x.

In total this is $2x + x + x - 29$, which the question says equals 131.

$4x - 29 = 131$, so $4x = 160$ and $x = 40$.

4 Call the daughter's age x. The father is then $5x$ and the mother is $5x - 9$.

> You could start by using some algebra.

Adding these up gives $11x - 9$, which is equal to 134 years.

Solve $11x - 9 = 134$ to get $x = 13$.

The mother is therefore $5 \times 13 - 9 = 56$ years old.

---

5 **a** $1 : 8$

    $x : 140$

    $140 \div 8 = 17.5$

    18 teachers

  b $21 \times 8 = 168$

    $168 - 140$

    28 more students

  c The ratio of students to teachers is

    $140 : 21$

    $20 : 3$

  d 21 teachers + 140 students = 161 seats needed.

    $4 \times 42 = 168$ seats.

    So 4 coaches are needed.

    4 coaches need 4 drivers.

    Total adults = 25.

    Students : Adults

    $140 : 25$

    $28 : 5$

  e $\dfrac{25}{165} = \dfrac{5}{33}$

> Ratio of teachers to students.
>
> Let number of teachers = x.
>
> Number of teachers must be a whole number.
>
> Every teacher can have 8 students to supervise.
>
> A total of 168 students can go.
>
> First find the number of coaches needed.
>
> Total adults = 25.
>
> Total in the group = 25 + 140 = 165.

6

OB = cos 36° × 7 cm = 5.663… cm

B: (5.66, 0)

A: (−5.66, 0)

A clear, well-labelled diagram will be useful. This one focuses on the important triangle.

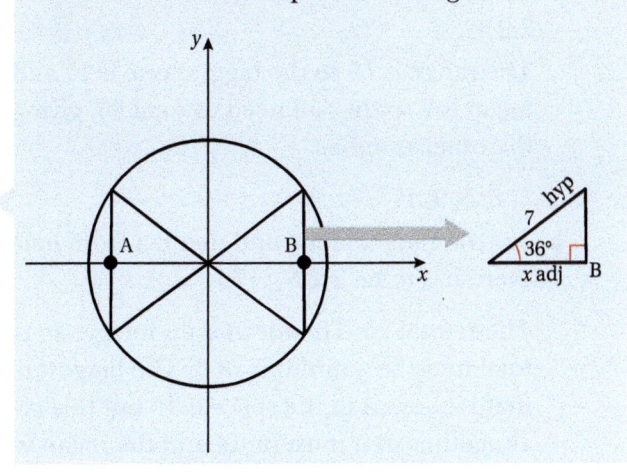

To work out x you need to use trigonometry.

Now interpret this in terms of the coordinates of point B (values rounded off to 2 d.p. as required).

Point A is a reflection of point B in the y-axis.

---

7 We know the following:

There are eight numbers.

The biggest is 16.

The range is 15, so the smallest is 16 − 15 = 1.

The mean is 7.5 so they all add up to 7.5 × 8 = 60.

The mode is 3 and 5 so there are the same number of 3s and 5s, and there must be two or three of each. The six numbers that must be included are 1, 3, 3, 5, 5, 16 and the others must be between 1 and 16. These ones add up to 33 so the other two add up to 27.

The possible solutions are therefore:

1, 3, 3, 5, 5, 12, 15, 16

1, 3, 3, 5, 5, 13, 14, 16

What does each piece of information tell you?

8 a The mode is 2 and the median is 5 so there must be:

2 2 5 _ _

The range is 15 so the biggest one is 17 and the mean is 7 so they all need to total 35, giving 9 as the other number:

2, 2, 5, 9, 17

b For the range, mode and median from before there has to be 2 2 5 _ 17

These total 26. The mean is an integer so the total must be a multiple of 5. The biggest number that is allowed in the space is 16 but this gives 42 altogether so it must be 14 and the mean is 8.

c This time the mean is not stated to be an integer.

2, 2, 5, 6, 17 gives the smallest mean of $32 \div 5 = 6.4$

> Write down the things you know and then see what you can work out.

9 a e.g. $3 = \frac{2}{1} + 1$, or $3 = \frac{3}{1} + 0$, etc.

b e.g. $3 = \frac{4}{2} + 1$, or $3 = \frac{8}{8} + 2$, etc.

c e.g. $3 = \frac{-2}{-1} + 1$, or $3 = \frac{6}{-3} + 5$, etc.

> Since c must be an integer, the fraction must be an integer, too.
>
> This means that a must be a multiple of b.
>
> The fraction will be positive if you use negative values for both a and b.

10

0.74 or $\frac{74}{100}$	0.46 or $\frac{46}{100} = \frac{23}{50}$	0.9 or $\frac{90}{100} = \frac{9}{10}$
0.86 or $\frac{129}{150} = \frac{43}{50} = \frac{86}{100}$	0.7 or $\frac{70}{100} = \frac{7}{10}$	0.54 or $\frac{54}{100} = \frac{27}{50}$
0.5 or $\frac{50}{100} = \frac{1}{2}$	0.94 or $\frac{94}{100} = \frac{47}{50}$	0.66 or $\frac{33}{50} = \frac{66}{100}$

> Remember that in a magic square all the rows and columns and both main diagonals add up to the magic number. The key idea here is to convert everything into the same type of number. It is easiest to work either in decimals or in fractions with a denominator of 100. The diagram shows possible answers: you only need one answer in each square.

11 There are 4 aces. The probability of picking 2 aces is:

$$\frac{4}{52} \times \frac{3}{51} = \frac{12}{2652}$$

There are two red kings, so the probability of picking 2 red kings is:

$$\frac{2}{52} \times \frac{1}{51} = \frac{2}{2652}$$

Picking two aces is 6 times as likely.

> You could start by writing down the probability of picking one ace. Then, if you are lucky and have picked an ace, write down the probability of picking an ace when there are only 51 cards left.

12

		Socks						
		G	G	B	B	B	BLU	STR
Ties	P	a	a					b
	BLU					d		
	PUR							
	G	c d	c d					

a $\frac{2}{28} = \frac{1}{14}$

b $\frac{1}{28}$

c $\frac{2}{28} = \frac{1}{14}$

d $\frac{3}{28}$

e $1 - \frac{3}{28} = \frac{25}{28}$

> In probability questions a diagram of some kind is often helpful. Here the letters refer to each part of the answer.

13

+	4	5	6	7	8
4			10		
5		10			
6	10				
7					
8					

P(4 kits and 6 kits) = 0.1 × 0.3 = 0.03

P(5 kits and 5 kits) = 0.2 × 0.2 = 0.04

P(6 kits and 4 kits) = 0.3 × 0.1 = 0.03

Any of these outcomes are possible, so add them together to get 0.1.

> The probability of 8 kits is not needed to answer the question as there is no combination with the other litters that gives a total of 10.

> A table might help but note that this shows the different possibilities and not the probabilities (because they are not all equally likely).

14 1 pint (imperial) is 0.568 litres (568 ml).

9 pints = 568 ml × 9 = 5112 ml

5112 ml = approximately 5000 ml

= 5×10^3 ml of blood in James's body.

There are 5×10^9 red blood cells per millilitre of blood, so in total James has about $5 \times 10^9 \times 5 \times 10^3$
= $25 \times 10^{12} = 2.5 \times 10^{13}$ red blood cells.
10% of $2.5 \times 10^{13} = 0.25 \times 10^{13}$.
The number of remaining blood cells is
$2.5 \times 10^{13} - 0.25 \times 10^{13} = 2.25 \times 10^{13}$.

> We know there are two different units in the question: millilitres and pints.
>
> Here we have converted pints into millilitres.
>
> The question asks you to work with approximate figures.

15

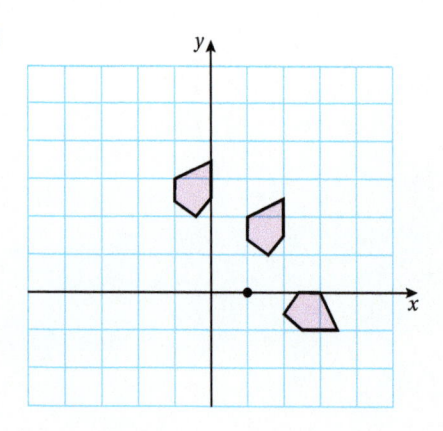

> It seems sensible to work backwards through the transformations.
>
> The question isn't clear as to whether the second, intermediate diagram is drawn, so you might not have the one starting from coordinate point (1, 2).

16 a

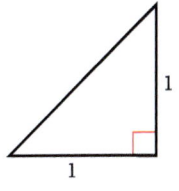

$\sqrt{1^2 + 1^2} = \sqrt{2}$

So the hypotenuse is $\sqrt{2}$.

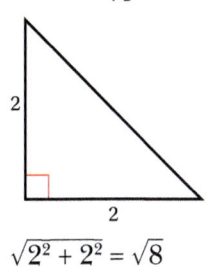

$\sqrt{2^2 + 2^2} = \sqrt{8}$

So the hypotenuse is $\sqrt{8}$.

These numbers are both used in the question.

However, the second triangle has sides that are double those of the first triangle.

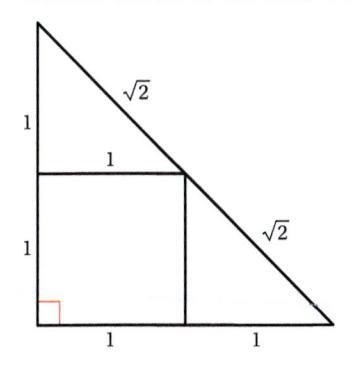

So $2\sqrt{2} = \sqrt{8}$

> It seems sensible to work out the length of each hypotenuse (because square roots are involved).

b $3 \times \sqrt{2}$ looks like a triangle with sides 3 times those of the small triangle.

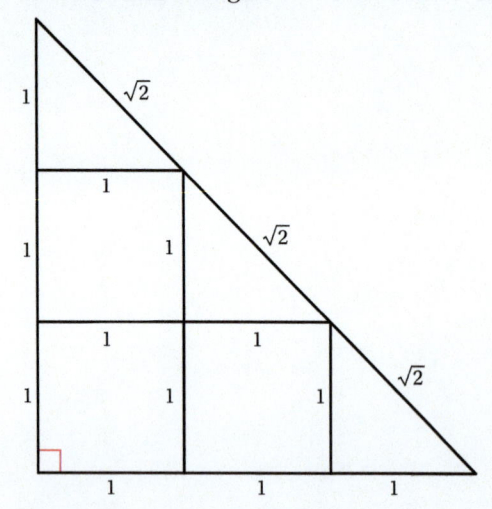

The big triangle above is identical to the triangle below.

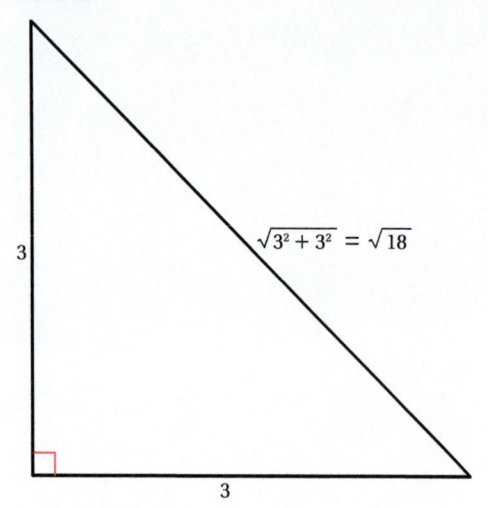

This shows that $\sqrt{18} = 3\sqrt{2}$

17

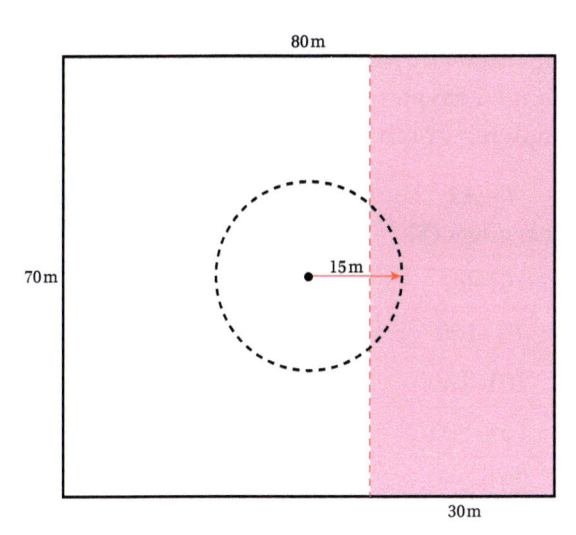

This is not easy to visualise, so a sketch is a good idea.

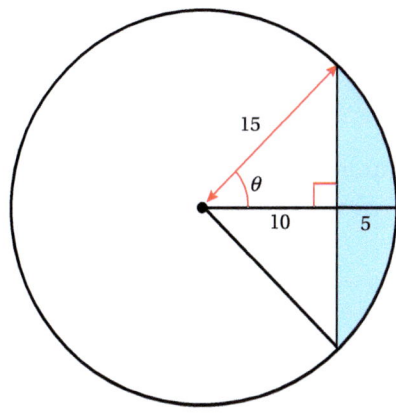

You need to know the shaded area that the goat can reach.

The angle is worked out by doing $\cos\theta = \frac{10}{15}$

so $\theta = 48.189\ldots$

The area of the sector is $\frac{96.379\ldots}{360} \times \pi \times 15^2$

The angle of the sector is $2 \times \theta$.

The area of the triangle is
$\frac{1}{2}ab \sin C = \frac{1}{2} \times 15 \times 15 \times \sin(2\theta)$

This gives the shaded, goat-eaten area as
$189.24\ldots - 111.80\ldots = 77.437\ldots$

The cost of planting the wheat is $30 \times \$65 = \$1950$

The takings are $\$4.50 \times (30 \times 70 - 77.437\ldots) = \$9101.53$

The farmer's profit is $\$9101.53 - \$1950 = \$7151.53$

18 a

Weekly earnings ($)	Frequency	Cumulative frequency
61–80	2	2
81–100	5	7
101–150	9	16
151–200	2	18
201–250	1	19
251–300	1	20

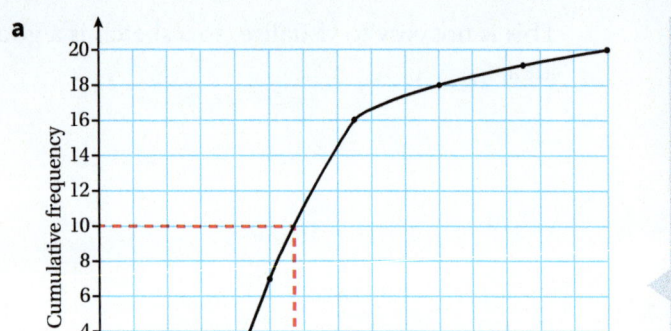

The usual way to work out the median from a grouped frequency table is to draw a cumulative frequency graph.

This gives a median of about $114, which is not helpful to the manager as it is below $130.

You might be interested to see what happens to the median when worked out in this way!

b The median won't increase.

The mean salary is $(7 \times 90.5 + 9 \times 125.5 + 2 \times 175.5 + 1 \times 225.5 + 1 \times 275.5) \div 20$.

This is $130.75, so you could say that the average is now above the national average.

---

19 a $30x + 20y \leqslant 350$

Each glass of lemonade needs 30 g sugar, so altogether the drinks needs $30x$ sugar.

Each brownie needs 20 g sugar, so altogether the snacks need $20y$ sugar.

In total this must be less than or equal to 350.

b Let n be number of friends.

$50n \leqslant 350$

so $n \leqslant 7$

If everyone has one of each, then that is 50 g per person.

20 $KE = \frac{1}{2}mv^2$, where m is the mass in kg and v is the speed in m/s.

The tennis ball has mass 56 g and velocity 120 miles per hour.

$56\,g = 0.056\,kg$ so $m = 0.056$

120 miles per hour $= 120 \times \frac{8}{5}$ km per hour

$\qquad\qquad\qquad\qquad = 192$ km per hour

$\qquad\qquad\qquad\qquad = \frac{192\,000}{3600}$ m/s $= 53.\dot{3}$ m/s

$KE = \frac{1}{2} \times 0.056 \times (53.\dot{3})^2$

$\quad\; = 79.6$ joules

Student 1 has not converted the units so that the mass is in kg and the speed is in m/s.

Student 2 appears to have worked out $(\frac{1}{2}mv)^2$ rather than $\frac{1}{2}mv^2$ (where only the v should be squared).

> The first thing you might want to do is to try to work this out for yourself.

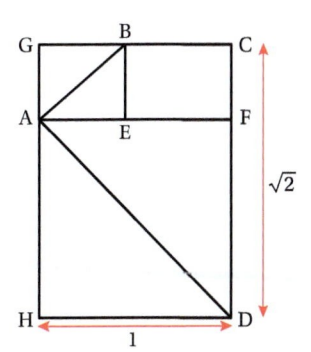

21

The question states that it is a kite, so AD = CD and AB = BC.

AD and CD are both $\sqrt{2}$.

AH = 1

> This question can be answered in lots of ways. Here is one that does not involve the use of Pythagoras' theorem.

> Because it is folded across the width of the rectangle, which is 1.

so GA = $\sqrt{2} - 1$

GA is folded to meet AE so AE = $(\sqrt{2} - 1)$ and
EF = $1 - (\sqrt{2} - 1) = 2 - \sqrt{2}$

BC is the same as EF, so sides AB and BC are both $2 - \sqrt{2}$

The four sides total: $\sqrt{2} + \sqrt{2} + 2 - \sqrt{2} + 2 - \sqrt{2} = 4$

22 $f(x) : g(x)$ is $3 : 4$, i.e. $\frac{3}{4} : 1$.

So $\dfrac{f(x)}{g(x)} = \dfrac{3}{4}$

$\dfrac{f(x)}{g(x)} = \dfrac{x^2 - 7x + 12}{2x^2 - x - 15}$

$= \dfrac{(x-3)(x-4)}{(2x+5)(x-3)}$

$= \dfrac{x-4}{2x+5}$

So $\dfrac{x-4}{2x+5} = \dfrac{3}{4}$

$\Rightarrow 4(x-4) = 3(2x+5)$

$\Rightarrow 4x - 16 = 6x + 15$

$\Rightarrow 2x = -31$

$\Rightarrow x = -\dfrac{31}{2}$

> By converting the ratio to the form $n\ 1$ it is easier to see that $f(x)$ must be the smaller value.

> When a fraction contains quadratic expressions, it is always helpful to factorise and simplify if possible.

23 **a** $y = 0.2 - 5 \times 0.2^2 + 4$

$ = 0.2 - 0.2 + 4$

$ = 4$ m

> The y-coordinate is the height above the ground.
>
> Substitute 0.2 into the formula for y.

b After $t = 0.8$ seconds

$x = 0.8$

$y = 0.8 - 5 \times 0.8^2 + 4$

$y = 1.6$ m

> Find the position of the keys after 0.8 seconds by substituting into both formulae.

[Diagram: right triangle with horizontal leg 0.8, vertical leg 1.6, and hypotenuse d from origin.]

> You can now find the distance from (0, 0) by using Pythagoras' theorem.

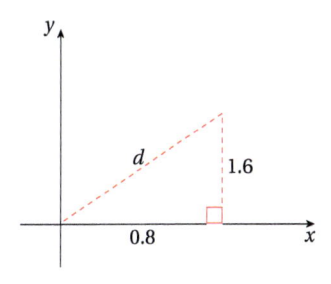

$d^2 = 0.8^2 + 1.6^2$

$ = 3.2$

$\Rightarrow d = \sqrt{3.2}$

$d = 1.79$ m

c At ground level, $y = 0$

$\Rightarrow t - 5t^2 + 4 = 0$

$\Rightarrow 5t^2 - t - 4 = 0$

$\Rightarrow (5t + 4)(t - 1) = 0$

$\Rightarrow t = -\dfrac{4}{5}$ or $t = 1$

Since $t \geqslant 0$ [time is greater than or equal to zero]

$t = 1$ second

> The keys will strike the ground when their height is zero.
>
> Solve the equation for $y = 0$.

24

```
D    1    F  x  C
┌────────┬──────┐
│        ┊      │
1        1      1
│        ┊      │
└────────┴──────┘
A    1    E  x  B
```

$\dfrac{AB}{BC} = \dfrac{1+x}{1}$

This ratio is the same as $\dfrac{EF}{CF}$, which is $\dfrac{1}{x}$

So $1 + x = \dfrac{1}{x}$

$\Rightarrow x^2 + x = 1$

$\Rightarrow x^2 + x - 1 = 0$

$\Rightarrow x = \dfrac{-1 \pm \sqrt{1^2 - 4 \times 1 \times (-1)}}{2 \times 1}$

$\Rightarrow x = \dfrac{-1 \pm \sqrt{5}}{2}$

$\therefore x = \dfrac{-1 + \sqrt{5}}{2}$

$\Rightarrow \dfrac{AB}{BC} = \dfrac{1 + \dfrac{-1+\sqrt{5}}{2}}{1}$

$= \dfrac{2 + -1 + \sqrt{5}}{2}$

$= \dfrac{1 + \sqrt{5}}{2}$

> The dimensions of the rectangle are not given, let the width be 1 m.
>
> [All rectangles with the same properties are similar, so pick a value that is easy to work with.]
>
> Let the width of the smaller rectangle be x, and work out what happens when you use the similarity property.

> Use the quadratic formula.

> Remember that x is a length, so must be positive.

11 Put it together

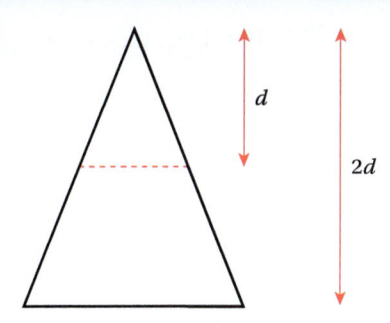

1

If you look at the cones from the side they will look like isosceles triangles.

The two cones are similar.

Scale factor of lengths = 2

∴ Scale factor of surface areas = 2^2 = 4

∴ Small cone has $\frac{1}{4}$ curved area of large cone.

⇒ Frustum accounts for $\frac{3}{4}$ of the curved surface area.

⇒ curved surface area of small cone : curved surface area of frustum is 1 : 3.

Remember that the scale factor of areas is found by squaring the scale factor of lengths.

When dealing with similar shapes you don't always need to find the actual areas.

2 a Option 1:

$$1 + \frac{2}{x-1}$$

$$= \frac{x-1}{x-1} + \frac{2}{x-1}$$

$$= \frac{x-1+2}{x-1}$$

$$= \frac{x+1}{x-1}$$

or Option 2:

$$\frac{x+1}{x-1}$$

$$= \frac{x-1+2}{x-1}$$

$$= \frac{x-1}{x-1} + \frac{2}{x-1}$$

$$= 1 + \frac{2}{x-1}$$

> You can start with either side of the equation. We will look at what happens in both cases.
>
> In Option 1 we start with the right hand side and use common denominators.
>
> In Option 2 we start with the left side, write the denominator on the top and adjust with the +2 (so that the numerator still has the same value. This enables us to divide by the term $(x-1)$.

b Largest value of $\frac{x+1}{x-1}$ = largest value of $1 + \frac{2}{x-1}$

> Use part **a** as a clue to help you solve part **b**.

This is found when $(x-1)$ is as small as possible (and positive).

i.e. $x - 1 = 4 - 1 = 3$

$\Rightarrow$ Largest value is $1 + \frac{2}{3} = \frac{5}{3}$

---

3 a If $a \oplus b = b \oplus a$

$\Rightarrow ab - \frac{a}{b^2} = ba - \frac{b}{a^2}$

$\Rightarrow \frac{a}{b^2} = \frac{b}{a^2}$

$\Rightarrow a^3 = b^3$

$\Rightarrow a = b$

> To work out the right hand side of this equation you need to swap a and b.
>
> Remember that $ab = ba$
>
> Take the cube root of both sides.

b

$$\frac{3}{c} \oplus c = \frac{3}{c} \times c - \frac{\left(\frac{3}{c}\right)}{c^2}$$

$$= 3 - \frac{3}{c^3}$$

$$= \frac{21}{8}$$

So $\frac{24}{8} - \frac{3}{c^3} = \frac{21}{8}$

$\Rightarrow \frac{3}{c^3} = \frac{3}{8}$

$\Rightarrow c^3 = 8$

$\Rightarrow c = \sqrt[3]{8} = 2$

> To divide the fraction $\frac{e}{f}$ by the number g you can multiply the denominator by g to get $\frac{e}{fg}$.
>
> Think about how this has been used in this question.

4

> Draw the diagram yourself and notice that the pentagon can be built from five identical isosceles triangles.
>
> Concentrate on one of these triangles, this will make up one fifth of the total angle at the centre of the shape.

$x° = \dfrac{360°}{5} = 72°$

> Draw the triangle and divide into two congruent right-angled triangles.
>
> Use the tangent ratio to find the height and then the area.

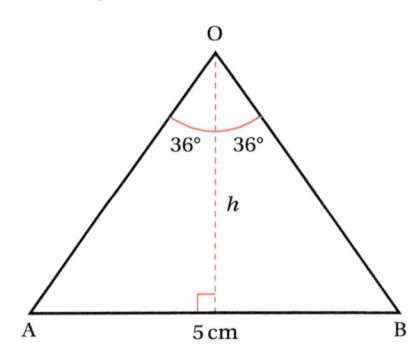

$\dfrac{2.5}{h} = \tan 36°$

So $h = \dfrac{2.5}{\tan 36°}$

Area of triangle ABO $= \dfrac{1}{2} \times 5 \times \dfrac{2.5}{\tan 36°}$

$= \dfrac{2.5 \times 2.5}{\tan 36°}$

$= \dfrac{6.25}{\tan 36°}$

Area of pentagon = 5 × area of triangle ABO

$= 5 \times \dfrac{6.25}{\tan 36°}$

$= 43.0 \text{ cm}^2$

5

$\sqrt[3]{xyz} = 6 \Rightarrow xyz = 6^3 = 216$

$x + y + z = 25$

So $xyz = 6 \times 6 \times 6$ [Sum 18]

$= 12 \times 3 \times 6$ [Sum 21]

$= 12 \times 18 \times 1$ [Sum 31]

$= 18 \times 4 \times 3$ [Sum 25]

> You need to find three numbers that multiply to give 216 and add together to give 25. What sets of three numbers multiply to give 216?

> You can trade factors to find other number combinations. In the second row, a factor of 2 has been borrowed from one of the sixes, making a 3 and a 12.

> Trade factors systematically until you find a set of three numbers that works. Be patient!

6

$\begin{pmatrix} 1 & 4 \\ 2 & 3 \end{pmatrix} \begin{pmatrix} x \\ y \end{pmatrix} = -1 \begin{pmatrix} x \\ y \end{pmatrix}$

And $\Rightarrow x + 4y = -x$

$\Rightarrow -2x = 4y$

$\Rightarrow x = -2y$

So, we need a vector $\begin{pmatrix} x \\ y \end{pmatrix}$ with $x = -2y$

Try $\begin{pmatrix} -2 \\ 1 \end{pmatrix}$

$\begin{pmatrix} 1 & 4 \\ 2 & 3 \end{pmatrix} \begin{pmatrix} -2 \\ 1 \end{pmatrix} = \begin{pmatrix} 2 \\ -1 \end{pmatrix}$

$= -1 \times \begin{pmatrix} -2 \\ 1 \end{pmatrix}$

So -1 is an eigenvalue and $\begin{pmatrix} -2 \\ 1 \end{pmatrix}$ is the associated eigenvector.

> See what happens when you assume that -1 is an eigenvalue. You don't know what the eigenvector might be so just use unknowns for now.

> Multiply the matrix and vector; make this equal to the right hand side.

> Now you just need a vector with the *x*-element equal to $(-2) \times$ the *y*-element.

7 a $ax + 3y = 5$ (1) $\Rightarrow 4ax + 12y = 20$

$3x + 4y = 8$ (2) $\Rightarrow 9x + 12y = 24$

$(4a - 9)x = -4$

$\Rightarrow x = \dfrac{-4}{4a-9} = \dfrac{4}{9-4a}$

> You need to multiply the equations so that either the x-terms or the y-terms are equal. Here we chose y.

> Substitute into equation 2.

$\Rightarrow 3 \times \dfrac{4}{9-4a} + 4y = 8$

$4y = 8 - \dfrac{12}{9-4a}$

$= \dfrac{8(9-4a)-12}{9-4a}$

$= \dfrac{72 - 32a - 12}{9-4a}$

$= \dfrac{60 - 32a}{9-4a}$

$y = \dfrac{15 - 8a}{9 - 4a}$

b $\dfrac{15-8a}{9-4a} = \dfrac{4}{9-4a}$

$\Rightarrow 15 - 8a = 4$

$\Rightarrow 8a = 11$

$\Rightarrow a = \dfrac{11}{8}$

$3b + 4b = 8$

$\Rightarrow b = \dfrac{8}{7}$

> Here the question just means that x and y are equal.

> Solve the equation for a.

> Use equation 2 with both x and y equal to b.

8

> You need to make x the subject. This means you need to get x out of the denominator.
>
> Multiply both sides by the denominator of the fraction.

$y = \dfrac{x+1}{x-1}$

$\Rightarrow (x-1)y = x+1$

$\Rightarrow xy - y = x + 1$

$\Rightarrow xy = x + 1 + y$

$\Rightarrow xy - x = 1 + y$

$\Rightarrow x(y-1) = 1 + y$

$\Rightarrow x = \dfrac{1+y}{y-1}$

> Expand the brackets.

> Now collect like terms: put the x terms on one side, and all other terms on the other.

> Factorise and solve for x.

9 a

> Put $x=0$ and $y=0$ into both equations and solve to find the intersections with the axes.
>
> Notice that the line $y=4x-7$ is steeper as the gradient is larger.

b Lines meet when $4x-7=2x+1$

$$\Rightarrow 2x=8$$
$$\Rightarrow x=4$$

$y=2x+1 \Rightarrow y=9$

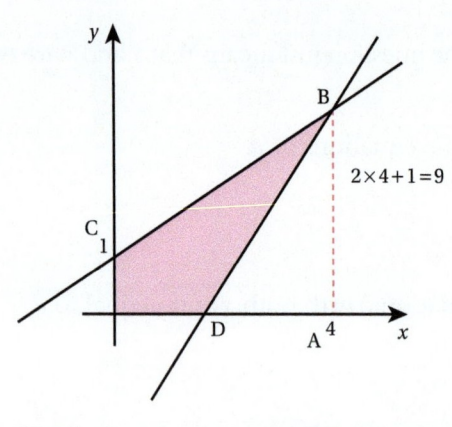

> Find out where the lines meet so that you know the size of the shape.

> Draw the extra line AB so that you can see a familiar shape (trapezium).

Shaded area = Area OABC − Area of traingle DAB

$$=\left(\frac{1+9}{2}\right)\times 4 - \frac{1}{2}\times\left(4-\frac{7}{4}\right)\times 9$$

$$= 20 - \frac{1}{2}\times\frac{9}{4}\times 9$$

$$= 20 - \frac{81}{8}$$

$$= \frac{160}{8} - \frac{81}{8}$$

So shaded area = $\dfrac{79}{8}$

10

$$x^2 - y^2 = 65$$
$$\Rightarrow (x-y)(x+y) = 65$$

Factorise when you see the difference of two squares.

$$\Rightarrow 5(x+y) = 65$$
$$\Rightarrow x+y = 13$$

We know that $x - y = 5$ so substitute this into the new equation.

$$(x+y)^2 = 13^2 = 169$$

The question asks about squared numbers; square the equations and see what happens.

So $x^2 + 2xy + y^2 = 169$ (1)

Similarly $(x-y)^2 = 5^2 = 25$

So $x^2 - 2xy + y^2 = 25$ (2)

(1) + (2) $\Rightarrow 2(x^2 + y^2) = 194$

So $x^2 + y^2 = 97$